Editors: Hin-cheung Lovell and Susan E. Leiper
Art Editor: Ma Kin-chuen
Photography: Zhang Ping
Measured Drawings: Ye Bofeng
Drawing Proofs: Yang Naiji and Zhong Xiaoqing
Line Drawings: Yuan Quanyou
Index: May Holdsworth
Designer: Oscar Lai

The original Chinese edition, *Ming shi jiaju zhen shang*, was co-published by
Joint Publishing Co. (HK) and Cultural Relics Publishing House, Beijing, China,
in 1985

Published by
Joint Publishing (H.K.) Co., Ltd.
9 Queen Victoria Street
Central District
Hong Kong

First Hong Kong English edition, 1986
Second impression, 1988
Fourth impression, 1994

Printed in Hong Kong by Ngai Kwong Printing Co., Ltd.

ISBN 962·04·0463·7

SE FURNITURE

— MING AND EARLY QING DYNASTIES

Translated by Sarah Handler and the Author

Joint Publishing (H.K.) Co., Ltd.

CLASSIC CHINESE FURNITURE

WANG SHIXIANG

CLASSIC CHINE

Introduction

I The Golden Age

The history of Chinese furniture has been marked by the gradual change from low pieces to pieces of the height to which we are accustomed today. From the 15th century BC to the 3rd century AD people conducted their daily lives on a low platform covered with a mat, on which they knelt or sat cross-legged and used low pieces of furniture. In the 3rd century ideas about the propriety of kneeling began to change, as did social customs, and people started to sit with legs extended and to adopt leaning positions. As a result armrests (Fig. 1.1) and cushions (Fig. 1.2) appeared.[1] The practice of sitting with legs pendent on hourglass-shaped stools made of straw and basketwork (Fig. 1.3)[2] began in the period of the Northern and Southern Dynasties (386-589). By the Tang dynasty (618-907) not only were stools and chairs quite common but high tables were also used. None the less, during this transitional period people still knelt or sat cross-legged on low platforms.

By the Northern Song (960-1127) all kinds of high furniture became prevalent and craftsmanship much more refined. In the Southern Song (1127-1279) most of the types of furniture found in Ming times had already appeared. These sowed the seed for the blossoming of the furniture tradition during the Ming dynasty (1368-1644) and early part of the Qing dynasty, up to 1735. By the Qianlong reign (1736-95) furniture had completely changed and become overly elaborate, although the materials and craftsmanship were still of excellent quality. In the latter part of the Qing dynasty China became a semi-feudal, semi-colonized society and the tradition of fine furniture, together with all the other arts, declined.

The style of living and the kinds of furniture used during the Song dynasty differed from those of earlier times. Undoubtedly there must have been some very good pre-Song pieces, but so little has survived that our knowledge of pre-Song furniture is very limited. It is only from Ming and early Qing times that pieces of furniture of high-quality material and craftsmanship have been preserved from the large numbers that were made. Thus this period is called the golden age of classic Chinese furniture.

Furniture reached such a level of perfection at this time as a result of the Song dynasty heritage, as well as for various other reasons. I shall now discuss two of the most important of these reasons. First, with the development of commerce and the consequent economic prosperity during the Ming dynasty, both city and country life flourished. This had an effect on social customs, and most people began to want good furniture. Second, the open-door policy led to the importation of many goods, including large quantities of hardwood which was so essential for fine furniture.

According to *Ming shu* (*Ming History*), in the Xuande reign (1426-35) thirty-three large cities, including Beijing and Nanjing, had customs houses.[3] After mid Ming another twenty or thirty were added to this list and the large cities became even more prosperous. For instance, in Nanjing after the Wanli reign (1573-1620) commerce flourished and the population increased. Xie Zhaozhe in his *Wu za zu* (*Compendium of Knowledge Classified into Five Parts*) says:

The streets of Nanjing are so wide that nine chariots can ride abreast. Recently there has been such an increase in population that shops are beginning to encroach upon these roads.[4]

In *Wu Qing Zhen zhi* (*Gazetteer of Wuzhen and Qingzhen* [in Zhejiang Province]) it is recorded that:

Wuzhen on the east and Qingzhen in Tongxiang on the west face each other. Since there has been a long period of peace the population is continually increasing. For three miles the houses almost touch each other and one can see the chimneys of 10,000 families ... the area is extensive, families are numerous, and there is nothing that the hundred kinds of craftsmen do not produce.[5]

In such towns as Zhenze, Pingwang, Shuangyang, Yanmu, Tanqiu and Meiyan in northern Zhejiang which were centres of silk manufacture as well as entrepôts, the population and trade volume increased by up to tenfold between the Jiajing (1522-66) and Wanli (1573-1620) reigns.[6] Although the gazetteers did not mention furniture manufacture, furniture is a necessity of daily life and so must have been one of the developing and prospering crafts.

In Ming dynasty texts there are records of the popular demand for hardwood furniture from mid Ming. A most important passage on the widespread fashion of using hardwood furniture is found in *Yunjian jumu chao* (*Record of Things seen in Yunjian*) by Fan Lian (born 1540):

When I was young I saw but a few pieces of furniture, such as writing tables and large chairs, made from fine wood. The common people only had pieces made from ginkgo wood and gold tinted lacquer square tables. Mo Tinghan and the young gentlemen of the Gu and Song families began the practice of bringing a few pieces of fine wood furniture to Yunjian [near present-day Shanghai] from Suzhou. During the Longqing [1567-72] and Wanli periods, even lower officials began to use fine wooden furniture, and cabinetmakers from Huizhou [in Anhui Province] opened shops in Yunjian where they made wedding furniture and other objects. At that time the wealthy families did not consider *ju* wood good enough and so it had become customary for them to have all their beds, cabinets and tables made from *huali* wood, burl wood, blackwood, *xiangsi* wood [*jichi* wood], and boxwood. This furniture is very fine and exorbitant, each piece costing 10,000 cash, a most extravagant custom. It is strange that even those policemen who had a home would arrange a comfortable place to rest, separated by wooden partitions. In the courtyard they raised goldfish and planted various kinds of flowers. Inside there were good-quality wooden tables and a horsetail whisk for dusting. They called it the study. However, I really do not know what books they studied![7]

Foreword

The author of this book, Wang Shixiang, is a native of Beijing and has long entertained a deep interest in Chinese furniture. By good fortune he has been able to carry on his research in a city that for 500 years, from the 15th century to the early years of the 20th, was the capital of two imperial dynasties. It is no wonder, then, that more masterpieces of furniture, of the widest variety, are concentrated in Beijing than in any other city of China.

Mr Wang has taken full advantage of his unique opportunity and has devoted years of careful study to this wealth of furniture, to the materials, methods of construction, types of pieces and variations in style. A rather particular aspect of Chinese furniture is that certain designs, such as the chair with a yoke-shaped top rail or the trestle table, have remained in favour for many centuries. From the broad range of examples available, the author has been able to show the multiple variation in proportions and discreet decoration which cabinetmakers have devised within the limitation of firmly established tradition.

But above all, the Western reader is introduced here to the widest possible range of domestic furniture, from simple stools and benches, chairs and tables, cabinets and bookcases to the great canopy beds. In addition, he cannot but be impressed by the structural integrity of Chinese joinery, so well demonstrated by detailed illustrations and precise drawings. The Occidental reader, confronted by the justness of proportion and the sophistication of joinery of Chinese furniture, will do well to recall that many centuries ago, early in their cultural history, the Chinese evolved the world's most beautiful and structurally lucid order of wooden architecture.

Those of us already interested in Chinese furniture, as well as those who encounter it here for the first time, should alike be grateful to the author for his meticulous research and his publication which, without doubt, will remain an authoritative reference work for many years to come.

Laurence Sickman
Director Emeritus
The Nelson-Atkins Museum of Art

Contents

List of Owners

Collections	Plate numbers
Beijing Cultural Relics Bureau	143, 145
Beijing Cultural Relics Store	116, 136
Beijing Hardwood Furniture Factory	17, 24, 26, 29, 54, 78, 80, 81, 94, 97, 99, 146, 148, 155, 158, 159, 164, 165
Beijing Timber Factory	12, 21, 22, 35, 66, 112
Central Academy of Arts and Crafts	13, 15, 42, 43, 47, 52, 61
Mrs Chen Mengjia (Professor Zhao Luorui)	37, 38, 40, 41, 45, 57, 65, 70, 74, 77, 85, 92, 98, 101, 106, 114, 118, 120, 130, 132, 135, 139, 140, 169
Fayuansi (Library and Museum of Chinese Buddhism)	119
Fei Boliang	16
Huang Zhou	28, 137
The Palace Museum	20, 27, 53, 56, 59, 62, 64, 76, 89, 91, 96, 110, 113, 117, 121, 126, 128, 129, 133, 138, 149, 150, 171
The Summer Palace	25, 49, 68, 69, 83, 93, 95
Tianjin Cultural Relics Store	147
Tianjin Museum of Art	32, 34
Tianjin Museum of History	156
Wang Shixiang	7, 8, 9, 10, 11, 14, 18, 19, 31, 33, 36, 39, 44, 46, 50, 51, 55, 58, 60, 63, 67, 71, 72, 73, 75, 79, 82, 84, 87, 88, 90, 100, 102, 103, 104, 105, 107, 108, 111, 115, 123, 124, 125, 127, 131, 134, 142, 144, 151, 152, 153, 154, 157, 160, 161, 162, 163, 166, 167, 168, 170, 172, 173, 174, 175
Yang Naiji	30
Ye Wanfa	48, 141
Zhang An	23, 86
Zhejiang Provincial Museum	109
Mrs Zhu Guangmu	122

Publisher's Note

Classic Chinese Furniture: Ming and Early Qing Dynasties is the result of Wang Shixiang's intensive research into the subject of Chinese furniture over a forty-year period, and we are delighted that he should have entrusted us with the publication of the book.

To the production of the book Wang Shixiang brought the same qualities that he did to his research and connoisseurship: boundless enthusiasm and energy, insight and discernment, meticulous care and attention to detail. Indeed, the assembling of 162 pieces from twenty public and private collections in China, the securing of permission to reproduce them, their preparation prior to photography, the actual photography sessions – all this could not have been accomplished if in his co-ordination Wang Shixiang had not been sustained by an intense interest in the subject, inexhaustible energy and the belief that no detail was too minor for his attention. In the book Wang Shixiang describes the makers of a number of pieces as "unsparing" of material, time and labour. The same epithet may be used of the author: he was unsparing of himself. Even during the photography sessions he could be seen lifting and moving pieces of furniture.

A volume such as *Classic Chinese Furniture* could not of course have been brought to fruition without the contribution of many others. The task of rendering the book into English was a collaborative effort on the part of the author and Dr Sarah Handler, a specialist in Chinese furniture from the United States. The glossary, consisting of terms culled from old texts, those used by craftsmen and those coined by the author, added considerably to the arduousness of the translation. Together Wang Shixiang and Sarah Handler worked in Beijing for over a year, and tribute must be paid to the latter's specialist knowledge and dedication to the task. Sarah Handler's sojourn in Beijing was made possible in part by a fellowship from the Committee for Scholarly Communications with the People's Rupublic of China (CSCPRC), which both the recipient and the publishers would like to acknowledge with appreciation.

We should like to thank Zu Lianpeng, the master craftsman who repaired, cleaned and generally prepared the pieces of furniture for photography, thereby restoring them to their former glory; Zhang Ping, who photographed the furniture and the interiors in a period stretching over a year; Yuan Quanyou (Mrs Wang Shixiang), who did the line drawings in the text section; Ye Bofeng, who did the measured drawings in the plate section; Yang Naiji and Zhong Xiaoqing, who checked the measured drawings against the furniture; and May Holdsworth for compiling the index.

We are most grateful to Mr Laurence Sickman, Director Emeritus of the Nelson-Atkins Museum of Art and a leading authority on Chinese art, for contributing the Foreword. Not only is Mr Sickman an old friend of the author, but he is also one of the few Western specialists who gained early in life a first-hand knowledge of Chinese furniture, which remains over the years a vital part of his many-faceted interest in Chinese art.

To the institutions and collectors who granted us permission to reproduce pieces in their collection, we wish to express our gratitude. Without their co-operation, it would not have been possible to include in *Classic Chinese Furniture* such a wide selection of both typical and unique pieces.

Dedicated to the memory of
Chen Mengjia

Wang Shixing in *Guang zhi yi* (*On a Variety of Subjects*) records that:

The people of Suzhou, being very clever and fond of antiques, were skilled at using old methods to make things ... such as small treasures for the study, tables and beds. Recently they have liked to use *zitan* and *huali* woods. They preferred plain to elaborately carved pieces; but if they used decoration it always followed the ancient patterns of the Shang, Zhou, Qin and Han dynasties. This fashion spread all over China and was especially popular during the Jiajing, Longqing and Wanli reigns.[8]

These quotations are very important for the history of Ming period furniture since they record that hardwood furniture became popular from the middle of the dynasty, and they mention Suzhou, the centre of the manufacture of fine furniture. The fashion for good furniture raised both the quality and the quantity to an unprecedentedly high level.

Wood is basic to the manufacture of furniture; if there is not enough local wood it must be imported. In the Longqing reign China instituted an open-door policy which is described by Zhou Qiyuan in his preface to Zhang Xie's *Dong xi yang kao* (*Studies on Countries to the East and West*):

At the end of the Longqing reign the Emperor abolished the law prohibiting trade with foreign nations. Since then merchants from all over have been trading on the seas and many valuable goods are imported, so that rare goods are becoming more common. Each year this commerce involves hundreds of thousands of cash, and both the government and private merchants depend upon it, almost as though it were the Emperor's Southern Storehouse.[9]

By abolishing the law prohibiting trade with foreign countries, the Emperor established an open-door policy permitting sea trade and private trade with foreign lands. Since Indochina produced quantities of precious hardwood, it is most likely that a great deal was imported and that the manufacture of furniture was thus stimulated.

The above quotations from contemporaneous texts show that within the golden age of Chinese furniture, the greatest flourishing of classic Chinese furniture occurred in the period from mid Ming, beginning with the Jiajing reign in the 1520s. This was not accidental but the result of circumstances closely related to the social and economic conditions of the time. From the discussion of different aspects of Ming and early Qing furniture in the following chapters, there will be no doubt that this period is indeed the golden age of classic Chinese furniture.

Notes

1. Armrests are curved pieces of wood with three legs which can be put on a bed for a person to lean on either forwards or backwards. A pottery armrest was found among the spirit goods in tomb number 1 at Zhaoshigang in Jiangning. It is illustrated by Jiangsu Sheng Wenwu Guanli Weiyuanhui 江蘇省文物管理委員會 (CPAM, Jiangsu Province), in "Nanjing jinjiao Liuchao mu de qingli 南京近郊六朝墓的清理 " ("The Excavation of Six Dynasties Tombs in the Suburbs of Nanjing"), *Kaogu xuebao,* 1957: 1, plate II.

    Large bag-like cushions (*yinnang* 隱囊) are also used for leaning against. In the Binyang Cave at Longmen, Vimalakirti is shown seated upon a bed and reclining against such a cushion. The drawing is traced from Fu Yunzi 傅芸子 , *Zhengcangyuan kaogu ji* 正倉院考古記 (*Notes on the Antiquities in the Shosoin*) (Tokyo: Bunkyūdō 文求堂 , 1941), p. 91, plate 23.

2. Hourglass-shaped stools (*quanti* 筌蹄 , literally bamboo fish trap) are high, narrow, waisted seats, such as that depicted in a Northern Wei dynasty wall painting in Dunhuang, Cave 285. See Dunhuang Wenwu Yanjiu Suo 敦煌文物研究所 (Dunhuang Research Institute), *Dunhuang bihua ji* 敦煌壁畫集 (*Dunhuang Wall Paintings*) (Beijing: Wenwu Press, 1975), plate 18, top. Hourglass-shaped stools can also be seen in a relief in the Lianhua Cave at Longmen (west side of niche no. 2 on the lower row of the south wall): Longmen Baoguan Suo 龍門保管所 (Longmen Preservation Institute), *Longmen shiku*

1.1 Pottery armrest unearthed from a Six Dynasties tomb in the suburbs of Nanjing

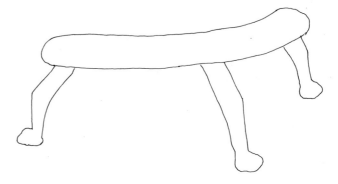

1.2 Cushion depicted in Northern Wei relief in the Binyang Cave, Longmen

1.3 Hourglass-shaped stool depicted in Northern Wei relief in the Lianhua Cave, Longmen

龍門石窟 (*The Longmen Caves*) (Beijing: Wenwu Press, 1980), plate 82.

3. Fu Weilin 傅維鱗, *Ming shu* 明書 (*Ming History*) (Jifu congshu 畿輔叢書, 1913 edition), *juan* 81, Shihuo zhi 食貨志, p. 10a.

4. Xie Zhaozhe 謝肇淛 (Ming), *Wu za zu* 五雜俎 (*Compendium of Knowledge Classified into Five Parts*) (Beijing: Zhonghua Press, 1959), p. 72.

5. Dong Shining 董世寧 (editor, Qing), *Wu Qing Zhen zhi* 烏青鎮志 (*Gazetteer of Wuzhen and Qingzhen*) (1760 edition), *juan* 2, p. 1.

6. Chen Hezhi 陳和志 (editor, Qing), *Zhenze Xian zhi* 震澤縣志 (*Gazetteer of Zhenze* Xian) (1893 edition), *juan* 4, pp. 1-2.

7. Fan Lian 范濂 (Ming), *Yunjian jumu chao* 雲間據目抄 (*Record of Things Seen in Yunjian*) (Biji xiaoshuo daguan 筆記小說大觀, lithographic edition), *juan* 2, p. 3b.

8. Wang Shixing 王士性 (Ming), *Guang zhi yi* 廣志繹 (*On a Variety of Subjects*) (Taizhou congshu 台州叢書, Jiaqing edition), *juan* 2, p. 24b.

9. Zhou Qiyuan 周起元, preface to Zhang Xie 張燮 (Ming), *Dong xi yang kao* 東西洋考 (*Studies on Countries to the East and West*) (Congshu jicheng chubian 叢書集成初編 edition), p. 1.

II The Best Furniture Woods

One important reason why Ming and early Qing furniture is of such high quality is that it was fashioned from hard, dense woods of good colour and beautiful grain. In this chapter only the main furniture woods will be discussed: *huanghuali*, *zitan*, *jichi*, *tieli*, *ju*, and burl wood.

A. *Huanghuali* wood 黃花梨

During the golden age most of the best furniture was made from *huanghuali* wood, as is evident from the fact that of the 162 pieces in this book over one hundred are fashioned from it. The colour of *huanghuali* is perfect, neither too subdued nor too showy, and its grain, which at times can be quite distinct, is very varied. It is no wonder that this wood is so favoured by connoisseurs.

The term *huanghuali* 黃花梨 is not found in early texts; only *huali*, written 花梨, and *hualü* 花櫚 are mentioned. Later the prefix *huang* was affixed to *huali* to distinguish it from the so-called *xinhuali* 新花梨 (new *huali*), the wood that became popular and which is still used in large quantities for making furniture today.

Hualü is mentioned in texts as early as in the Tang dynasty, in Chen Cangqi's *Bencao shiyi* (*Addendum to the Materia Medica*):

Hualü is found in Annam and Hainan. When made into beds and tables it resembles *zitan*, but is somewhat redder. It is very hard and attractive.[1]

In the 1462 edition of Cao Zhao's *Gegu yaolun* (*The Essential Criteria of Antiquities*) (1388) revised and enlarged by Wang Zuo, it is said:

Huali is found in Guangdong and southern lands. It is purplish red and has a fragrance very much resembling that of truth-bringing incense. *Huali* with a devil's-face grain is very valuable, while that with a coarse grain and light colour is inferior.[2]

The Qing edition of *Qiongzhoufu zhi* (*Gazetteer of Qiongzhoufu* [Hainan Island]) has the following entry under wood in the section on natural products:

Huali wood is purplish red in colour with a slight fragrance resembling that of truth-bringing incense. It grows in the Li mountains.[3]

Other sources tell us that Hainan Island is the main source for *huanghuali* wood. In *Guangzhou zhiwu zhi* (*Record of the Plants of Guangzhou*) compiled by Hou Kuanzhao and published in 1956, under the genus *Dalbergia* is included a species called *huali* produced in Hainan. To this is given the new name *Dalbergia hainanensis* (*Hainantan*, or *huali* wood from Hainan Island). It is described as follows:

This is a special wood from Hainan Island ... The tree grows in forests, especially in rather wet ravines sheltered from the sun. The wood is excellent. The outer wood is rather light in colour with a loose grain. The middle part, being more reddish, much harder, and with a fine, attractive grain, is suitable for sculpture and furniture ... In Hainan the wood is called *huali*, but this confuses it with the *huali* wood of an entirely different species, which is still very popular among Guangdong timber merchants. Therefore, I had to give it a new name.[4]

From this discussion we know that *huanghuali* wood still exists and that it was given the scientific name *Dalbergia hainanensis* only as recently as in 1956. In 1980 Cheng Junqing, the principal compiler of *Zhongguo redai ji yaredai mucai* (*Tropical and Sub-tropical Woods of China*), revised

Hou Kuanzhao's classification, giving it the new name of *Dalbergia odorifera* (*jiangxiang huangtan* 降香黃檀) He reasons that:

This kind of *Dalbergia* is the only one yet known in China in which the colours of the pith and the outer wood are quite distinct ... The unevenly coloured pith is dark red, even purplish, and often has a black grain ... The outer wood is a greyish-yellow or light yellow. Thus the difference is very clear.

Originally it was grouped with *Dalbergia hainanensis* whose colour varies but insignificantly:

However, on account of this distinctive characteristic we now give it a new name.[5]

This variation of colour is evident on some furniture made from *huanghuali* wood.

B. *Zitan* wood 紫檀

Zitan wood is mentioned as early as in the 3rd century in Cui Bao's *Gu jin zhu* (*Explanation of Ancient and Modern Matters*).[6] Thereafter it appears in Su Gong's *Tang bencao* (*Tang Materia Medica*),[7] Su Song's *Tujing bencao* (*Illustrated Materia Medica*),[8] Ye Tinggui's *Xiang fu* (*Book of Incense*),[9] Zhao Rukua's *Zhufan zhi* (*Record of Foreign Lands*),[10] *Da Ming yitong zhi* (*Record of the Ming Empire*),[11] Wang Zuo's revised and enlarged edition of *Gegu yaolun* (*The Essential Criteria of Antiquities*),[12] Li Shizhen's *Bencao gangmu* (*Compendium of Materia Medica*),[13] Fang Yizhi's *Tong ya* (*Compendium of My Knowledge*),[14] Qu Dajun's *Guangdong xinyu* (*New Remarks on Guangdong Province*),[15] and Li Tiaoyuan's *Nanyue biji* (*Notes on Nanyue*).[16] In these books *zitan* wood is said to come from various places which are mostly in Indochina, as well as from the Chinese provinces of Yunnan, Guangdong and Guangxi.

According to Chen Rong's *Zhongguo shumu fenlei xue* (*A Classification of Chinese Woods*),[17] *zitan* wood belongs to the *Pterocarpus* genus, which itself is a member of the *Leguminosae* family. And within this genus there are about fifteen species, most of which grow in the tropics. Two species grow in China: *zitan* (*Pterocarpus santalinus*) and rosewood (*Pterocarpus indicus*). According to Chen, *Pterocarpus santalinus* is a large tree. However, the *zitan* wood used in cabinetmaking is rarely found in large pieces and thus one cannot equate it, as he does, with *Pterocarpus santalinus*. *Zitan* wood is in fact much closer to rosewood (*Pterocarpus indicus*). The American scholar E.H. Schafer has studied the *zitan* problem and believes that the *zitan* wood which the Chinese imported from Indochina is rosewood.[18] Therefore, since what we call *zitan* is not a single species, at least one of the species included in our term *zitan* must be rosewood.

From very ancient times the Chinese have considered *zitan* the most precious wood. Perhaps precisely because it is so precious, fewer pieces were made from it than from *huanghuali* wood. Occasionally we find large pieces of *zitan* wood furniture, such as those illustrated in Plates 110 and 115, which, because of the scarcity of large *zitan* trees, are treated as exceptional treasures.

Zitan wood is the hardest and heaviest of all hardwoods. Most examples are purplish-black, but some pieces are as black as lacquer, so that the grain is virtually invisible. Although its grain is not as colourful and attractive as that of *huanghuali* wood, its subtlety and antique appearance are incomparable.

C. *Jichi* wood 鸂鶒

Jichi wood can be written 鸂鶒木, 鷄翅木 (chicken-wing wood), or *qizimu* 杞梓木. All Beijing craftsmen recognise two kinds, an old and a new. New *jichi* wood is coarse and purplish-black in colour, some of the grain lines being purple, others black. The grain is not very clear, and because it is rigid, straight and coarse, the wood has a tendency to split. Old *jichi* wood is denser and of a purplish-brown colour. The grain, especially in straight cuts, forms very good patterns suggesting the feathers near the neck and wings of a bird. After the middle of the Qing dynasty few pieces were made from old *jichi* wood. However, many pieces were made from new *jichi* wood in later times and it is still being used today. In this book the pieces in Plates 70, 71, 102 and 161 are made from old *jichi* wood.

The most detailed account of *jichi* wood was written by the Qing author Qu Dajun in *Guangdong xinyu*. Qu says that some *jichi* wood is white with a black grain, while some is yellow with a purple grain. If it is cut diagonally there will be fine cloud-like designs. The seeds of the tree are called red beans or love beans, and can be made into jewellery. Thus the wood is also called love wood.[19] The kind of *jichi* wood mentioned by Qu which is yellow with a purple grain is very similar to old *jichi* wood.

Jichi is one of the genera of wood belonging to the *Ormosia* family. According to Chen Rong in his *Zhongguo shumu fenlei xue*[20] there are about forty species under the genus. However, Hou Kuanzhao in *Guangzhou zhiwu zhi* states that there are more than sixty species, twenty-six of which are found in China.[21] In order to determine which of these species are the old *jichi* wood used in cabinetmaking, it would be necessary to have samples from furniture analysed by botanists.

D. *Tieli* wood 鐵力

Tieli wood is written 鐵力木, 鐵梨木 or 鐵栗木. *Tieli* is the largest of all hardwood trees and the timber is the least expensive. In the revised and enlarged edition of *Gegu yaolun* it is recorded that "in Dongguan 東莞 [a district of Guangdong Province near Hong Kong] it is used to build houses".[22] In *Guangdong xinyu* it is noted that "the Cantonese use it for beams, pillars and screens".[23] In *Nanyue biji* we find the statement: "People in the Li 黎 Mountains [on Hainan Island] use it for fuel but people in Wu 吳 [Jiangsu Province] and Chu 楚 [Hubei and Hunan Provinces] pay high prices for it."[24]

From these quotations we know that *tieli* wood is cheaper than other hardwoods. Many very large pieces of furniture are made from it, such as the table in Plate 92. It is frequently used for the backs of furniture, shelves, and interiors of drawers. For example, the back and inside of the drawers of the shelves in Plate 135 are all of *tieli* wood. The grain of *tieli* wood is similar to that of *jichi* wood, only coarser, and furniture merchants would sometimes pass off *tieli* pieces as being made of *jichi* wood.

The scientific name for *tieli* wood is *Mesua ferrea*. According to Chen Rong,

It is a large evergreen with a straight trunk which can be more than 100 feet [approximately 30 metres] high, with a diameter of 10 feet [approximately 3 metres] ... it originally came from the East Indies. *Guangxi tong zhi* 廣西通志 [*Gazetteer of Guangxi*] records that it can be found in the Rong 容 and Teng 藤 Districts [in eastern Guangxi]. The wood is very hard and durable with a dark red centre and a fine, beautiful grain. It is used for buildings in the tropics. In Guangdong it is fashioned into very durable tables, chairs and other kinds of furniture.[25]

This accurately describes the *tieli* wood used in Ming and early Qing furniture.

E. *Ju* wood 櫸

Ju is written 櫸 , and often simplified to 椐 . In north China the name *ju* is unknown and people call the wood southern elm (*nanyu* 南榆). It is harder than most woods and, although not exactly a hardwood, it plays an important role in Ming and early Qing furniture. It has been valued since Ming times and was discussed by such scholars as Li Shizhen[26] and Fang Yizhi.[27] Ming and early Qing *ju* wood furniture can still be found in towns and villages of south China and the pieces in Plates 33, 36, 105, 123 and 142 were all recently brought from the area around Lake Tai. We also find many pieces of *ju* wood, so-called southern elm, furniture in north China. These pieces were made in Ming and early Qing times and are identical to *huanghuali* wood pieces in form, style and craftsmanship. It is evident therefore that cabinetmakers and true connoisseurs of Chinese furniture greatly valued them, believing that their aesthetic and historical merits should not be disregarded simply because they were fashioned from a somewhat inferior wood.

According to Chen Rong, the scientific name of the *ju* genus is *Zelkova*. The species found in Jiangsu and Zhejiang Provinces is a large-leaf elm, having various other names such as *juyu* 櫸榆 and *dayeyu* 大葉榆 . Its wood is hard and dense, with a beautiful colour and grain; it has many uses and is quite precious. The old trees of a reddish colour are known as blood *ju* (*xueju* 血櫸).[28] *Ju* wood has a particularly beautiful large grain suggesting mountains piled upon mountains, called pagoda pattern by Suzhou cabinetmakers. This can be seen clearly on the southern official's hat armchair in Plate 52.

F. Burl wood (*ying mu* 癭木 or 影木)

Burl is not the name of a specific tree but refers to wood cut from a large knot or twisted root. Beijing craftsmen call it *yingzi* 癭子 ; they say that it can come from any kind of tree and that it always has circular patterns. I once saw a *zitan* wood drum-shaped stool with a top made from *zitan* burl wood. However, *nan*[29] burl wood is most common as many large trees have great knots at their base which can be cut into sizeable boards. The section on *nan* wood in Wang Zuo's revised and enlarged edition of *Gegu yaolun* mentions *toubainan* 骰柏楠 and *doubainan* 鬬柏楠 , the burl wood of *nan* which is described as having an allover grape pattern.[30] In the Palace Museum there is a set of four *zitan* wood armchairs with curved rests with splats made in three sections, the middle one having a burl wood panel (Pl. 56).

Notes

1. Chen Cangqi 陳藏器, *Bencao shiyi* 本草拾遺 , quoted in Li Shizhen 李時珍 , *Bencao gangmu* 本草綱目 *(Compendium of Materia Medica)* (Shanghai: Commercial Press, 1930), *juan* 35, Lü mu 欄木, p. 60.
2. Wang Zuo 王佐 , *Xinzeng Gegu yaolun* 新增格古要論 *(A Revised and Enlarged Edition of The Essential Criteria of Antiquities* by Cao Zhao 曹昭, 1388) (1462; Xiyinxuan congshu 惜陰軒叢書, 1846 edition), *juan* 8, Yi mu lun 異木論, pp. 5-9.
3. Ming Yi 明誼 *et al.* (Qing), *Qiongzhoufu zhi* 瓊州府志 *(Gazet-teer of Qiongzhoufu* [Hainan Island]) (1841 edition), *juan* 5, p. 26a.
4. Hou Kuanzhao 侯寬昭 *et al.*, *Guangzhou zhiwu zhi* 廣州植物誌 *(Record of the Plants of Guangzhou)* (Beijing: Science Press, 1956), pp. 344-5.
5. Cheng Junqing 成俊卿, *Zhongguo redai ji yaredai mucai* 中國熱帶及亞熱帶木材 *(Tropical and Sub-tropical Woods of China)* (Beijing: Science Press, 1980), pp. 260-2.
6. Cui Bao 崔豹 (Jin), *Gu jin zhu* 古今註 *(Explanation of Ancient and Modern Matters)* (Sibu congkan 四部叢刊 , 1935 edition), San bian 三編, *juan* b, p. 2.
7. Quoted in Li Shizhen, *op. cit.*, *juan* 34, Tanxiang 檀香 , p. 104.
8. Li Shizhen, *loc. cit.*
9. Li Shizhen, *loc. cit.*
10. Zhao Rukua 趙汝适 (Song), *Zhufan zhi* 諸藩志 *(Record of Foreign Lands)* (Xuejin taoyuan 學津討原 , 1805 edition), *juan* b, Tanxiang 檀香 , p. 6.
11. Li Shizhen, *loc. cit.*
12. Wang Zuo, *loc. cit.*
13. Li Shizhen, *op. cit.*, *juan* 34, p. 104.
14. Fang Yizhi 方以智 (Ming), *Tong ya* 通雅 *(Compendium of My Knowledge)* (Qing, Fushancizangxuan 浮山此藏軒 edition), *juan* 43, p. 10.
15. Qu Dajun 屈大均 (Qing), *Guangdong xinyu* 廣東新語 *(New Remarks on Guangdong Province)* (1700 edition), *juan* 25, Muyu, Hainan wenmu 木語·海南文木, pp. 48-50.
16. Li Tiaoyuan 李調元 (Qing), *Nanyue biji* 南越筆記 *(Notes on Nanyue)* (1882 edition), *juan* 13, Zitan huali tieli zhu mu 紫檀花梨鐵力諸木, pp. 5-6.
17. Chen Rong 陳嶸, *Zhongguo shumu fenlei xue* 中國樹木分類學 *(A Classification of Chinese Woods)* (Shanghai: Science and Technology Press, 1959, 2nd revised edition), p. 539.
18. Schafer, Edward H., "Rosewood, Dragon's Blood and Lac", *Journal of the American Oriental Society*, vol. 77:2 (1957), pp. 129-36.
19. Qu Dajun, *loc. cit.*
20. Chen Rong, *op. cit.*, p. 529.
21. Hou Kuanzhao, *op. cit.*, p. 343.
22. Wang Zuo, *loc. cit.*
23. Qu Dajun, *loc. cit.*
24. Li Tiaoyuan, *loc. cit.*
25. Chen Rong, *op. cit.*, p. 849.
26. Li Shizhen, *op. cit.*, *juan* 35 b, p. 44.
27. Fang Yizhi, *loc. cit.*
28. Chen Rong, *op. cit.*, p. 222.
29. *Ibid.*, p. 345.
30. Wang Zuo, *op. cit.*, *juan* 8, p. 6a.

III The Origins of the Principal Furniture Forms

In classic Chinese furniture there are two basic forms: that without an inset panel between the top and apron and that with an inset panel, known in China as the waistless and the waisted forms respectively. Waistless furniture, such as the narrow table and the recessed-leg table, is very ancient and already existed in Shang (16th-11th century BC) and Zhou (11th century-221 BC) times. Waisted furniture appeared much later.

As a result of the change in the style of living during the Tang and Song dynasties, new kinds of furniture developed, including different types of high table. Some high tables adopted the pillar-and-beam construction from wooden architecture and became waistless furniture. Others, taking over the box construction from beds and tables, and the form of Buddhist pedestals, became waisted furniture. Gradually other types of furniture besides tables became waisted, and by Southern Song times there was about as much waisted as waistless furniture. In the Ming and early Qing dynasties many types of furniture fell into either of these two basic categories. If we look carefully at pieces from this time and attempt to trace the origin of their forms, we can begin to understand the difference between the two categories. We can perhaps also determine the principles governing the different forms of furniture.

Wooden architectural construction is the origin of waistless furniture. In architecture, most pillars are round, vertical and placed on stone bases. In order to make the structure more stable, pillars usually slant inwards[1] so that the building is wider at the base than at the top. The pillars have spandrels at the top and are connected by beams. On waistless high tables, such as the Northern Song example excavated at Julu 鉅鹿 in Hebei Province (Fig. 3.1), the legs are round, straight, splayed slightly outwards towards the base, and without horse-hoof feet. These tables have spandrels and the legs are connected by stretchers, equivalent to beams in architecture. Thus the form of the table is almost identical to that of wooden architectural construction.

The predecessors of high-waisted tables are the box-construction bed, the box-construction table, and the Buddhist pedestal. In the Tang dynasty there were both low and high examples of the box construction; low ones may be seen in Dunhuang paintings (Fig. 3.2) and a high one in the painting entitled "The Court Musicians 宮樂圖 " (Fig. 3.3). They all have a box-like form with panels with ornamental openings on four sides. All Buddhist pedestals, from the base of the Northern Wei (386-534) pagoda with relief decoration at Yungang 雲崗 (Fig. 3.4) to the coffin platform in Wang Jian's 王建 tomb (Fig. 3.5) of the Five Dynasties period (907-960), are waisted. The waisted sections of Buddhist pedestals often have panels reminiscent of those on box-construction furniture.

After the Tang dynasty the box construction became simpler, with one ornamental opening instead of several on each side. This is very similar to the beds and high tables of Southern Song times which have a continuous base stretcher. A bed of this type is depicted in Li Song's 李嵩 painting "Listening to the *Ruan* 聽阮圖 " (Fig. 3.6) and a high table may be seen in Ma Yuan's 馬遠 "Elegant Gathering in the West Garden 西園雅集圖 " (Fig. 3.7). If we go one step further and remove the base stretchers, we then have the

3.1 High table unearthed from a Northern Song site at Julu, Hebei Province

3.2 Bed of box-like form depicted in Tang wall painting at Dunhuang

3.3 Table of box-like form depicted in the painting "The Court Musicians"

3.4 Northern Wei pagoda with pedestal base at Yungang

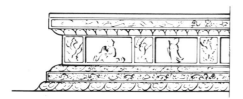

3.5 Coffin platform in the tomb of Wang Jian, Five Dynasties period

3.6 Bed depicted in "Listening to the *Ruan*" by Li Song, Southern Song

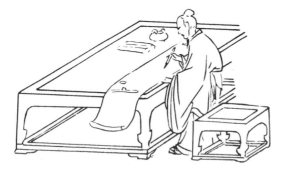

3.7 High table depicted in "Elegant Gathering in the West Garden" by Ma Yuan, Southern Song

straight form of Ming furniture (Fig. 3.8). The straight form adopted the waistless simplified shape of the box construction. However, other types of furniture evolved from Buddhist pedestals and were waisted.

With the advent of high furniture, in order for tables to be convenient for everyday use, it was necessary for them to have enough space underneath to accommodate the legs of a seated person. At the same time, with the increase in height tables became less stable. To create more leg room and increase stability one can either use a continuous base stretcher or strengthen the connection between the legs. Since stretchers interfere with sitting, the best solution is to strengthen the connection by adding a waist, or an inset panel between the top and the apron. Waisted tables, especially those with a high waist (Fig. 3.9), are very similar to Buddhist pedestals. This close relationship is immediately apparent when they are seen together. The waisted form of furniture which appeared in Northern Song was undoubtedly derived from Buddhist pedestals.

The Tang dynasty box construction and the Buddhist pedestal are both straight-sided rectangles and their vertical members are not splayed. The legs of many waisted tables are also square in section and are not splayed. When the ornaments disappeared from the side panels of the box construction, the lower corner of the panels remained and became the horse-hoof feet of waisted furniture. Thus it is evident that the form and construction of waisted furniture are in many ways similar to those of the box construction and the Buddhist pedestal.

The main point of the above discussion is that waisted and waistless furniture have different origins and therefore different forms and constructions. On the basis of many examples of Ming and Qing furniture it is clear that because waistless furniture is derived from wooden architectural construction it has neither horse-hoof feet nor base stretchers, which are vestigial features from the box construction. However, the straight waistless table may have horse-hoof feet and a base stretcher because it developed from the box construction. These guiding principles may even explain the form of that rather rare type of waisted furniture called the low table with extended legs[2] (Pls 84 and 91). The craftsman's aim was to make a waisted table with round legs. However, such a form would have gone against the basic principles of his craft, since waisted furniture had its origins in the box construction and round legs originated from the pillar-and-beam construction in architecture. The craftsman's ingenious solution was to make a complete low square-leg table on top and change that into a high table by extending the square legs to round terminations.

The principles were also always observed when craftsmen made tables with recessed legs. On both narrow rectangular tables and wide painting tables (Pls 102 and 103) there may be a base stretcher connecting the legs on the short sides but there is never a continuous base stretcher on all four sides. This is because in ancient times there was always a base stretcher (known then as *huangfu* 橫跗)[3] along the sides (Fig. 3.10). Yet, since the continuous base stretcher is the bottom part of a box-construction frame it will not appear on a table with recessed legs. The numerous different forms of furniture remain faithful to their respective origins and between them there is a distinct demarcation. With extremely few exceptions the two basic forms of furniture are never interchangeable and examples made many years and great distances apart remain quite similar within their respective tradition. This is why I have called these traditions the principles governing the forms of Chinese furniture.

At first glance Ming and early Qing furniture appears to have many forms and variations, seemingly reflecting the imagination and creativeness of many craftsmen. A careful study of the furniture, however, reveals that the principles governing each form were quite strict and that craftsmen could not combine at will features from different forms. It was from the middle of the Qing dynasty that craftsmen, in their efforts to please their patrons, tried their utmost to outdo their competitors in producing furniture of original, curious and ornate designs. In so doing they abandoned the strict principles which governed furniture design in Ming and early Qing, thus bringing the golden age of classic furniture to a close.

Notes

1. Inward slant (*cejiao*側脚) is the term used to describe the slight splay of pillars at the base. Li Jie 李誡 (Song), *Yingzao fashi* 營造法式 (*Building Standards*) (Shanghai: Commercial Press, 1954 reprint of Wanyou wenku 萬有文庫 edition), *juan* 5, Zhu 柱, p. 103.
2. Although I have asked many cabinetmakers, I have found none who can provide me with a name for this form of table. I therefore invented this name.
3. Low recessed-leg lacquered wood tables of the Warring States period have side floor stretchers, called *fu* 跗 in ancient times. See Shang Chengzuo商承祚, *Changsha chutu Chu qiqi tulu* 長沙 出土楚漆器圖錄 (*Illustrated Catalogue of the Chu Lacquer Excavated at Changsha*) (Shanghai: Chinese Classical Art Press, 1957), caption to plate 3.

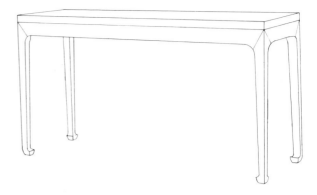

3.8 Narrow rectangular table with corner legs, Ming dynasty

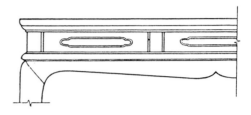

3.9 Detail of narrow rectangular table with corner legs, showing its high waist

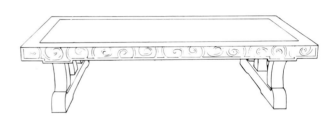

3.10 Table with base stretcher along the narrow sides, unearthed from a Warring States period tomb at Xinyang, Henan Province

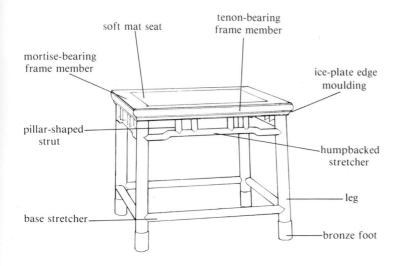

4.1 Waistless square stool with base stretchers

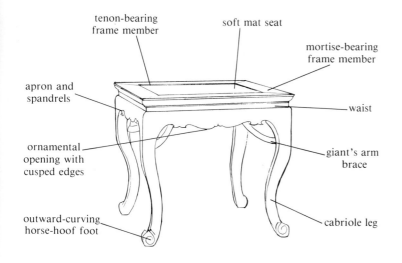

4.2 Waisted square stool with cabriole legs and giant's arm braces

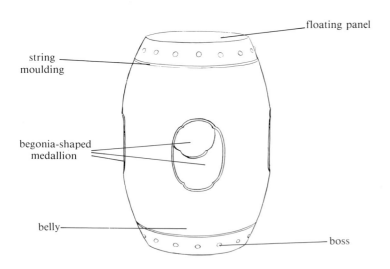

4.3 Drum stool with four openings

IV The Types and Forms of Furniture

The types of Ming and early Qing furniture, although less numerous than those since the mid Qing dynasty, comprise quite a full range compared to that found in the Song and Yuan dynasties. Furniture can be classified according to its function into four groups: stools and chairs; tables; beds; shelves and cabinets. A fifth group comprises a relatively small number of miscellaneous pieces.

It is of course impossible to include every kind of furniture, but I have endeavoured to be as comprehensive as possible. The pieces are arranged according to their forms, usually starting with the basic form and proceeding to its variants. However, the simplest forms of different types are often identical. Thus, to avoid monotony and to include more unusual examples, I have sometimes left out the basic form. Accompanying the descriptions of some types are drawings in which the component parts of the furniture are labelled. A reader who refers to these while reading the text will gain a certain familiarity with the cabinetmaker's technical terminology.

A. Stools and chairs

This group includes: (1) square, rectangular and round stools; (2) drum stools; (3) folding stools; (4) benches; (5) chairs; and (6) thrones.

(1) Square, rectangular, and round stools (*wudeng* 杌櫈)

The original meaning of the character *wu* is a tree without branches.[1] Therefore *wudeng* means a backless seat, or a stool. It is a term used in north China.

The basic forms of waistless stool have straight legs and stretchers. They may be square or rectangular and vary greatly in dimensions (Pls 9, 10 and 11). Many variations of spandrels occur, including plain ones and those carved with cloud-like motifs. When there is no apron, short pillar-shaped struts may be added (Pl. 12). Besides straight stretchers there are humpbacked stretchers. The ends of the stretchers are joined to the legs by a double mitre (Pl. 14), or they may go around the outside of the legs as if wrapped around them (Pls 12 and 13), a construction which simulates bamboo furniture. Some waistless stools have base stretchers (Fig. 4.1 and Pl. 14).

The basic form of the waisted stool has straight legs terminating in inward-curving horse-hoof feet, with either straight or humpbacked stretchers (Pl. 15). Stools with crossed stretchers (Pl. 16) can only be considered a variation of this simple form. Besides straight legs there are cabriole, or almost S-shaped legs (Fig. 4.2 and Pls 17, 18 and 19). The outward curve of the apron and leg can end in an inward-curving horse-hoof foot (Pls 20 and 21). Base stretchers may be found on waisted stools (Pl. 23). Sometimes the legs stand on a continuous floor stretcher with separate small feet (Pl. 24).

Round stools are comparatively rare and in this book there are only two examples (Pls 25 and 26), one of which (Pl. 26) bears a strong resemblance to the drum stool.

(2) Drum stools (*zuodun* 坐墩)

The drum stool is also called an embroidery stool *(xiudun* 繡墩) because many have on them a square piece of embroidery weighted with coins at the corners. Most Ming and early

Qing drum stools still bear vestiges of rattan stools and wooden drums. The openings in the sides are derived from the circular openings in rattan stools. The string mouldings and round bosses are reminiscent of the hide and the nails by which the hide was attached on drums (Fig. 4.3 and Pls 27 and 28). The example with vertical rods (Pl. 29) no longer shows any evidence of its derivation from a rattan stool, and by mid Qing times there is no hint of the drum.

(3) Folding stools (*jiaowu* 交杌)

Folding stools, commonly known as *mazha* 馬閘, are direct descendants of the ancient cross-legged stool called a barbarian seat (*huchuang* 胡牀). The folding stool was imported from the Western Region in the Eastern Han period (AD 25-220) and has been widely used in China for more than a thousand years. Its basic form, consisting of eight straight pieces of wood, has barely changed through the ages. Although such an example as that illustrated in Plate 30 dates from the Qing dynasty, it is almost exactly the same as the one depicted in the painting "Collating the Texts 北齊校書圖" in the Museum of Fine Arts, Boston,[2] which is generally considered to be a Northern Song copy of a Tang painting. A folding stool of unquestionable Ming date (Pl. 31) is more elaborate and has a removable footrest. Another folding stool has a frame seat which is folded by being pulled upwards (Pl. 32), hence it is called an upward-folding type.

(4) Benches (*changdeng* 長橙)

There were many forms of bench in Ming and early Qing times. Here only three examples will be considered: one small bench with recessed legs (Pl. 33), and two examples of two-seater benches with corner legs (Pls 34 and 35, and Fig. 4.4). The small recessed-leg bench was used by country people and is similar to the miniature furniture excavated from the 1589 tomb of Pan Yunzheng 潘允徵.[3] The two-seater benches (*errendeng* 二人橙) are called spring benches (*chundeng* 春橙) in the south.

(5) Chairs (*yi* 椅)

Ming and early Qing chairs may be divided into four types: side chairs (*kaobeiyi* 靠背椅); armchairs (*fushouyi* 扶手椅); armchairs with curved rests (*quanyi* 圈椅); and folding chairs (*jiaoyi* 交椅). All chairs with a back but no arms are called side chairs. One kind, of which there are quite a few Ming and early Qing examples, is also known as a lamp-hanger chair (*dengguayi* 燈掛椅) because of the resemblance of its rather high, narrow back to the hanger of a bamboo lamp hanger (Fig. 4.5). In this book a large (Pl. 37) and a small example (Pl. 36) are included. There are also two examples of other types of side chairs. One is quite simple in form but rather late in date (Pl. 39); the other is much more elaborate in design but earlier in date (Pl. 40). The question of whether the latter is a piece that has been reworked is still unresolved.

All chairs with a back and armrest, except for the armchair with curved rest and the folding chair, are known as armchairs. There are three main forms. One is quite low, with back and armrests at right angles to the seat (Pls 41, 42 and 43 and Fig. 4.6). In north China this form is called a rose chair (*meiguiyi* 玫瑰椅); the reason for the name is obscure. In the south it is called a writing chair (*wenyi* 文椅) because the literati liked to use it for that purpose. Since it is a rather light, easily portable chair with a back which does not obstruct one's vision, it can be put anywhere in a room. Its disadvantage is that the top rail is across the user's back so

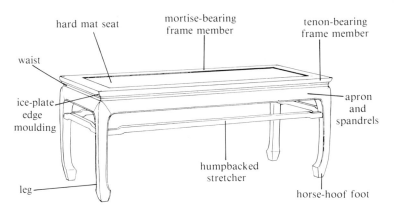

4.4 Waisted two-seater bench with humpbacked stretchers

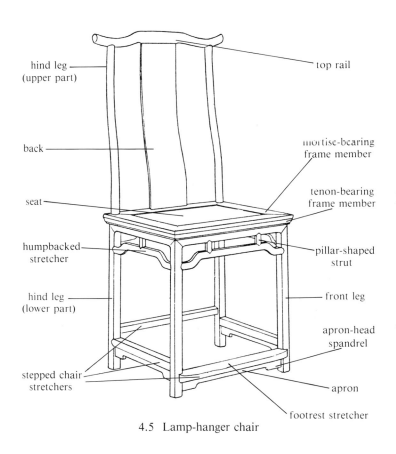

4.5 Lamp-hanger chair

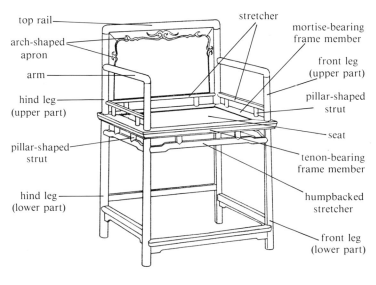

4.6 Rose chair

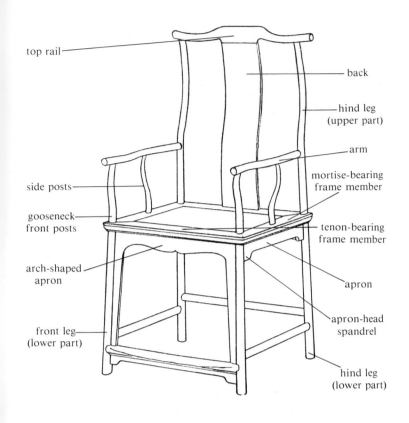

top rail

back

hind leg
(upper part)

arm

mortise-bearing
frame member

side posts

gooseneck
front posts

tenon-bearing
frame member

arch-shaped
apron

apron

apron-head
spandrel

front leg
(lower part)

hind leg
(lower part)

4.7 Official's hat armchair with four protruding ends

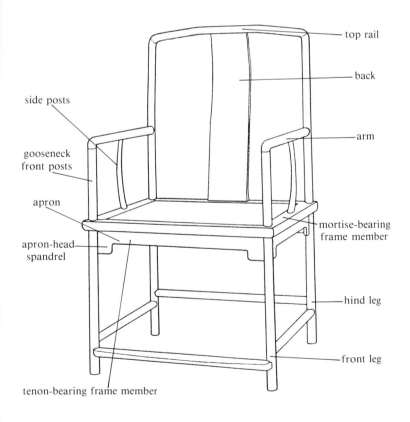

top rail

back

side posts

arm

gooseneck
front posts

apron

mortise-bearing
frame member

apron-head
spandrel

hind leg

front leg

tenon-bearing frame member

4.8 Southern official's hat armchair

that the chair is only suitable for use while writing and is not comfortable for resting.

If the top rail and arms both have protruding ends the chair is called an official's hat armchair (*guanmaoyi* 官帽椅) or an official's hat armchair with four protruding ends (*sichutou guanmaoyi* 四出頭官帽椅) (Fig. 4.7). If the top rail and arms do not protrude, it is called a southern official's hat armchair (*nanguanmaoyi* 南官帽椅) (Fig. 4.8). These names have been used by craftsmen for many years.

We have three examples of the official's hat armchair with four protruding ends (Pls 44, 45 and 46). They are of the same basic form, but vary in the size of their members, the degree of their curvature, and in whether they are decorated or undecorated. Of the six examples of the southern official's hat armchair only one, that with the relief carving of a hornless dragon on its splat (Pl. 48), is close to the basic form. The others — a low-backed one resembling a rose chair (Pl. 47), one similar to an armchair with curved rest (Pl. 49), one with a fan-shaped seat and with peony blossom carved on the splat (Pl. 50), one about only half the height of an ordinary chair (Pl. 52), and one with a hexagonal seat (Pl. 53) — are all rather special and some are unique.

The name for an armchair with curved rest (Fig. 4.9), *quan-yi* 圈椅 , appears in the Qing Regulations[4] and is commonly used by Beijing cabinetmakers. In Ming times this type of chair was simply known as a *yuanyi* 圓椅 , literally round chair.[5] Westerners have given it the name horseshoe armchair. The back of the chair flows down to form the arms in a smooth and graceful curve. This type of chair is very comfortable since the user's upper arm as well as the elbow is supported. The example with a low-relief medallion on the splat (Pl. 54) represents the basic form. Another example, with exceptionally fine decoration in the form of openwork carving of a *qilin* on the splat (Pl. 55), is an outstanding piece of Ming furniture. The waisted example with a continuous floor stretcher and ornate decoration (Pl. 56) is believed to be an early 18th-century imperial piece.

When a back is added to a folding stool it becomes a folding chair. There are two kinds: one with a straight back and one with a curved back. The former resembles a lamp-hanger chair and the latter (Fig. 4.10) is similar to the armchair with curved rest; in Song times it was called a basket back (*kaolaoyang* 栲栳樣).[6] Most have metal reinforcements at the joints which are both functional and very decorative. In this book there are two examples of the folding armchair with curved rest (Pls 57 and 58) which are of similar form but different date.

(6) Thrones (*baozuo* 寶座)

Thrones were made only for the emperor and are elaborate versions of large chairs intended to show his superiority. In the Palace Museum there are many thrones but as far as we know only one, that carved with lotus motifs (Pl. 59), is datable to the Ming dynasty.

Most thrones had a matching footstool. One such footstool, with mother-of-pearl inlay, made in the early Qing dynasty (Pl. 60) has long been separated from its throne; it is only logical to append it here.

B. Tables

There are seven types of table: (1) wide *kang* tables (*kangzhuo* 炕桌), narrow *kang* tables (*kangji* 炕几), and narrow *kang* tables with recessed legs (*kang'an* 炕案); (2) incense stands

(*xiangji* 香几); (3) wine tables (*jiuzhuo* 酒桌) and half tables (*banzhuo* 半桌); (4) square tables (*fangzhuo* 方桌); (5) waistless narrow rectangular tables (*tiaoji* 條几), narrow rectangular tables with corner legs (*tiaozhuo* 條桌), and narrow rectangular tables with recessed legs (*tiaoan* 條案); (6) painting tables with corner legs (*huazhuo* 畫桌), painting tables with recessed legs (*huaan* 畫案), wide writing tables with drawers and corner legs (*shuzhuo* 書桌), and writing tables with drawers and recessed legs (*shu'an* 書案); and (7) others.

(1) Wide *kang* tables, narrow *kang* tables and narrow *kang* tables with recessed legs

A feature of houses in north China is the *kang*, a chair-level bed which is also used for daytime sitting. Built-in against the wall, *kang* are hollow and made of wood, bricks, or, in poorer households, unbaked clay with a brick top. Brick and clay *kang* can be heated from within. If a *kang* is made of wood, as for example in the palace, the floor of the entire room would be specially made of brick and heated from underneath. *Kang* have their own low furniture consisting of tables, cupboards and shelves.

There are three kinds of *kang* table. The wide *kang* table, the ratio of whose length to width is about three to two, is most often placed in the middle of a *kang* or bed. Narrow *kang* tables and narrow *kang* tables with recessed legs are much narrower and tend to be used on the two sides of the *kang*. Narrow tables, made of three pieces of wood joined together at right angles or with corner legs, are called narrow *kang* tables.

The basic form of the wide *kang* table has straight legs and straight or humpbacked stretchers. The waisted form has straight legs with horse-hoof feet and straight or humpbacked stretchers. Since exactly the same forms are found in stools (Pls 9 and 15) it is not necessary to show examples. Among the illustrated *kang* tables there is one very special waistless table which is square rather than rectangular, with a floating panel inserted into grooves under the water-stopping moulding (Pl. 61).

Unusual waisted examples include: a table with an openwork apron (Pl. 62); a table with unmitred joint of apron and leg (*qiyatiao* 齊牙條) (Pl. 63); a table with an extremely exaggerated curve to its apron and legs (*gutuipengya* 鼓腿彭牙) and very large horse-hoof feet (Pl. 64 and Fig. 4.11); a table with a unique form of cabriole leg (*sanwantui* 三彎腿) (Pl. 65); and an elaborately decorated high-waisted example (*gaosuoyao* 高束腰) (Pl. 66).

We illustrate two typical narrow *kang* tables. The black lacquer piece consists of three solid boards meeting each other at right angles (Pl. 67). The other is a *zitan* wood corner-leg example (Pl. 68).

Our first example of a narrow *kang* table with recessed legs (Pl. 69) has a very basic form, which is also found on long benches and narrow rectangular tables with recessed legs. On a narrow *kang* table with recessed legs and everted flanges, the apron-head spandrels are not very pronounced but the manner in which the legs curve outwards gives it an individual character (Pl. 70). The narrow three-drawer *kang* table with recessed legs (Pl. 71) is fairly large and could only have been placed on a sizeable *kang*; it was thus probably used in an official building.

(2) Incense stands

Incense stands derive their name from their use as supports

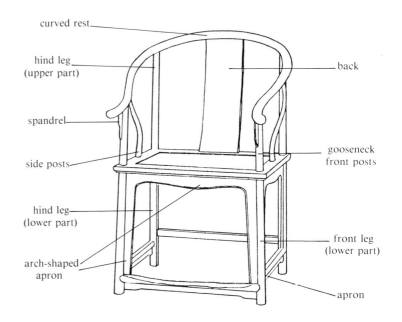

4.9 Armchair with curved rest

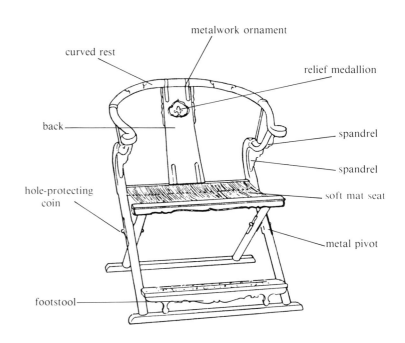

4.10 Folding chair with curved back

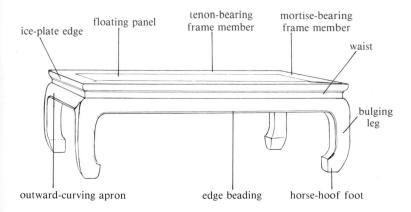

4.11 Waisted wide *kang* table with convex apron and bulging legs with horse-hoof feet

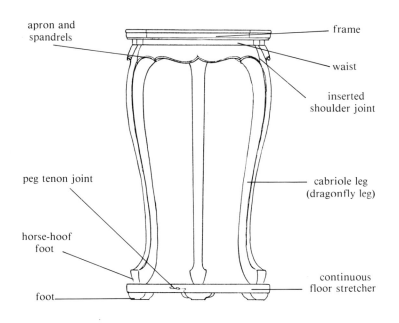

4.12 Round incense stand with three legs

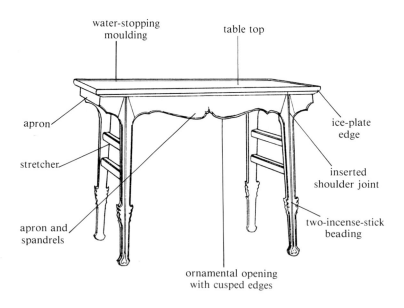

4.13 Wine table with inserted shoulder joints

for incense burners. Most furniture is square or rectangular, but incense stands, because of their function, tend to be round and have exaggeratedly curved legs. Irrespective of whether an incense stand is used indoors or outdoors, it is always placed away from walls and other furniture. It is intended to be seen from all sides and so a round form with beautiful flowing lines is more appropriate. From the beginning of the Qing dynasty, incense stands became less popular and tea tables, derived from square and rectangular incense stands, became prevalent.

We have three examples of round incense stands, the one with three legs (Pl. 72 and Fig. 4.12) being the most common type. Of the two five-legged round stands one is a very heavy piece and perhaps originally belonged to a temple (Pl. 73). The other example is round, smooth and shaped like a quince (Pl. 74). The four-legged piece has an octagonal top, a most ingenious shape (Pl. 75). The maker of the six-legged piece (Pl. 76) spared neither materials nor effort. The form of the stand may have been influenced by lacquered wood furniture from Song and Yuan times.

(3) Wine tables and half tables

Wine tables and half tables are two kinds of comparatively small rectangular table. Wine tables can be traced back to the Five Dynasties period and the Northern Song, when they were often used at social gatherings. On most, along the edge of the top there is a water-stopping moulding to prevent wine and food from spilling on to the user's clothes. It must be pointed out that although this type of table is undeniably of recessed-leg construction, it is for some inexplicable reason always called a corner-leg table by Beijing craftsmen. Half tables derive their name from the fact that they are half the size of an Eight Immortals table. They are also called extension tables (*jiezhuo* 接桌), as they are used to extend Eight Immortals tables that are not large enough for their intended use. The terms half table and extension table are both found in ancient texts[7] and are also used by Beijing cabinetmakers.

In this book there are four examples of wine table and they are constructed in two different ways. The first two examples (Pls 77 and 78) have elongated bridle joints (Fig. 5.6), with the surfaces of the legs protruding slightly from the aprons and apron-head spandrels. The other two examples (Pls 79 and 80) use the inserted shoulder joint (Figs 4.13 and 5.7) so the legs are flush with the aprons. Both large and small recessed-leg pieces are usually made according to one of these two methods.

We have four examples of half tables, including two examples each of the waistless and the waisted types. The two waisted pieces are exceedingly rare and although I have made enquiries among many craftsmen I have not discovered names for them. Thus I have created new names: the bracket-shaped table (*dougongshi* 斗拱式) (Pl. 83) and the low table with legs extended (*aizhuozhantuishi* 矮桌展腿式) (Pl. 84).

(4) Square tables

There are many extant square tables. They may be large, medium-sized or small, and are known as Eight Immortals tables (*baxianzhuo* 八仙桌), Six Immortals tables (*liuxianzhuo* 六仙桌) and Four Immortals tables (*sixianzhuo* 四仙桌). Among the five waistless examples selected for this book the one with humpbacked stretchers and ornamental struts (Pl. 85) is closest to the basic form.

Although those in Plates 86, 87 and 88 are of the same type, they are not identical. One of the standard Ming dynasty forms of square table is the type with three spandrels to one leg and a humpbacked stretcher (*yitui sanya luoguocheng* 一腿三牙羅鍋根) (Fig. 4.14). It is so named because each leg joins the apron-head spandrels of two long aprons as well as a corner spandrel, and there is a humpbacked stretcher below. The examples in Plates 86, 87 and 88 are variations of this type. The square table with an apron made by joining the straight (Pl. 89) is a form also found in narrow rectangular tables with corner legs and in painting tables. The two waisted square tables (Pls 90 and 91) are rather unusual pieces.

(5) Waistless narrow rectangular tables, narrow rectangular tables with corner legs, and narrow rectangular tables with recessed legs

There are three types of long narrow table. They vary a great deal in size but only the narrow rectangular tables with recessed legs, such as that in Plate 104, are more than 3 metres long. The reason for the length restriction is that, even though the top of such tables can be considerably longer, the space between the legs is always about 3 metres or less. All the weight of waistless narrow rectangular tables and narrow rectangular tables with corner legs is supported at the corners. Thus, if the length is more than 3 metres the top is likely to sag.

The waistless narrow rectangular table (Pl. 92 and Fig. 4.15) consists of three boards meeting at right angles, just like the narrow *kang* table discussed above (Pl. 67).

Five examples of the waistless narrow rectangular table with corner legs are illustrated here. The one with humpbacked stretcher and pillar-shaped struts (Pl. 93) is an example of the basic form of this type. Another resembles a waistless stool, except that the apron-head spandrels have more decoration (Pl. 94). An example of the type with three spandrels to one leg has hollow spandrels framed by rods (Pl. 96). The straight-form example with everted flanges, hidden drawers and giant's arm braces (Pl. 97) is very rare. The high-waisted example with cusped apron and carpenter's square legs (Pl. 99) still preserves traces of the ornamental openings with cusped upper edges that are found on box-construction beds.

Beijing craftsmen classify narrow rectangular tables with recessed legs into those with flat tops and those with everted flanges. They use either the elongated bridle joint or the inserted shoulder joint, any other type of construction being unusual.

Tables with elongated bridle joints exist in a variety of forms and can be subdivided in the following way: (a) those with four legs touching the ground and no stretchers (Pl. 100); (b) those with four legs touching the ground and base stretchers (Pl. 104); and (c) those with four legs not touching the ground and side floor stretchers (Pls 102 and 103). Often above the base or side floor stretchers there is a four-sided inner frame (Pls 103 and 104) or inset panel, which can have many variations (Pl. 102). All tables with inserted shoulder joints have four legs resting on the ground without base or side floor stretchers (Pl. 107). It is only in the decorations on the legs and their mouldings that there are many variations. There are several rare variant forms of the narrow rectangular table with recessed legs. One small flat-top narrow table with recessed legs has a shelf (Pl. 101). The tables in Plates 105 and 106 appear to have elongated bridle joints, but actually the apron tenons into the legs.

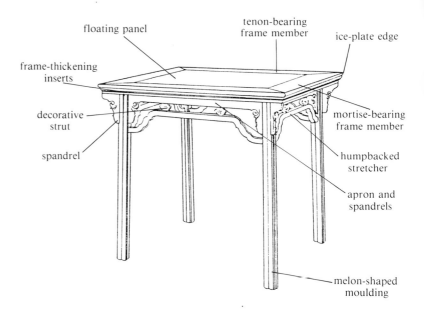

4.14 Square table with three spandrels to one leg and with humpbacked stretchers and decorative struts

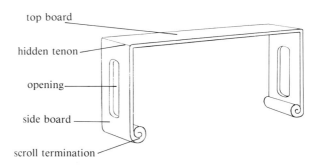

4.15 Narrow rectangular table with oval openings on the solid board legs

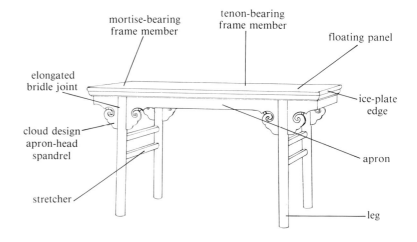

4.16 Painting table with recessed legs and elongated bridle joints

(6) Painting tables with corner legs, painting tables with recessed legs, wide writing tables with drawers and corner legs, and writing tables with drawers and recessed legs

There are four kinds of large table, the smallest of which is larger than the half table. In construction and form many are identical to narrow rectangular tables with corner legs and narrow rectangular tables with recessed legs, but they are wider. If these tables were narrower, they would not be convenient for the user to wield his brush while painting or doing calligraphy, or to open his books while reading, and could not be called painting or writing tables. Beijing craftsmen make a clear distinction between the four kinds of large table. Painting tables with corner legs and painting tables with recessed legs are designed so that the user can easily stand at them to paint and write; they therefore have no drawers. Their names indicate their different constructions. Tables with drawers are also named according to their construction: wide writing tables with drawers and corner legs, or writing tables with drawers and recessed legs.

The basic form of the waistless painting table with corner legs has humpbacked stretchers and pillar-shaped struts. The example in Plate 108 is rather extraordinary in that it has no pillar-shaped struts and an exceptionally large humpbacked stretcher. The table in Plate 109 is quite elaborately decorated with hornless dragons, but it is a simple straight-form piece. The waisted painting table with corner legs (Pl. 110), whose form is basically that of a narrow table, is almost completely covered with rounded relief carving; it has long been considered a unique piece.

Four of our five examples of painting table with recessed legs have elongated bridle joints. The one with cloud motif spandrels (Pl. 111 and Fig. 4.16) is another fairly common form. A most attractive piece has addorsed phoenixes on its spandrels (Pl. 112). Some have unusual designs on their inset side panels (Pl. 113). The smallest type of painting table (Pl. 114) is only slightly larger than a half table and has a high humpbacked stretcher and a rather antique air. In this book the only example of a painting table with recessed legs with inserted shoulder joints (Pl. 115) is made in such a way that it can be easily taken apart and put together again; it is so large and heavy that otherwise it would be very difficult to move. It is one of the most important pieces of *zitan* wood furniture.

Ming dynasty tables with drawers are very rare and here we have only one example (Pl. 116), a wider version of a trestle table.

(7) Others
There are many other kinds of table such as half-moon tables, fan-shaped tables, chess tables, lute tables, narrow tables with drawers, altar tables with corner legs, and altar tables with recessed legs. Since there are many kinds and many extant examples of each kind, here we can only illustrate a narrow table with drawers (Pl. 117), a lute table (Pl. 118) and an altar table with corner legs (Pl. 119).

C. Beds

There are three kinds of bed: (1) daybeds (*ta* 榻); (2) Luohan beds (*luohanchuang* 羅漢牀); and (3) canopy beds (*jiazichuang* 架子牀).

(1) Daybeds
Beds without railings are called daybeds by Beijing craftsmen. Both examples in this book are waisted (Pls 120 and 121). The folding one (Pl. 121) is very rare.

(2) Luohan beds
Beds with back and side railings are known as Luohan beds (Fig. 4.17). This term is not used in the south, nor can it be found in old texts. Stone balustrades, called Luohan railings (*luohan lan'gan* 羅漢欄杆), are often seen in Beijing gardens and even more commonly on bridges; these railings have no posts between the panels. Similarly, the railings of a Luohan bed, unlike those of a canopy bed, have no posts between the panels. Thus it is quite possible that the name Luohan bed was derived from the term Luohan railings.

The base of the Luohan bed can be made in different ways and may be waisted or waistless. It not only resembles a daybed but also has some similarities to *kang* tables and even rectangular stools. The railings of Luohan beds exist in many variations. When the railing is formed of three pieces the bed is called a three-panel screen bed (*sanpingfengshi* 三屏風式). When the railing is formed of five pieces, three on the back and one on each side, the bed is known as a five-panel screen bed (*wupingfengshi* 五屏風式). There are even some seven-

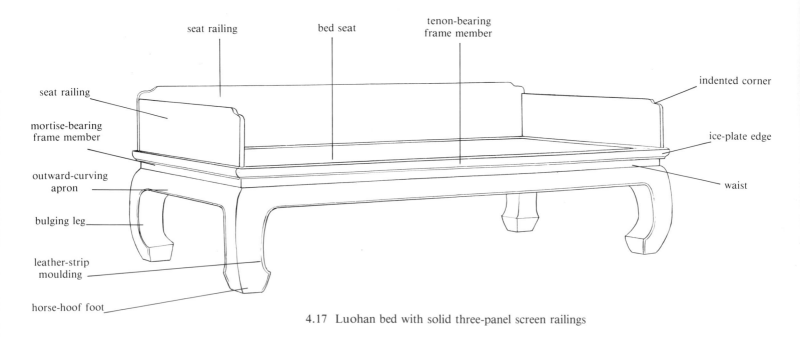

4.17 Luohan bed with solid three-panel screen railings

panel screen beds (*qipingfengshi* 七屏風式), with three on the back and two on each side. The railings can be constructed from a single board (Pl. 122), from frames with inset panels (Pl. 123), by joining the straight (Pl. 124), or by assembling the curved. The only variation not illustrated in this book is that made by assembling the curved. However, the decorative effect of this method can be easily imagined by looking at the doors of the cabinet in Plate 146 and the clothes rack in Plate 167. The bed in Plate 125 is a very rare example since it is waistless, has base stretchers, and struts are used to secure the ornamental panels.

(3) Canopy beds

Jiazichuang is a general term for canopy beds, which can be further divided into: (a) four-post canopy beds (*sizhuchuang* 四柱牀), with a post at each corner; and (b) six-post canopy beds (*liuzhuchuang* 六柱牀), with two additional posts in front. Since the front posts are used to support the front railings, this bed is also called a canopy bed with front railings (*menweizi jiazichuang* 門圍子架子牀) (Fig. 4.18). Very large beds stand on platforms and some have a narrow alcove in front, in which case they are called alcove bedsteads (*babuchuang* 拔步牀). In this book there is only one example of a canopy bed with six posts (Pl. 126) and one of a canopy bed with full-moon opening (Pl. 128).

Footstools were usually placed in front of Ming dynasty beds. In front of Luohan beds a pair of short footstools was used, while with a canopy or alcove bedstead single rather long and narrow footstools were preferred. Almost all the footstools have long since been separated from their beds. One of these (Pl. 129) has been selected to complete the section on beds.

D. Shelves and cabinets

There are four kinds of shelves and cabinets: (1) shelves (*jiage* 架格); (2) display cabinets (*lianggegui* 亮格櫃); (3) round-corner cabinets (*yuanjiaogui* 圓角櫃); and (4) square-corner cabinets (*fangjiaogui* 方角櫃).

(1) Shelves

Shelves are also called bookshelves (*shuge* 書格 or *shujia* 書架). However, since they are not necessarily used to hold books, it would be better to refer to them simply as shelves.

The basic form has four legs and open shelves without ornamental openings or drawers. The three-tiered shelf open on four sides with two drawers (Pl. 130) is close to the basic form. In order to decorate the shelves, ornamental railings are frequently added to the back and sides (Pl. 131). The back may consist of a board or occasionally be left open. Sometimes a four-sided inner frame or arch-shaped inner frame may be added on the back and sides, or just the sides (Fig. 4.19). Although in this book there is no example of a shelf with solid back and three-sided inner frames, the type may be envisaged by looking at the open shelf in the Wanli display cabinets (Pls 136 and 137). Some shelves have a latticed back (Pl. 132), and others have lattice on three sides

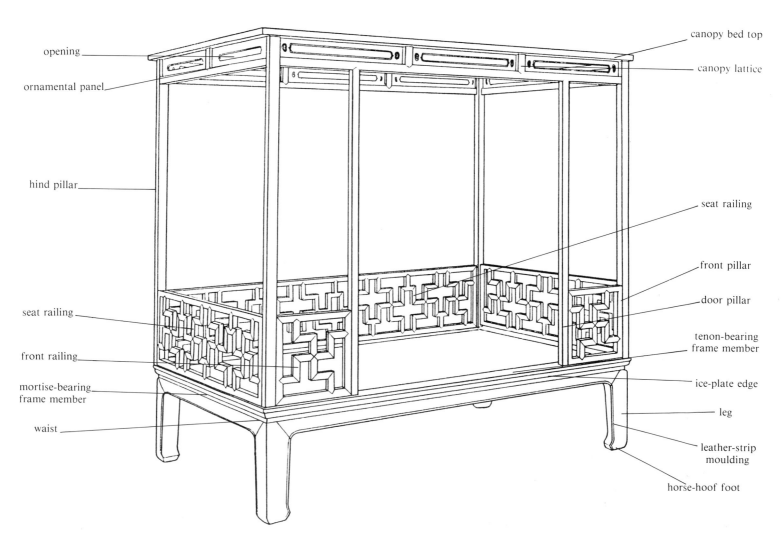

4.18 Canopy bed with front railings

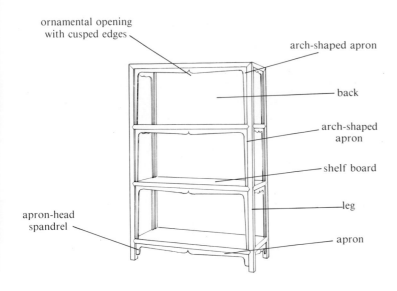

ornamental opening
with cusped edges

arch-shaped apron

back

arch-shaped
apron

shelf board

leg

apron-head
spandrel

apron

4.19 Three-tiered shelf

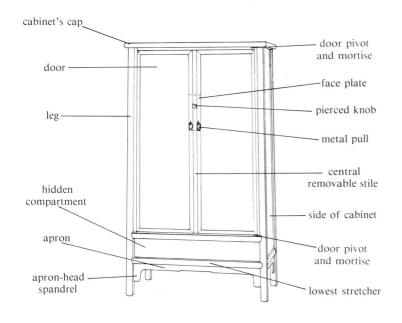

cabinet's cap

door

leg

hidden
compartment

apron

apron-head
spandrel

door pivot
and mortise

face plate

pierced knob

metal pull

central
removable stile

side of cabinet

door pivot
and mortise

lowest stretcher

4.20 Round-corner cabinet

(Pl. 133). When there is lattice on four sides, or on three sides with a solid back, the shelves serve as a food cupboard. In Beijing the colloquial term for such a cupboard is *qisimao* 氣死猫 (vexing the cat). Food cupboards are everyday kitchen cabinets which are usually made of unfinished wood, but there are also de luxe models which are used for treasured books and antiques.

(2) Display cabinets

The display cabinet is a combination of shelves and a cabinet. In most Ming dynasty display cabinets the shelf is above the cabinet, so that the piece functions as both a display and a storage cabinet.

Display cabinets have a standard form which consists of a cupboard with open shelf above resting on a separate low stand. The form has a special name, Wanli display cabinet (Wanli *gui* 萬曆櫃), whose connection with the Wanli reign is obscure. We have no alternative but to adopt this name commonly used by Beijing craftsmen. The two examples illustrated here are quite different in the way they are decorated, one being fairly simple (Pl. 136), the other elaborately decorated (Pl.137). The example in Plate 138 evolved from the basic form of the Wanli cabinet: it has two open shelves, the space above each shelf being rather limited, so that for display purposes it is not as convenient as the cabinet with a single shelf. This may be the reason why so few examples of this type have been passed down through the ages.

(3) Round-corner cabinets

For some inexplicable reason round-corner cabinets are also called noodles cabinets (*miantiaogui* 面條櫃). The top of this type of cabinet, which protrudes slightly on three sides, is called the cabinet's cap (*guimao* 櫃帽) and usually has rounded corners. The reason why the top protrudes is so that there is enough space for the door pivot mortises. Therefore round-corner cabinets are also known as wood-hinged door cabinets (*muzhumengui* 木軸門櫃). All round-corner cabinets have a clear splay, and when placed together with waistless furniture, which is similarly splayed, the effect is most pleasing. Small round-corner cabinets which are less than one metre high and placed on the *kang* are called *kang* cabinets (*kanggui* 炕櫃) (Pl. 139). Large ones are about the same size as bookshelves (Fig. 4.20) and there are a few even larger examples.

Round-corner cabinets without a central removable stile are called *yingjimen* 硬擠門 . Some have a central stile (Pls 139, 141, 142 and 143) and when a lock is added it is secured with the doors. The doors of the small round-corner cabinet (Pl. 139) extend right to the base stretchers without any hidden compartment. When there is a hidden compartment it is placed under the doors (Pls 142 and 143), thus providing additional interior space. A door may be made from one piece of wood or divided into sections and named according to the number of horizontals, or mortise-bearing frame members. For instance, a door made in four segments requires five mortise-bearing frame members and can be called a door with five horizontal members (*wumomen* 五抹門) (Pl. 143).

(4) Square-corner cabinets

Square-corner cabinets have no splay and may or may not (Pl. 146) have a central removable stile. Those with no upper part are called square-corner cabinets (Pls 145 and 147). If there is an upper part they are known as compound wardrobes in four parts (*dingxiang ligui* 頂箱立櫃 or *sijiangui*

四件櫃), because a pair consists of four pieces (Fig. 4.21). This kind of cabinet varies greatly in size. Small ones (Pl. 148) can be placed on a *kang*; large ones may be 3 or 4 metres high, and if placed in a large hall will reach the rafters.

E. Miscellaneous

All types of furniture which do not belong under any of the preceding four headings are placed here. They comprise many different categories, most of which are illustrated in the plates. Miscellaneous pieces include: (1) screens (*pingfeng* 屏風); (2) coffers (*menhuchu* 悶戶櫥); (3) chests (*xiang* 箱); (4) picnic boxes (*tihe* 提盒); (5) desk trays (*duchengpan* 都承盤); (6) mirror platforms (*jingtai* 鏡台) and dressing cases (*guanpixiang* 官皮箱); (7) clothes racks (*yijia* 衣架); (8) washbasin stands (*mianpenjia* 面盆架); (9) roller stools (*gundeng* 滾櫈); (10) sugar-canc squeezers (*ganzhechuang* 甘蔗牀); and (11) miniature furniture.

(1) Screens
Pingfeng 屏風 is the general term for all kinds of screen, including folding screens made from many panels which can be arranged in different configurations (*weiping* 圍屏) and those set in a stand (*zuopingfeng* 座屏風). In addition, there is a small screen (Fig. 4.22) derived from Song dynasty pillow screens (*zhenping* 枕屏) and inkstone screens (*yanping* 硯屏). By Ming and Qing times such small screens had become mere decorations placed on long tables in main halls.

Most of the extant folding screens are made by what *Xiushilu* (*A Record of Lacquer Art*) calls the *kuancai* 款彩 technique,[8] that is, the design is engraved on the surface of the screen and then filled in with colours. Lacquer having such decoration was known in the West first as Bantam work, then as Coromandel lacquer.[9] I know of no extant examples of hardwood folding screens that are datable to earlier than the mid Qing dynasty.

Screens set in stands may have one, three or five panels. Such pieces were not used in ordinary households and it is possible that examples may in future be found in temples. In single-panel screens set in a stand, the panel may be fixed on to the base or be removable. Among the many examples of screens set in a stand in the Palace Museum, only one pair, decorated with openwork carving of hornless dragons (Pl. 150), is Ming in style. We illustrate two examples of small screens, one with a fixed panel (Pl. 151) and the other with a removable panel (Pl. 152). After the Qianlong period large mirrors replaced single-panel screens.

(2) Coffers
The coffer has a closed or hidden compartment beneath the drawers, hence its name *menhuchu* 悶戶櫥, closed-compartment cupboard. Its interior can be used for storage while objects can be placed on top of it. Beijing craftsmen use *menhuchu* as a general term for this kind of furniture regardless of whether the coffer has one, two or three drawers. However, since those with two drawers are also

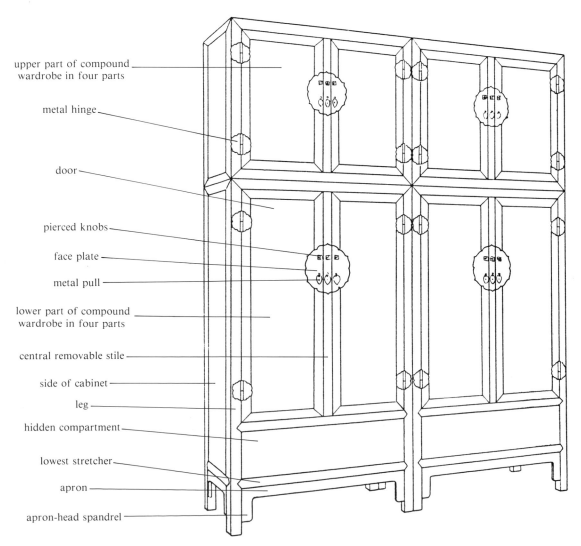

upper part of compound wardrobe in four parts

metal hinge

door

pierced knobs

face plate

metal pull

lower part of compound wardrobe in four parts

central removable stile

side of cabinet

leg

hidden compartment

lowest stretcher

apron

apron-head spandrel

4.21 Compound wardrobe in four parts

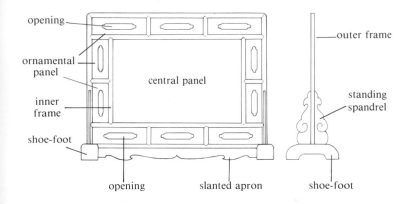

4.22 Small screen set in a stand

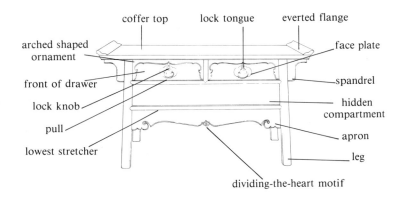

4.23 Two-drawer coffer

called two-drawer coffers (*lianerchu* 聯二櫥) and those with three drawers, three-drawer coffers (*liansanchu* 聯三櫥), the term *menhuchu* is most often used for one-drawer coffers. Most one-drawer coffers are not very long and when placed between the two halves of a compound wardrobe in four parts, the entire wall of the bedroom is filled; for this reason the one-drawer coffer is also known as the plug between two cabinets (*guisai* 櫃塞). Moreover, when a daughter is about to be married, various items of her trousseau are tied with red strings to the top of a coffer; for this reason it is commonly referred to as a trousseau coffer (*jiadi* 嫁底). Coffers are thus a type of furniture used in ordinary households and usually placed in bedrooms to store jewellery and clothing. In this book there are four coffers (Pls 153, 154, 155 and 156) illustrating the one-drawer, two-drawer (Fig. 4.23) and three-drawer versions, as well as various kinds of style ranging from plain to decorated.

(3) Chests

The Ming dictionary *Zheng zi tong* 正字通 (*Dictionary of Correct Characters*) defines a chest in this way: "All furniture with a bottom and lid that can be used for storage is called a chest". In *Lu Ban jing jiangjia jing* 魯班經匠家鏡 (*Lu Ban's Classic, a Mirror for Craftsmen*) chests with many drawers which can be used for herbs and prepared medicines are called medicine chests (*yaoxiang* 藥箱).[10] There are many types of Ming-style chest, but here we show only three examples: the small chest (Pl. 157) and the medicine chests (Pls 158 and 159). Small chests are used for money, precious objects and documents.

The two examples of medicine chest both have doors in front of the drawers, and thus are more complicated than the examples mentioned in *Lu Ban jing jiangjia jing*. This is because *Lu Ban jing* records the furniture of the common people which is of course different from hardwood furniture in quality and in the degree of refinement.

(4) Picnic boxes

Picnic boxes are divided into tiers and have a handle. There are large, medium-sized and small examples. The large ones are carried on a pole by two people. Two medium-sized ones can be carried on a pole by one person. Picnic boxes are called by different names in *Lu Ban jing jiangjia jing*: large picnic boxes are called *dafang gangxiang* 大方杠箱 , literally, large square boxes carried on a pole; medium-sized picnic boxes are called *shige* 食格 , literally, food boxes.[11] Small picnic boxes that can be carried in one hand are called *tihe* 提盒 , literally, hand-carried boxes (Pl. 160). The Ming dynasty author Tu Long in his *You ju jian* (*Notes on Equipment for Excursions*) also discusses hand-carried boxes, or small picnic boxes.[12] Designed by scholars, these differ somewhat from picnic boxes sold in shops, but basically they are the same type of container.

(5) Desk trays

There are several ways of writing the name for desk tray: *duchengpan* 都承盤 , *duchengpan* 都丞盤 , *dushengpan* 都盛盤 , and *duzhenpan* 都珍盤 . All these terms refer to a tray that can hold the various implements and articles found on a scholar's desk (Pl. 161). Such trays were more popular in the Qing than in the Ming dynasty, and after the Qianlong period their forms and decorative schemes became increasingly ornate.

(6) Mirror platforms and dressing cases

There are three kinds of Ming and early Qing mirror platform. The folding mirror platform (*zhedieshi jingtai* 折叠式鏡台) (Pl. 162), commonly called the collapsible mirror platform (*paizishi jingtai* 拍子式鏡台), is derived from the mirror stands (*jingjia* 鏡架) prevalent in Song times, as may be seen in the painting "Lady at her Dressing Table 靚妝仕女圖 ".[13] The throne-type mirror platform (*baozuoshi jingtai* 寶座式鏡台) (Pl. 163) evolved from the Song armchair, such as the one depicted in the Song dynasty painting "Enjoying Autumn in the Banxian Hall 半閑秋興圖 ",[14] to which drawers were added. The five-panel screen-type mirror platform *wupingfengshi jingtai* 五屏風式鏡台 (Pl. 164), is a form which came into vogue later than the other types, and extant examples are more numerous. It is illustrated in *Lu Ban jing jiangjia jing*.

Within this category there is a piece of furniture consisting of a base with drawers and a top in the form of a lidded tray, called a *guanpixiang* 官皮箱 (Pl. 165). The name, which means literally official's leather chest, suggests that it was used in official quarters, but as yet we cannot ascertain its exact function. However, since there are so many extant examples, it seems likely that such pieces were used in homes. Moreover, most of them are decorated with auspicious designs and so do not look like official pieces. The form, with a tray and drawers, would be most convenient for a mirror and toilet articles. Its antecedent is a mirror box (*jingxiang* 鏡箱) excavated from a Southern Song tomb at Changzhou 常州 (Figs 4.24a and b). Moreover, it resembles a mirror box mentioned in *Lu Ban jing jiangjia jing*, and it seems reasonable to suggest that the *guanpixiang* is a mirror box and thus has the same function as the mirror platform. We might call it a dressing case in English.

(7) Clothes racks

Clothes racks, over which garments are placed, are usually found at the end of a bed. *Lu Ban jing jiangjia jing* mentions plain ones and those with carved decoration.[15] A comparison of the miniature pieces excavated from Ming tombs with extant examples reveals the great difference between the two types. Both examples illustrated here (Pls 166 and 167) are elaborately carved and can be regarded as typical Ming pieces.

(8) Washbasin stands

Washbasin stands may be low (*aimianpenjia* 矮面盆架) or high with a towel rack (*gaomianpenjia* 高面盆架). The low ones have three, four or six legs. Some of the four-legged and six-legged (Pl. 168) forms can be folded. Most washbasin stands with towel racks have six legs (Fig. 4.25) while some have four legs, and as a rule they cannot be folded. Our three examples (Pls 169, 170 and 171) illustrate the different ways in which washbasin stands may be decorated.

(9) Roller stools

Roller stools (*gundeng* 滾櫈) (Pl. 172) resemble footstools but are in fact a type of medical apparatus. The Ming dynasty author Gao Lian in *Zun sheng ba jian* (*Eight Volumes on Nourishing Life*) writes:

Take a footstool of ordinary height, two feet long and six inches wide. Make a top with a frame divided down the centre with a roller on each side. On the round rollers make pivots at each end fitting into holes in the stool. Then you can roll them with your feet, rubbing the gushing spring (*yong quan*

4.24a Mirror box (with cover missing) from a Southern Song tomb in Changzhou, Jiangsu Province

4.24b Mirror box with mirror support in place

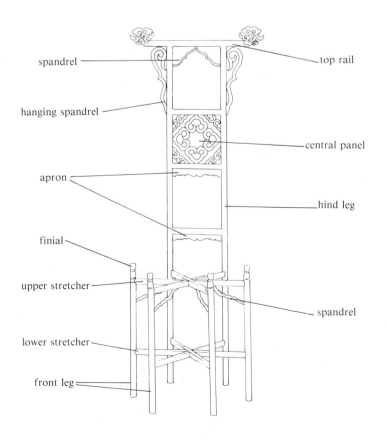

4.25 Washbasin stand with towel rack

湧泉) acupuncture point. Since you can rub them all day it will be most convenient.[16]

In Ming dynasty woodblock illustrations, we can see that roller stools are placed under the table in front of a chair[17] and are not used in the same way as ordinary footstools which are placed in front of beds.

(10) Sugar-cane squeezers

The sugar-cane squeezer (*ganzhechuang* 甘蔗牀) is a small utensil used to squeeze the juice out of sugar-canes (Pl. 173). It is popular in south China.

(11) Miniature furniture

Miniature furniture consists of miniature replicas of larger pieces. The miniature *zitan* wood long table with everted flanges (Pl. 175) can be used for decoration on a long table. The small bench (Pl. 174) can be used as a plaything and if a padded cotton cushion is placed on top and tied to the four legs, it can serve as a pillow. Thus it is also known as a bench-shaped pillow (*zhendeng* 枕櫈). Chinese doctors support a patient's wrist on it while feeling his pulse.

Notes

1. Chen Pengnian 陳彭年 (revised by, Song), *Yu pian* 玉篇 (*The Jade Book*, a lexicon) (privately published in 1850 by the Deng 鄧 family after the Song edition), *juan* 12, Mu bu 木部 , 157.
2. Tomita Kojiro, *Portfolio of Chinese Paintings in the Museum of Fine Arts, Boston* (*Han to Sung Periods*) (Cambridge, Mass.: Harvard University Press, 1938), plate 47.
3. Shanghaishi Wenwu Baoguan Weiyuanhui 上海市文物保管委員會 (CPAM, the City of Shanghai), ''Shanghaishi Luwan Qu Ming Pan Shi mu fajue baogao 上海市盧灣區明潘氏墓發掘報告 '' (''Report on the Excavation of the Ming Dynasty Tomb of the Pan Family in the Luwan District, Shanghai''), *Kaogu*, 1961:8, pp. 425-34.
4. Bao Liang 保亮 *et al.* (Qing), *Gongbu xuzeng zuofa zeli* 工部續增做法則例 (*Additional Manufacturing Regulations for the Ministry of Works*) (Beijing: Ministry of Works, 1819), *juan* 81, p. 7.
5. Wang Siyi 王思義 (Ming), *San cai tu hui* 三才圖會 (*Pictorial Encyclopaedia of Heaven, Earth and Man*) (Ming edition), Qiyong 器用 , Zaqi lei 雜器類 , p. 146.
6. ''Today's folding chairs are the barbarian seats of ancient times. There is only the basket-back type.'' Zhang Duanyi 張端義 (Song), *Gui er ji* 貴耳集 (*Precious Ear Collection*) (Congshu-jicheng chubian edition), Wenxue lei 文學類 , p. 64.
7. The term *banzhuo* 半桌 (half table) appears in Bao Liang, *op. cit.*, *juan* 81, p. 1. The term *jiezhuo* 接桌 (extension table) is found in He Shijin 何士晉 (compiler, Ming), *Gongbu changku xuzhi* 工部廠庫須知 (*What One Ought to Know about the Workshops and Storehouses of the Ministry of Works*) (Xuanlantang congshu xubian 玄覽堂叢書續編 , 1947 edition), p. 13.
8. See Wang Shixiang, *Xiushilu jieshuo* 髹飾錄解說 (*Commentary on A Record of Lacquer Art* by Huang Cheng 黃成 , preface 1625) (Beijing: Wenwu Press, 1983), item 129.
9. The former was named after the Dutch East India Company's port in Java, the latter after the port on the southeast coast of India, through which the screens passed on their way to Europe.
10. See Wang Shixiang 王世襄 , ''*Lu Ban jing jiangjia jing* jiaju tiaokuan chushi 魯班經匠家鏡家具條款初釋 '' (''Preliminary Explanatory Notes on the Furniture Entries in *Lu Ban's Classic, A Mirror for Craftsmen*''), *Gugong Bowuyuan yuankan* 故宮博物院院刊 , 1981:1, p.87.
11. *Ibid.*, p. 83.
12. Tu Long 屠龍 (Ming), *You ju jian* 遊具箋 (*Notes on Equipment for Excursions)* (Meishu congshu edition, Part II, Section 9), p. 36.
13. Tomita, *op. cit.*, plate 74.
14. See *Tianlaige jiu cang Songren huace* 天籟閣舊藏宋人畫册 (*Album of Song Paintings Formerly in the Tianlaige Collection*) (n.p., n.d.), no. 11.
15. Wang Shixiang, *op. cit.*, p. 78.
16. Gao Lian 高濂 (Ming), *Zun sheng ba jian* 遵生八箋 (*Eight Volumes on Nourishing Life*) (Qing woodblock edition), Qiju anle jian 起居安樂箋 , pp. 15-16.
17. Yang Dingjian 楊定見 (editor, Ming), *Zhongyi shuihu quanzhuan* 忠義水滸全傳 (*The Complete Story of the Loyal Heroes of the Water Margin*) (Ming edition), Fig. 56.

V The Precision and Ingenuity of Joinery

The art of joinery in classic Chinese furniture reached its climax in the Ming and early Qing period. This achievement was the combination of the tradition of fine carpentry transmitted from Song times and the Ming knowledge of hardwoods. Since hardwood is very dense, a craftsman can make all kinds of very complicated and ingenious joints. When joining members, metal nails are never used and glue is always secondary to the joinery. Joinery is the sole method by which members can be connected one to another on any surface regardless of whether they are thick or thin, slanted or vertical. It is the means by which members are connected so judiciously that a piece looks well from any angle, and with such consummate skill that not even a hair can be inserted. This achievement on the part of Ming and early Qing cabinetmakers fully merits our close study; it is an art which has already exerted a great influence on furniture-making in other countries and will be still more influential in the future.

To describe joinery systematically and in detail would require an entire book. Thus, only a few representative joints are described here in an attempt to facilitate the reader's understanding of the pieces illustrated in this book.

A. Tongue-and-groove joint with penetrating transverse brace (*longfengsun jia chuandai* 龍鳳榫加穿帶) (Fig. 5.1)

When one board is not wide enough for the intended purpose, two or more must be used together. They are joined by the tongue-and-groove joint with penetrating transverse brace. (The Chinese term for the joint, *longfengsun*, is literally dragon-and-phoenix joint.) First a long dovetailed tenon is made on the edge of one board and is pushed from one end into a groove of the same shape in the adjoining board. With a tongue-and-groove joint the extent of the glued surface is greater than if smaller tenons are used, and thus the boards will neither warp nor separate.

After the boards have been glued together, vertical grooves are made on the back and penetrating transverse braces are pushed in. Since penetrating transverse braces taper slightly towards one end, they are inserted beginning with the narrower end and are thus tightened. Each end of the brace extends beyond the board, forming a tenon fitting into a mortise in the tenon-bearing frame member. The number of penetrating transverse braces depends on the length of the boards and there is usually one about every 40 centimetres. Finally, on all four sides of the floating panel a tongue is made to fit into the groove on the frame.

B. Method of assembling a mortised-and-tenoned frame with floating panel (*cuanbian dacao zhuangban* 攢邊打槽裝板) (Fig. 5.2).

Once boards have been connected by a tongue-and-groove joint with penetrating transverse brace, they can be inserted into a frame as a floating panel. The frame is composed of four members, two long tenon-bearing members and two short mortise-bearing members. Along the inside of the frame grooves are made to accept the tongue of the floating panel, and the ends of the penetrating transverse braces are fitted into mortises in the tenon-bearing frame members.

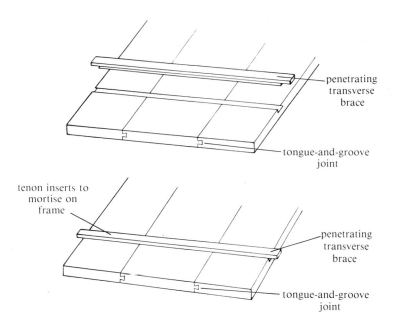

penetrating transverse brace

tongue-and-groove joint

tenon inserts to mortise on frame

penetrating transverse brace

tongue-and-groove joint

5.1 Tongue-and-groove joint with penetrating transverse brace

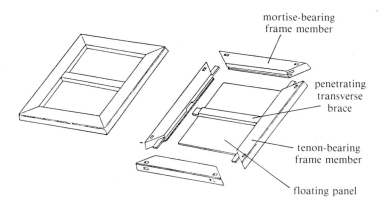

mortise-bearing frame member

penetrating transverse brace

tenon-bearing frame member

floating panel

5.2 Assembling a mortised-and-tenoned frame with floating panel

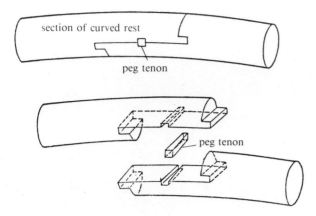

section of curved rest

peg tenon

peg tenon

5.3a Peg tenon joint

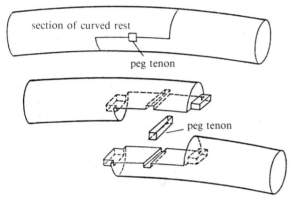

section of curved rest

peg tenon

peg tenon

5.3b Peg tenon joint

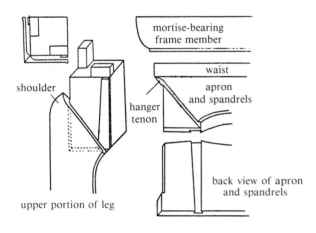

mortise-bearing frame member

shoulder

waist

apron and spandrels

hanger tenon

back view of apron and spandrels

upper portion of leg

5.4 Embracing-shoulder tenon

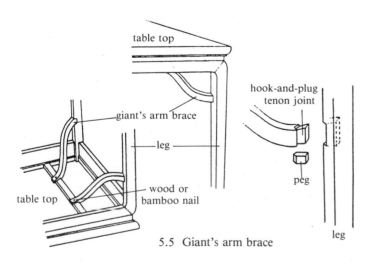

table top

hook-and-plug tenon joint

giant's arm brace

leg

peg

table top

wood or bamboo nail

leg

5.5 Giant's arm brace

This method of construction is used because it allows a thin piece of board to be used in place of a thick one for the floating panel. Moreover, the unsightly end grains of the floating panel are hidden by the groove in the frame, and those of the frame are also concealed, so that only the beautiful grains of the wood are exposed. This is therefore a logical and aesthetic method, which is also sparing in its use of materials. It is used predominantly for table tops as well as for doors, and the sides and backs of cabinets.

C. Peg tenon joint (*xiedingsun* 楔釘榫)
(Figs 5.3a and 5.3b)

This is an ingenious joint used for curved members such as curved rests on armchairs (Pls 54, 55 and 56) and for round tables, stools, stands and continuous floor stretchers. The joint consists of two overlapping pieces with the addition of a tongue at the tip of each which fits into a groove in the other member. This prevents warping by locking the members vertically. A square groove is made in the centre to receive a peg tenon, thus securing the members horizontally and making the connection firm.

D. Embracing-shoulder tenon (*baojiansun* 抱肩榫)
(Fig. 5.4)

The embracing-shoulder tenon is used to connect the leg, apron and waist of waisted furniture. For example, in the waisted square table (Pl. 90) a mitre is cut in the leg under the waist so that the upper part of the leg is recessed. A triangular mortise is then made in the leg behind the shoulder. A dovetailed hanger tenon is next made on the top of the leg which fits into a mortise on the back of the apron and waist. The waist and apron of Ming and early Qing waisted furniture are usually made from a single piece of wood, and so when they are attached to the leg in this manner the joint is neat and firm. After the middle of the Qing dynasty a very inferior version of this joint is used with the hanger tenon omitted and the apron and waist often made from two pieces of wood. By late Qing the joint deteriorates further and not only is the hanger tenon lacking, but also the triangular mortise and tenon, so that the joint is merely mitred and glued. These omissions so weaken a table that when it is moved the apron is easily pulled out.

E. Giant's arm brace (*bawangcheng* 霸王棖)
(Fig. 5.5)

Craftsmen in the past created the giant's arm brace in order to make table legs strong enough to bear the weight of the table top. In this way they could dispense with stretchers which interfered with the legs of a seated person. The upper part of the giant's arm brace supports the penetrating transverse brace, to which it is fastened with wood or bamboo nails. The lower tip is connected to the upper part of the leg by the hook-and-plug tenon joint. Such a hook-and-plug tenon joint, already in use in coffins in the Warring States period,[1] is ideally suited for the purpose. For this joint the end of the dovetailed tenon curves slightly upwards so that it hooks into the mortise in the leg. This mortise is longer than the tenon, so that after the tenon has been pushed up into the mortise it must be secured by a small block of wood inserted beneath it. To take the joint apart, all that has to be done is remove the plug, lower the tenon and pull it out. The term giant's arm brace is an allusion to the famous 3rd-century BC hero Xiang Yu 項羽, who is said to have used his arm to support heaven. The joint can be seen on several tables (Pls 84, 97, 98, 108 and 119), and on a square stool (Pl. 18).

F. Elongated bridle joint (*jiatousun* 夾頭榫)
(Fig. 5.6)

The elongated bridle joint is the most commonly used joint in the recessed-leg construction. On top of each of the four legs there are two tenons fitting into mortises in the tenon-bearing frame members. A slot is made at the top of the leg to contain the apron and apron-head spandrel; thus, instead of being flush, the leg protrudes. When the aprons are inserted into the four legs, they form a continuous frame supporting the table top. This construction ensures that the members meet in un-shifting right-angle joins and that the weight of the table top is evenly supported. Examples of this construction are the painting tables with recessed legs (Pls 100, 101, 102, 103, 104, 111, 112, 113 and 114), the wine tables (Pls 77 and 78), and the long narrow bench (Pl. 33).

G. Inserted shoulder joint (*chajiansun* 插肩榫)
(Fig. 5.7)

The inserted shoulder joint is also used in the recessed-leg construction. Although it differs markedly in appearance from the elongated bridle joint, the two are quite similar in construction. Like the elongated bridle joint the inserted shoulder joint has tenons on top of the legs which fit into mortises in the tenon-bearing frame members. Behind the double mitre there is a slot into which the double-mitred indentation of the apron is inserted. Once in place, all the surfaces are flush. This joint is tightened by the weight of the table top. The inserted shoulder joint is found on wine tables (Pls 79 and 80), a narrow rectangular table with recessed legs (Pl. 107), and a painting table with recessed legs (Pl. 115).

H. Running horse tenon (*zoumaxiao* 走馬銷)
(Fig. 5.8)

This is one kind of planted tenon which is not made of the same piece of wood as the member but of a separate piece inserted into the member. It is generally used in situations where it may be necessary to take apart the joint of the members. Half of the tenon is rectangular and is inserted into a similarly shaped mortise in one member. The other half of the tenon is stepped and tapered. It is inserted into the larger end of the mortise and then pushed to the small end, thereby locking the joint. To take apart the two members, it is necessary to push the tenon back to the position in which it entered the mortise. The concept is somewhat similar to the giant's arm brace but there is no plug. This kind of tenon is used in the railings on all the Luohan beds (Pls 122, 123 and 124).

Note

1. Zhongguo Shehui Kexue Yuan Kaogu Yanjiusuo 中國社會科學院考古研究所 (Institute of Archaeology, Central Academy of Social Sciences), *Huixian fajue baogao* 輝縣發掘報告 (*Report on the Excavations at Huixian*) (Beijing: Science Press, 1958), Figure 84.

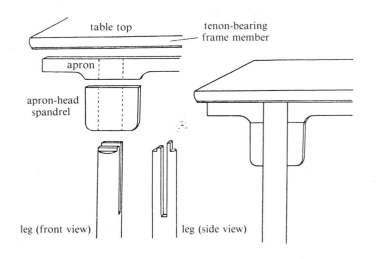

5.6 Elongated bridle joint

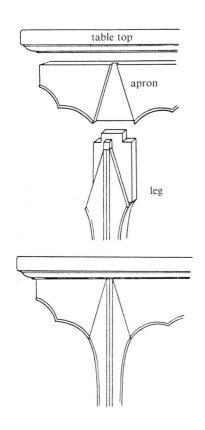

5.7 Inserted shoulder joint

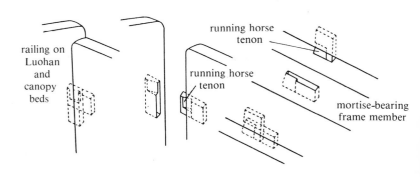

5.8 Running horse tenon

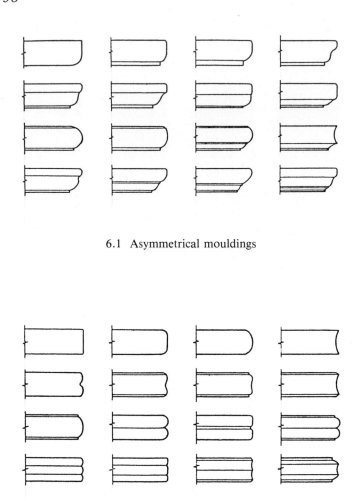

6.1 Asymmetrical mouldings

6.2 Symmetrical mouldings

VI The Richness and Variety of Decorative Techniques

Ming and early Qing craftsmen were able to make the already superbly formed and constructed furniture even more beautiful by means of embellishing devices. These devices can be discussed under six headings: the selection of materials; mouldings; latticework; carving; inlay; and the role of secondary components.

A. The selection of materials (*xuanliao* 選料)

Since very early times the Chinese people have loved beautifully grained wood. The "Prose Poem on the Beauty of Wood Grains",[1] written by Liu Sheng 劉勝 , King of Zhongshan 中山王 in the late 2nd century BC, contains the lines:

If you make lovely wood into a cane or armrest, it will be superbly beautiful. If used for a pillow or low table, the grain will be dazzling.

As large quantities of hardwoods were used in Ming times, craftsmen were more and more able to avail themselves of the opportunity to exploit the aesthetic qualities of grains. The great natural beauty of grain patterns may be regarded as superior to all man-made decoration; their attraction never palls and will last forever. In many pieces of furniture one can see how the cabinetmaker has carefully selected the material and put those parts with the most beautiful grain patterns in the most obvious positions. In the *huanghuali* wood table with recessed legs and everted flanges (Pl. 103), a grain suggestive of floating clouds and running water ornaments the floating panel and tenon-bearing frame member. On this floating panel and on the doors of the mirror platform (Pl. 162), there are dark circular formations and dots which are termed devil's face in *Gegu yaolun* and leopard's spots in *Guangdong xinyu*.[2] The grain of *jichi* wood is very fine and has a zigzag pattern, as may be seen on the fronts of the two drawers of the desk tray (Pl. 161), for which the most beautiful parts of the wood have been selected. The burl wood panels forming one section of each of the three panelled splats on the southern official's hat armchair with high arms (Pl. 49) and the *zitan* wood waisted armchair with curved rest (Pl. 56) also show the superb use of woods for decorative effects.

B. Mouldings (*xianjiao* 線脚)

Mouldings, which ornament the surfaces and edges of pieces of furniture, play an important role in decoration. Although in Chinese there are many terms for specific mouldings there is no general term, and so I have borrowed the modern architectural expression *xianjiao*. At first glance the mouldings of traditional furniture seem relatively simple, with either flat, convex or concave surfaces combined with convex or concave beading. However, close scrutiny of actual pieces reveals that mouldings are in fact very complex. Even on two members of approximately the same size and same type of surface, the beading may vary slightly in depth or width, or the curves may be soft or sharp, resulting in a different appearance in the piece of furniture. There are innumerable combinations and variations.

Mouldings usually appear on the frame of the top and the legs of furniture such as stools, chairs, tables, beds and cabinets. They can be divided into two types: the symmetrical and the asymmetrical. Craftsmen call the latter ice-plate edge (*bingpanyan* 冰盤沿), which suggests their resemblance to the edge of a tray. The armchair with curved rest and openwork splat (Pl. 55) has an asymmetrical ice-plate edge while the southern official's hat armchair with peony design (Pl. 50) has a symmetrical moulding. Figures 6.1 and 6.2 show examples of both types drawn from actual pieces.

Furniture legs can be divided into four kinds according to their shape when seen in section (round, square, oval and rectangular), each of which can be embellished with one of several types of mouldings (Figs 6.3 and 6.4). For example, the square tables (Pls 88 and 89) both have square legs with what craftsmen call melon-shaped mouldings (*tiangualeng* 甜瓜稜), but the legs are not identical. The mouldings of the large narrow rectangular table with recessed legs (Pl. 104) and the small narrow rectangular table with recessed legs (Pl. 113) are not alike although both tables have rectangular legs. Furthermore, the shape, curves and dimensions of the legs of the incense stands (Pls 72, 73, 74, 75 and 76) and the altar table (Pl. 119) vary from top to bottom, resulting in extremely complex mouldings.

Figures 6.1, 6.2, 6.3 and 6.4 illustrate but a fraction of the mouldings found on Ming and early Qing dynasty furniture. The figures serve to emphasize the importance of mouldings in furniture decoration.

C. Latticework (*cuan dou* 攢鬥)

Another way of decorating furniture is the use of latticework. The term *cuan dou* is a contraction of *cuanjie* 攢接 (joining the straight) and *doucu* 鬥簇 (assembling the curved). *Cuan* is a term used by Beijing craftsmen meaning to mortise and tenon straight pieces of wood together so that they form a vertical, horizontal, or slanted geometric lattice design. *Doucu* is a term that I have invented to describe the making of a lattice with round motifs from curved pieces of wood joined together by loose tenons. It also refers to the making of a lattice by carving each round motif from a single piece of wood and then joining the motifs with separate tenons to form a complete design.

The advantages of joining the straight and assembling the curved are that the wood can be used in such a way as to avoid its splitting, and openwork patterns can be created. When pieces made by joining the straight and assembling the curved are compared with pieces carved from a single block, it is obvious that carving can never be a complete substitute. Joining the straight lattice, which allows the openwork to be neat in appearance and spacious in feeling, is found on the square table (Pl. 89) and the flat-top narrow table with recessed legs (Pl. 106), as well as in the lattice of the three shelves (Pls 131, 132 and 133), the lattice railings of the Luohan bed (Pl. 124), and the *wan* 卍 character motif railings of the canopy bed (Pl. 126). Good examples of assembling the curved occur on the wondrously elaborate lattices of the doors with four-cloud motif (Pl. 146) and the phoenix-and-cloud patterned central panel of the clothes rack (Pl. 167). In the canopy bed with full-moon opening (Pl. 128), the railings, which consist of four-cloud motifs connected by crosses, are made by the two techniques: that of assembling the curved and that of joining the straight, a combination that results in a dazzling *tour de force* of decorative effect.

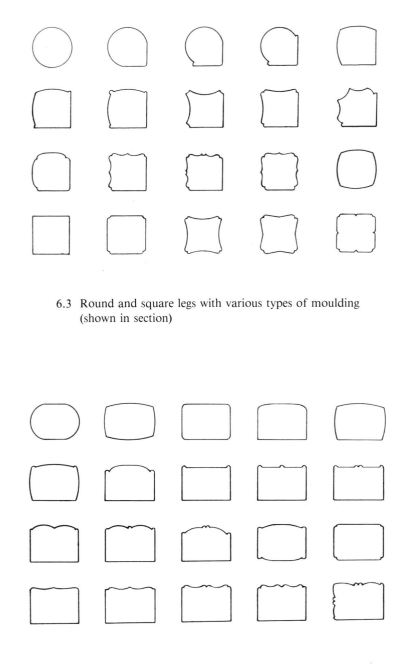

6.3 Round and square legs with various types of moulding (shown in section)

6.4 Oval and rectangular legs with various types of moulding (shown in section)

D. Carving (*diaoke*雕刻)

Carving is the most common, and therefore the most important, method of decorating furniture. Even when joining the straight and assembling the curved some carving is necessary. Carving can be divided into four types on the basis of technique: relief carving; openwork carving; a combination of relief and openwork carving; and three-dimensional carving.

Relief carving, the type most often used on furniture, can be further differentiated according to the degree of relief. The curling tendril pattern on the folding stool (Pl. 31), the peony motif on the armchair (Pl. 50), and the *lingzhi* fungus and hornless dragon design on the Luohan bed (Pl. 123) all have varying depths of relief carving. Most relief carving is done on a ground from which the background areas have been shaved and smoothed away, the carving and background each occupying about equal space. The half table (Pl. 84) and the square table (Pl. 91) are examples of this. In a number of examples, such as the armchair with curved rest (Pl. 54), the ground of the medallion is not smooth, but patterned. Sometimes the design covers the entire surface and there is no ground, as on the lotus throne (Pl. 59) and on the painting table with corner legs and *lingzhi* fungus (Pl. 110).

In openwork carving, because the ground is entirely removed, the solid design shows up vividly by contrast and the empty spaces give a feeling of airiness. There is one-sided openwork and double-faced openwork. Among the many one-sided examples, the *qilin* design on the armchair with curved rest (Pl. 55) is the most splendid. Double-faced carving is found on the clothes rack (Pl. 166) and the throne-type mirror platform (Pl. 163).

Relief and openwork carving are combined on the apron-head spandrels of the narrow rectangular table with corner legs (Pl. 94) and on the painting table (Pl. 112).

Three-dimensional carving is usually found on top rails; examples are the *lingzhi* fungus on the washbasin stand with towel rack (Pl. 169), and the dragon heads on the washbasin stand with towel rack (Pl. 170). Although the lotus flowers surmounting the legs of the washbasin stand (Pl. 168) are simple in execution, they should also be regarded as carvings in the round.

E. Inlay (*xiangqian*鑲嵌)

Inlay is named according to the material used, such as wood inlay, mother-of-pearl inlay and ivory inlay. When many kinds of precious materials such as jade, stone, ivory, horn, agate, amber, and various kinds of wood are combined to make the inlay, the effect is especially gorgeous; this type is called one-hundred-precious-material inlay.

In wood inlay there must be a contrast in both colour and texture between the wood of the inlay and the wood of the ground, so that the design will be clear. A good example is the *nan* wood altar table (Pl. 119) inlaid with *huanghuali* wood elephant design. Other examples are the mother-of-pearl inlay on the *zitan* wood throne stool (Pl. 60), and the one-hundred-precious-material inlay on the large compound wardrobe in four parts (Pl. 149) and on the washbasin stand with towel rack (Pl. 171).

F. The role of secondary components

This section deals with such secondary components as the various types of marble used on cabinet doors, Luohan bed railings, and the tops of stools and tables; soft furnishing such as silk matting and woven cane seats; and different kinds of metalwork fixtures. Some of these have natural patterns and some are fashioned by man, each contributing a different decorative effect.

The best marble comes from Dali 大理 in Yunnan Province. A greyish piece with a yellow tint, used for the top of the small painting table with recessed legs (Pl. 112), has a pattern resembling mountain ranges covered with lush forests which is most pleasing to the eye. The green marble on the wine table with inserted shoulder joints (Pl. 80) is also very beautiful, but the provenance of the stone has yet to be ascertained.

Very finely woven cane seats are so soft that they resemble silk cloth. Some have subtle patterns, such as that on the *zitan* wood armchair with curved rest (Pl. 56), which can be seen only in a good light.

Metalwork is used mainly on chests, boxes, cabinets and coffers; examples are too numerous to be discussed in detail here. The face plate used on the large compound wardrobe in four parts (Pl. 149) is especially intricate. Metal used for reinforcement, usually on the corners of tops and stepped apron mouldings, is both functional and decorative, as may be seen on the elaborately decorated high-waisted *kang* table (Pl. 66). Many folding chairs have gold or silver designs hammered into iron, which resemble gold or silver inlay and create a pleasing effect of antiquity.[3] An excellent example of silver designs hammered into iron can be seen on the *huanghuali* wood folding chair (Pl. 57).

Notes

1. Liu Sheng 劉勝, "Wen mu fu 文木賦" ("Prose Poem on the Beauty of Wood Grains"), in Yan Kejun (editor), *Quan shanggu Sandai Qin Han Sanguo Liuchao wen* 全上古三代秦漢三國六朝文 *(Complete Collection of Essays from Earliest Times through the Six Dynasties Period)* (Beijing: Zhonghua Shuju, 1958), Han wen, *juan* 12, pp. 190-1.

2. Wang Zuo, *op. cit.*, vol. 9, Yi mu lun 異木論, p. 6b; and Qu Dajun, *op. cit.*, Hainan wenmu 海南文木.

3. For the techniques of gold and silver designs hammered into iron, see Wang Shixiang 王世襄, "Tan Qingdai de jiangzuo zeli 談清代的匠作則例" ("On the Qing Dynasty Regulations for Various Craftsmen"), *Wenwu*, 1963:7, pp. 19-25.

VII The Appreciation and Use of Furniture

In 1980 I wrote an article entitled "Ming shi jiaju de pin yu bing" ("The Merits and Defects of Ming and early Qing Furniture"),[1] in which I enumerated sixteen merits and eight defects of classic Chinese furniture in an attempt to separate the good from the bad, and the beautiful from the ugly. At that time I had two aims. First, I wanted to point out that the furniture of that period is renowned for its simplicity *(jianlian* 簡練) and purity *(shunpo* 淳樸). However, these characteristics do not fully describe the furniture and there are many other features worthy of appreciation and criticism. All these features are evident in the furniture and can be seen and appreciated even by the uninitiated. Second, I wanted to make clear that although the period of the Ming and early Qing is the golden age of traditional furniture, this does not mean that every piece made in that period is good; there are examples of inferior pieces.

After the article was published, I was glad to have the comments of old and new friends. Most agreed with me concerning the defects, but there was some disagreement about the merits. One critic said that to list as many as sixteen merits was to make too many fine distinctions which he himself was unable to recognize. Another felt that even sixteen merits were insufficient to take account of all the qualities, such as the innocence *(tianzhen* 天眞) and the naïveté *(hanzhi* 憨稚) of Ming dynasty furniture, which I did not mention.

Actually, when writing the article I had anticipated that readers would have different opinions and so stated at the beginning:

It is very difficult to be precise in words when criticizing the decorative arts, especially when talking about their artistic value which is rather subjective. Moreover, people vary in their ability to judge quality and of course have different interpretations. Thus one person's opinion may not be acceptable to another.

In the aesthetic evaluation of Chinese furniture, disagreement is inevitable. But that should not deter us from discussion. The ideal opportunity for lively discussion would be to display all the furniture in a suitable place and invite a large number of people to examine it and offer their views. As this is impossible at present, the next best solution is to publish the pieces in an illustrated book so that they can be presented to others for appreciation. This is one of the main reasons why I have compiled this volume. After all, each furniture lover must with his own eyes form his own opinions about the good and bad qualities of a piece, and its beauty or ugliness. One person's opinion is only a point of reference for others.

Originally I intended to put my entire article in an appendix. Later I changed my mind and decided simply to outline the merits discussed therein.

The sixteen merits can be divided into the following five groups.

A. Seven qualities which pertain to naturalness and directness, which are the most important elements of Ming furniture style:
   (1) simplicity (*jianlian* 簡練);
   (2) purity *(shunpo* 淳樸);
   (3) awkwardness *(houzhuo* 厚拙);
   (4) dignity *(ningzhong* 凝重);
   (5) massiveness *(xiongwei* 雄偉);
   (6) wholeness *(yuanhun* 圓渾); and
   (7) stillness *(chenmu* 沉穆).
B. Three features which contrast with the qualities in the previous group:
   (8) rich decoration *(nonghua* 穠華);
   (9) refined decoration *(wenyi* 文綺); and
   (10) elegant decoration *(yanxiu* 研秀).
C. Two seemingly contradictory qualities which I purposely put together in order to clarify them:
   (11) sharpness *(jingting* 勁挺); and
   (12) fluidity *(rouwan* 柔婉).
D. Two mutually dependent characteristics:
   (13) emptiness *(kongling* 空靈); and
   (14) tracery-like articulation of spaces *(linglong* 玲瓏).
   These are two sides of the same coin, so to speak, the former referring to the empty spaces in the whole structure while the latter refers to the vivid effect derived from the articulation of the details of the pattern carved against a background of empty spaces.
E. Two qualities:
   (15) classic refinement *(dianya* 典雅); and
   (16) tasteful originality *(qingxin* 清新).
   By the former we mean strict adherence to traditional principles and methods without being enslaved by them into merely copying antique pieces. By the latter we mean the ability to create original designs boldly, but not merely for the sake of striving after effect.

Most of the sixteen pieces of furniture which I used in the article to illustrate these merits are also found in this volume. The interested reader will find them listed in the notes.[2]

A study of the relationship between people and furniture and of how pieces are placed and used in daily life would be most interesting. However, to be treated thoroughly such a subject needs its own book and here I can only briefly comment on how antique furniture may be used today. This should be of interest not only to collectors and lovers of old furniture, but also to cabinetmakers and those who use Ming-style furniture.

In many Ming dynasty paintings we can see that interiors were quite simple and furnishings rather sparse. It was not until the Qing dynasty that rooms became increasingly crowded and furniture more elaborate. Today when furniture of Ming and early Qing style is to be used it is better to have a few rather than a great many pieces. Three or five pieces will transform a room, and it is best to limit the pieces to this number in order to allow the real spirit of the furniture to communicate itself. If more pieces are crowded in one room the effect will be entirely spoilt.

Needless to say the most suitable place for Ming and early Qing furniture is a traditional Chinese building. Yet, to my surprise, I have seen some very modern European and American homes in which it was used most harmoniously. Why does Ming-style furniture fit so well with modern Western life and furnishings? It is simply because modern Western taste favours a simplicity akin to that of the Ming and early Qing dynasty furniture. This shows the universality of the forms and artistry of classic Chinese furniture, which has become part of the cultural heritage not only of the Chinese, but also of the rest of the world.

In former times the arrangement of furniture depended on the function of the room in which it was to be used. In large halls it was usually placed in a symmetrical, somewhat rigid, arrangement. In studios and living quarters it was found in freer, more varied and more practical arrangements. Thus there was a contrast between the symmetrical and the asymmetrical, the prescribed and the flexible. I believe that contrast is important for emphasis and variety. However, it is quite impossible to imagine a house today with a large hall containing symmetrically placed furniture. None the less, we can still consciously make use of contrast by creating a static symmetrical arrangement in some areas and a less rigid, more informal, arrangement in other areas.

In Chapter III I discussed the origins and development of waistless and waisted furniture. Among waistless pieces there are many types, such as the straight-leg rectangular stool (Pl. 9), the lamp-hanger chair (Pls 36 and 37), the southern official's hat armchair (Pls 46, 48 and 50), the square corner-leg table of the type with three spandrels to one leg and a hump-backed stretcher (Pls 87 and 88), the table with recessed legs and everted flanges (Pl. 100), the painting table with recessed legs (Pls 111 and 112), the round-corner cabinet (Pls 141 and 142), and the coffer (Pl. 153). But all these types belong to the same family. On the other hand waisted and straight-form furniture as, for example, the rectangular stool (Pl. 15), the two-seater bench (Pl. 35), the wide *kang* table (Pl. 63), the half table (Pl. 83), the large square table with corner legs (Pl. 90), the narrow rectangular table with corner legs (Pl. 97), the painting table with corner legs (Pl. 109), the square-corner cabinet (Pl. 145), and the compound wardrobe in four parts (Pls 148 and 149), all belong to another family. If we put pieces of the same family together, no matter how different they are in type and appearance, there will still be certain similarities which make them harmonious. These similarities have to do with both form and spirit. Thus, I suggest that the best effect may be obtained by arranging furniture of the same origin together. If this consideration is borne in mind by collectors when displaying their pieces, by manufacturers in reproduction, and by users when purchasing furniture, the effect will be harmonious and the beauty of individual pieces enhanced.

I would like to conclude with some remarks about the use of a few particular types of furniture. Many people consider the chair to be the most uncomfortable of Ming pieces and so manufacturers of Ming-style chairs try to reduce the height of its seat. Originally the Ming chair, especially the southern official's hat armchair (Pl. 50) and the armchair with curved rest, was an extremely comfortable seat if provided with a footstool. Some were indeed provided with footstools but over the years they have become separated from their chairs. Today few large Ming-style chairs, and almost none with footstools, are made. I believe that if such chairs were made together with their footstools, they would be quite popular.

A wide, long table with drawers under the top board and stands of drawers at each end is a Qing-style desk. A Ming-style painting table has no drawers and so much leg room that those who have used one tend to prefer it to a Qing-style desk, whose drawers drastically curtail the freedom of movement necessary when painting or doing calligraphy. Thus a table with no drawers is better than one with drawers. Of course there is a certain inconvenience in the absence of drawers, but that can be remedied by the placement of a cabinet or shelf behind the table and a multi-drawered dressing case or medicine chest at its side. Then no matter in which direction the user turns all will be within reach.

Lengthy use of a Western-style bed with a soft mattress can be the cause of backache. Classic Chinese beds have mattresses woven from palm fibre and cane which provide ventilation and the correct degree of softness, so that no matter how long a person sleeps on them he should not develop back trouble. I consider the Luohan bed with railings on three sides and cane seat (Pls 123-5) to be the ideal bed.

The merits of the roller stool (Pl. 172) are still not generally recognized. If one puts one's feet on it and rolls, the rubbing action on the so-called gushing spring acupuncture point will improve the circulation. It is, therefore, an excellent piece of equipment for physiotherapy which, I predict, will become as popular as the iron balls that are so beneficial when rotated in the palm.

Notes

1. ''Ming shi jiaju de pin yu bing 明式家具的'品'與'病' '' (''The Merits and Defects of Ming and early Qing Furniture''), *Wenwu*, 1980:4, pp. 74-81; 1980:6, pp. 75-9; and *Artist*, 1980, overall no. 13, pp. 44-51; overall no. 15, pp. 75-9.
2. The following is a list of the sixteen merits and the respective pieces which exemplify them.
   (1) simplicity: the Luohan bed (Pl. 122);
   (2) purity: the painting table with corner legs (Pl. 94);
   (3) awkwardness: the five-legged incense stand (Pl. 73);
   (4) dignity: the southern official's hat armchair (Pl. 50);
   (5) massiveness: a throne, now in Bishushanzhuang 避暑山莊, Chengde 承德 (not illustrated);
   (6) wholeness: a drum stool, now in Bishushanzhuang, Chengde (not illustrated);
   (7) stillness: the black lacquer narrow *kang* table (Pl. 67);
   (8) rich decoration: the canopy bed (Pl. 128);
   (9) refined decoration: the painting table with corner legs (Pl. 110);
   (10) elegant decoration: the half table (Pl. 84);
   (11) sharpness: the square table (Pl. 86);
   (12) fluidity: the official's hat armchair (Pl. 46);
   (13) emptiness: a side chair illustrated by Ecke in *Chinese Domestic Furniture* (Peking: Henri Vetch, 1944), Pl. 100;
   (14) tracery-like articulation of spaces: the screen set in a stand (Pl. 150);
   (15) classic refinement: part of the clothes rack (Pl. 167); and
   (16) tasteful originality: the hexagonal southern official's hat armchair (Pl. 53).

The Plates

1 Interior view of Shufangzhai, the Palace Museum

2 Interior view of Shufangzhai,
the Palace Museum

4

3 Interior view of Chuxiugong, the Palace Museum

4 West Hall of Paiyundian, Zixiaoge,
   the Summer Palace

**8 Ming dynasty *huanghuali* wood table
with recessed legs and everted flanges,
incense stand, and rectangular stool**
Wang Shixiang Collection

**5 Corner of
Huang Zhou's studio**

6 Corner of Wang Shixiang's studio

7 Ming dynasty *huanghuali* wood lute
table, incense stand and square stool

Wang Shixiang Collection

Stools
and
Chairs

9

9 Ming dynasty _huanghuali_ wood waistless rectangular stool
Height 51 cm, seat 51.5 cm × 41 cm
① Bottom view showing rattan seat and braces

Wang Shixiang Collection

①

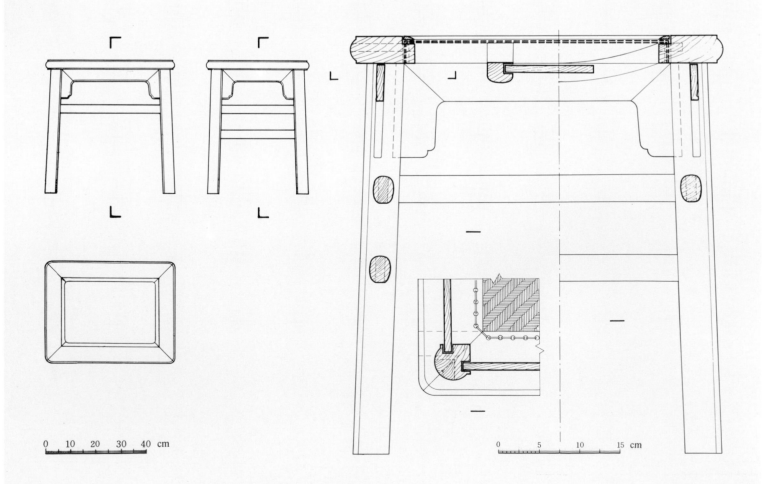

0 10 20 30 40 cm

0   5   10   15 cm

10

10 **Ming dynasty** *huanghuali* **wood waistless small square stool**
Height 26 cm, seat 28 cm × 28 cm
Wang Shixiang Collection

11 **Ming dynasty** *huanghuali* **wood rectangular stool and small square stool**
Wang Shixiang Collection

11

12

13

12 **Ming dynasty *huanghuali* wood waistless square stool with humpbacked leg-encircling stretcher and pillar-shaped struts**
Height 51 cm, seat 52.5 cm × 52.5 cm
Beijing Timber Factory Collection

13 **Ming dynasty *huanghuali* wood waistless square stool with humpbacked leg-encircling stretcher and decorative struts**
Height 46.5 cm, seat 50.5 cm × 50.4 cm
Central Academy of Arts and Crafts

①

14

15

14 Qing dynasty *zitan* wood waistless square stool with base stretchers
Overall height 47 cm, seat 52.5 cm × 52.5 cm, height of bronze foot 5.5 cm
① Bronze foot
Wang Shixiang Collection

15 Ming dynasty *huanghuali* wood waisted rectangular stool with humpbacked stretchers
Height 50 cm, seat 48.5 cm × 42.5 cm
Central Academy of Arts and Crafts

16

16 **Ming dynasty *huanghuali* wood**
waisted rectangular stool with
crossed stretchers
Height 48.5 cm, seat 55.2 cm × 46.3 cm
① Side view
② Bottom view

Fei Boliang Collection

①

②

17

17 **Ming dynasty *huanghuali* wood waisted rectangular stool with cabriole legs and humpbacked stretchers**
Height 51 cm, seat 51 cm × 42 cm
Beijing Hardwood Furniture Factory Collection

20 **Ming dynasty *zitan* wood waisted square stool with convex aprons and bulging legs ending in horse-hoof feet**
Height 52 cm, seat 57 cm × 57 cm
The Palace Museum

20

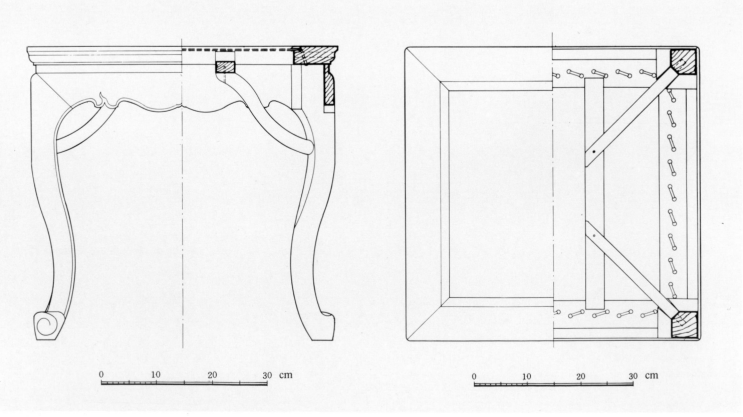

21

19

**18 Ming dynasty *huanghuali* wood waisted square
stool with cabriole legs and giant's arm braces**
Height 52 cm, seat 55.5 cm × 55.5 cm
Wang Shixiang Collection

**19 Ming dynasty *huanghuali* wood waisted square
stool with cabriole legs, humpbacked stretchers
and pillar-shaped struts**
Height 54 cm, seat 48 cm × 47.7 cm
Wang Shixiang Collection

**21 Ming dynasty *huanghuali* wood waisted large
square stool with convex aprons and bulging legs
ending in horse-hoof feet**
Height 55 cm, seat 64 cm × 64 cm
Beijing Timber Factory Collection

22

23

22 **Ming dynasty *huanghuali* wood small painting table and two waisted large stools**
Beijing Timber Factory Collection

23 **Qing dynasty *hong* wood waisted square stool with base stretchers**
Height 52 cm, seat 54.5 cm × 54.5 cm
Zhang An Collection

24 Ming dynasty *huanghuali* wood waisted square stool with humpbacked stretchers and continuous floor stretcher

Height 52 cm, seat 53 cm × 53 cm

① One corner of stool

Beijing Hardwood Furniture Factory Collection

24

①

25

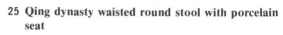

25 Qing dynasty waisted round stool with porcelain seat

Height 49 cm, diameter of seat 41 cm

① Top view showing porcelain seat

The Summer Palace

①

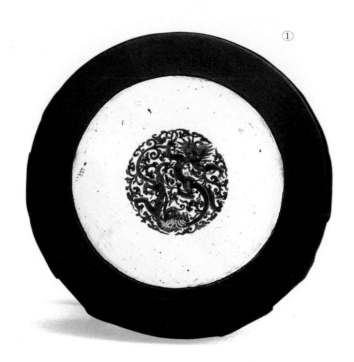

27

26

28

29

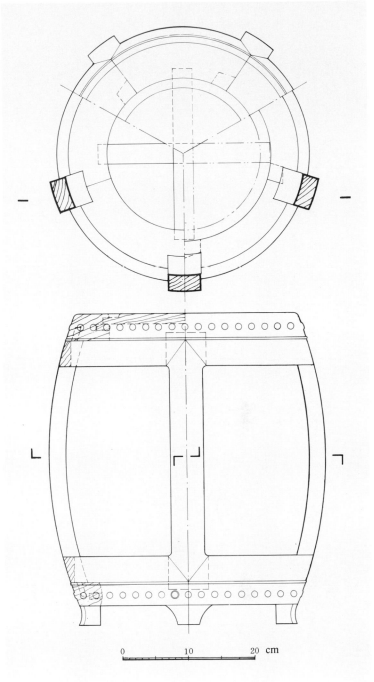

0   10   20 cm

26 Ming dynasty *huanghuali* wood eight-legged round stool
Height 49 cm, diameter of seat 38 cm, diameter of widest part 45 cm
Beijing Hardwood Furniture Factory Collection

27 Qing dynasty *zitan* wood drum stool with five openings
Height 52 cm, diameter of seat 28 cm
The Palace Museum

28 Qing dynasty *zitan* wood drum stool with five openings
Height 48 cm, diameter of seat 34 cm, diameter of widest part 42 cm
Huang Zhou Collection

29 Qing dynasty *zitan* wood drum stool with straight rods
Height 47 cm, diameter of seat 29 cm
Beijing Hardwood Furniture Factory Collection

30

31

30 Qing dynasty *huanghuali* wood folding stool
Height 43 cm, level seat and frame
47.5 cm × 39.5 cm

Yang Naiji Collection

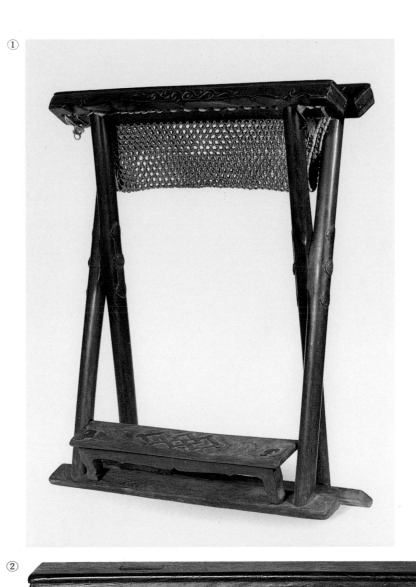

31 Ming dynasty *huanghuali* wood folding stool with footrest

Height 49.5 cm, level seat and frame 55.7 cm × 41.4 cm
① Stool folded
② Front of seat member

Wang Shixiang Collection

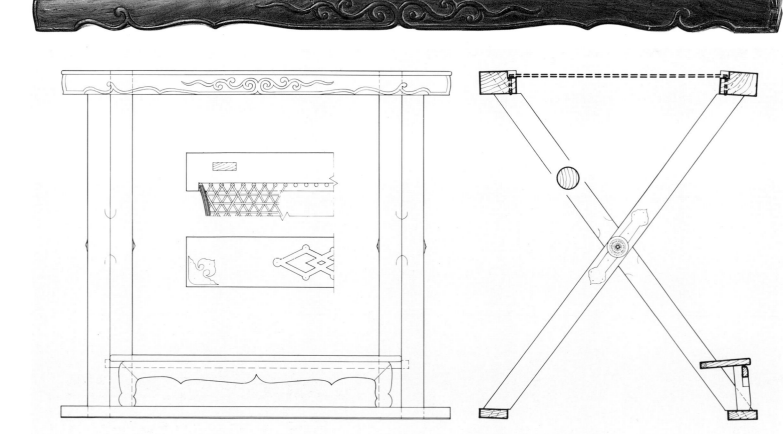

0   10   20 cm

72

32

①

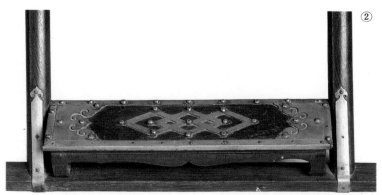

②

33

①

32 Qing dynasty *huanghuali* wood upward-folding stool

Height 49 cm, seat 56 cm × 49 cm
① Stool partially folded
② Footrest

Tianjin Museum of Art

33 Qing dynasty *ju* wood small bench with elongated bridle joints

Height 40 cm, seat 49.5 cm × 15 cm
① Side view

Wang Shixiang Collection

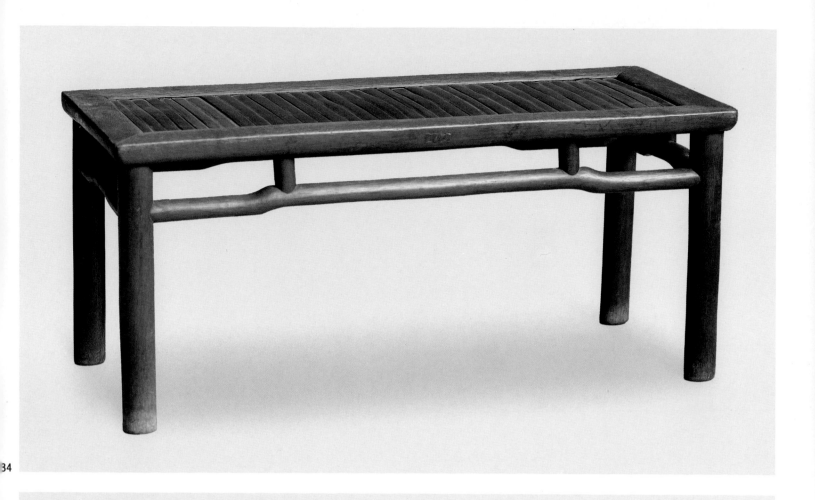

34

35

**34 Qing dynasty *zuo* wood waistless two-seater bench
with humpbacked stretchers and pillar-shaped struts**
Height 39 cm, seat 83 cm × 31 cm
Tianjin Museum of Art

**35 Ming dynasty *huanghuali* wood waisted two-seater
bench with humpbacked stretchers**
Height 49 cm, seat 102 cm × 42 cm
Beijing Timber Factory Collection

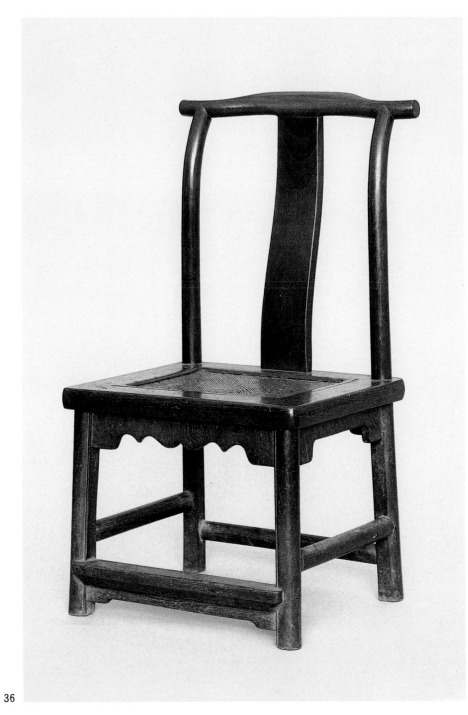

36

②

36 Qing dynasty *ju* wood small lamp-hanger chair

Overall height 83.5 cm, seat 43 cm × 37 cm, height of seat 37 cm

① Side view
② Top view of cane seat
③ Bottom view of cane seat

Wang Shixiang Collection

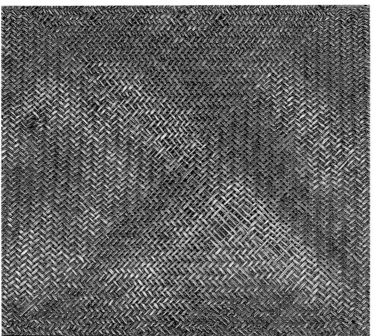

①

③

37

39

37 Ming dynasty *huanghuali* wood large lamp-hanger chair
Height 117 cm, seat 57.5 cm × 41.5 cm
Mrs Chen Mengjia Collection

39 Qing dynasty *hong* wood small side chair
Height 85 cm, seat 48 cm × 44 cm
Wang Shixiang Collection

38 Ming dynasty *huanghuali* wood square table and large lamp-hanger chairs

Mrs Chen Mengjia Collection

40 Ming dynasty *huanghuali* wood carved side chair

Height 99.5 cm, seat 62.5 cm × 42 cm

① Back view

② Front view of chair back

Mrs Chen Mengjia Collection

41

①

41 Ming dynasty *huanghuali* wood rose chair
Height 85.5 cm, seat 56 cm × 43.2 cm
① Front view of chair back
Mrs Chen Mengjia Collection

42

42 Ming dynasty *huanghuali* wood rose chair
Height 69 cm, seat 58 cm × 45 cm
Central Academy of Arts and Crafts

①

②

**43 Ming dynasty *huanghuali* wood rose chair with
openwork carving**
Height 87 cm, seat 61 cm × 46 cm
① Side view of arm
② Chair back

Central Academy of Arts and Crafts

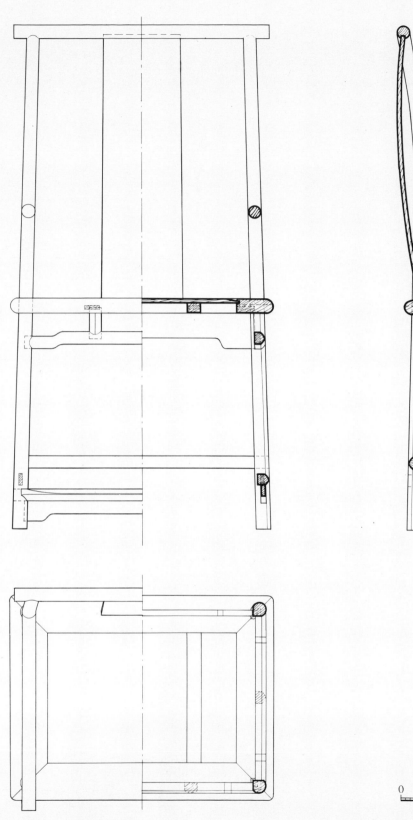

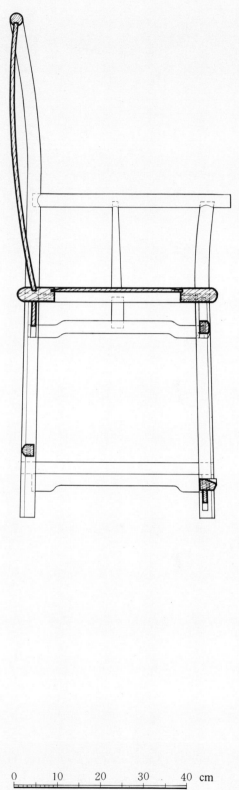

0   10   20   30   40 cm

**44 Ming dynasty *tieli* wood official's hat armchair
with four protruding ends**
Height 116 cm, seat 74 cm × 60.5 cm

Wang Shixiang Collection

**45 Ming dynasty *huanghuali* wood official's hat
armchair with four protruding ends**
Height 120.4 cm, seat 55.5 cm × 43.4 cm
Mrs Chen Mengjia Collection

**47 Ming dynasty *huanghuali* wood low-back
southern official's hat armchair**
Height 82 cm, seat 59 cm × 47 cm
Central Academy of Arts and Crafts

①

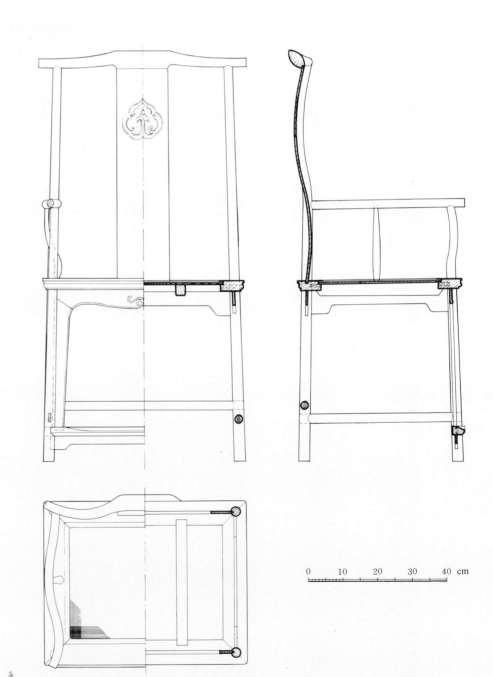

**46 Ming dynasty *huanghuali* wood
official's hat armchair with four
protruding ends**
Height 119.5 cm, seat 58.5 cm × 47 cm
① Cloud motif on splat

Wang Shixiang Collection

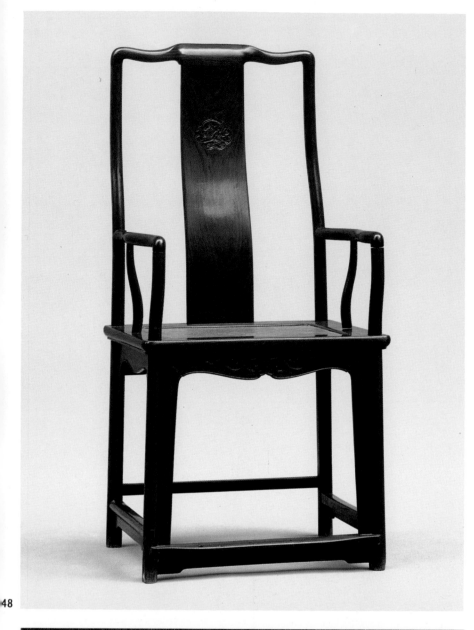

①

48

②

**48 Ming dynasty *huanghuali* wood high-back
southern official's hat armchair**
Height 119.5 cm, seat 57.5 cm × 44.2 cm
① Side view
② Hornless dragon motif on splat

Ye Wanfa Collection

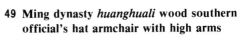

49 **Ming dynasty** *huanghuali* **wood southern official's hat armchair with high arms**
Height 93.2 cm, seat 56 cm × 47.5 cm
① Side view
② Jade plaque on splat
The Summer Palace

①

②

49

①

②

50 Ming dynasty *zitan* wood fan-shaped southern official's hat armchair
Height 108.5 cm, dimensions of seat: width of front 75.8 cm, width of back 61 cm, depth 60.5 cm
① Side view
② Peony medallion on splat

Wang Shixiang Collection

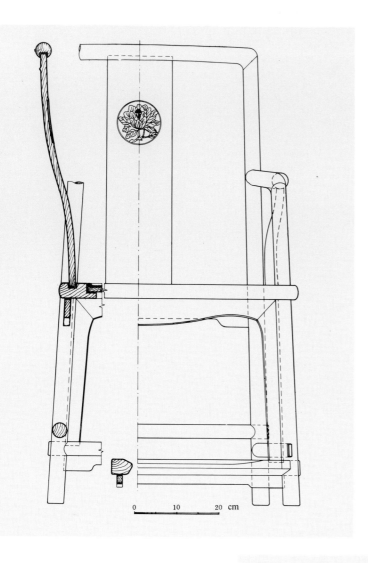

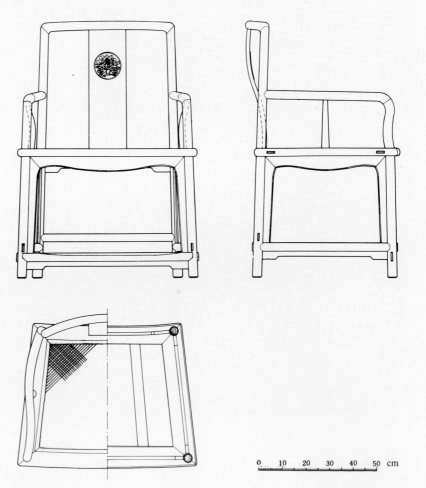

0   10   20 cm

0   10   20   30   40   50 cm

**51 Qing dynasty *ju* wood small lamp-hanger chair
and Ming dynasty *zitan* wood southern official's
hat armchair**

Wang Shixiang Collection

52 Ming dynasty *ju* wood low southern official's hat armchair

Overall height 77 cm, seat 71 cm × 58 cm; height of seat 31.5 cm

① Rectangular panel on splat

Central Academy of Arts and Crafts

53

①

53 Ming dynasty *huanghuali* **wood hexagonal**
southern official's hat armchair
Overall height 83 cm, seat 78 cm × 55 cm,
height of seat 49 cm
① Side view

The Palace Museum

54

54 Ming dynasty *huanghuali* wood armchair with curved rest

Height 93 cm, seat 54.5 cm × 43 cm

① Dragon medallion on splat

Beijing Hardwood Furniture Factory Collection

①

①

55 Ming dynasty *huanghuali* wood armchair with curved rest and openwork splat

Height 107 cm, scat 60.7 cm × 48.7 cm

① Openwork *qilin* motif on splat

② Side view

Wang Shixiang Collection

②

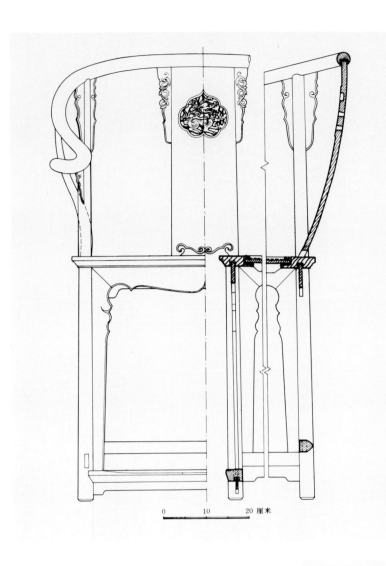

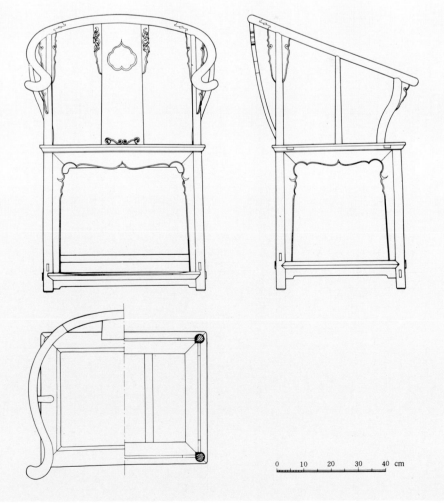

① Side view

③④

56 Qing dynasty *zitan* wood waisted armchair with curved rest and floor stretcher

Overall height 99 cm, seat 63 cm × 50 cm, height of seat 49 cm

① Side view
② Splat
③ Openwork tendril design at bottom of leg
④ Openwork tendril design at end of arm
⑤ Side view of openwork tendril design at end of arm

The Palace Museum

②

⑤

7

①

②

③

④

⑤

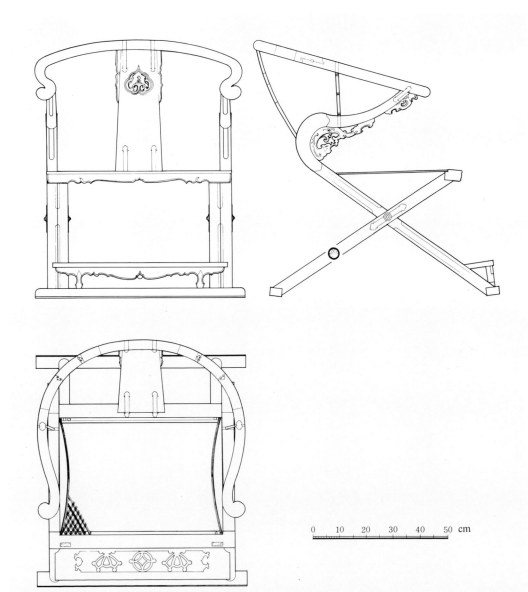

**57 Yuan dynasty *huanghuali* wood
folding armchair with curved rest**

Height 94.8 cm, seat 69.5 cm × 53 cm

① Side view
② Back view
③ Cloud motif on splat
④ Spandrel and iron reinforcement
hammered with silver design
⑤ Footrest

Mrs Chen Mengjia Collection

**58 Ming dynasty _huanghuali_ wood folding armchair
with curved rest**

Height 112 cm, seat 70 cm × 46.5 cm

① Side view

② Openwork rectangular spandrel on splat

Wang Shixiang Collection

①

②

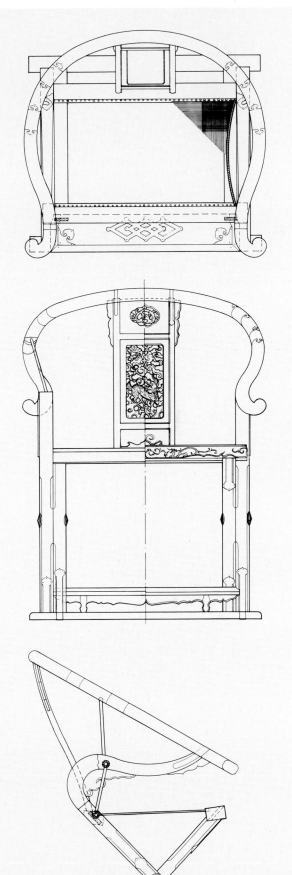

10　20　30　40　50 cm

59 Ming dynasty *zitan* wood waisted throne with continuous floor stretcher

Height 109 cm, seat 98 cm × 78 cm

The Palace Museum

①

60 Qing dynasty *zitan* wood waisted footstool with mother-of-pearl inlay
Height 11.5 cm, top 117 cm × 38 cm
① Central mother-of-pearl inlaid medallion
② Top view

Wang Shixiang Collection

60

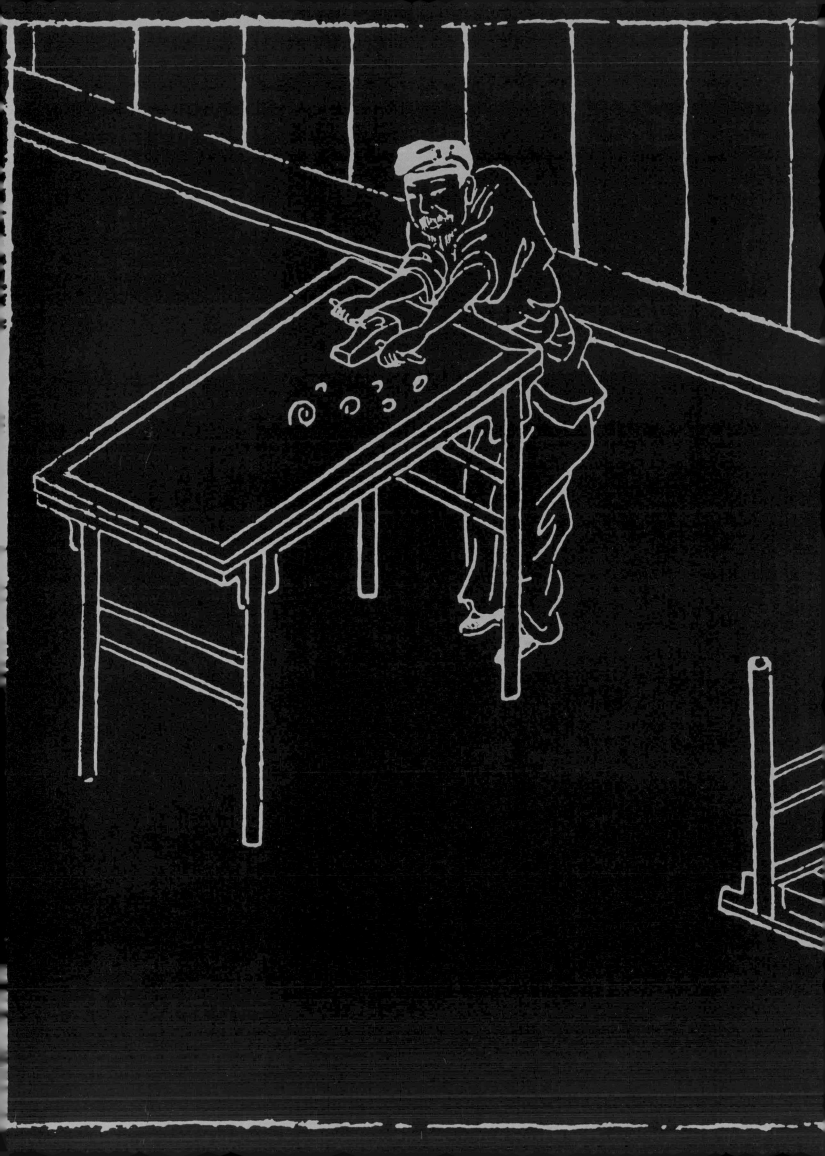

Tables

61

61 Qing dynasty *huanghuali* wood bamboo-style waistless square *kang* table
Height 24 cm, top 80.5 cm × 80.5 cm
Central Academy of Arts and Crafts

62 Qing dynasty *huanghuali* wood waisted wide *kang* table with openwork aprons
Height 31.8 cm, top 99.5 cm × 67 cm
The Palace Museum

63

①

63 Ming dynasty *huanghuali* wood waisted wide *kang* table with unmitred joint of apron and legs
Height 29.5 cm, top 108 cm × 69 cm
① Side view
② One corner of *kang* table
Wang Shixiang Collection

②

64

①

②

64 Ming dynasty *huanghuali* wood waisted wide *kang* table with convex apron and bulging legs ending in horse-hoof feet

Height 29 cm, top 84 cm × 52 cm

① Apron carved with dragons and lotus

② One corner of *kang* table

The Palace Museum

①

65

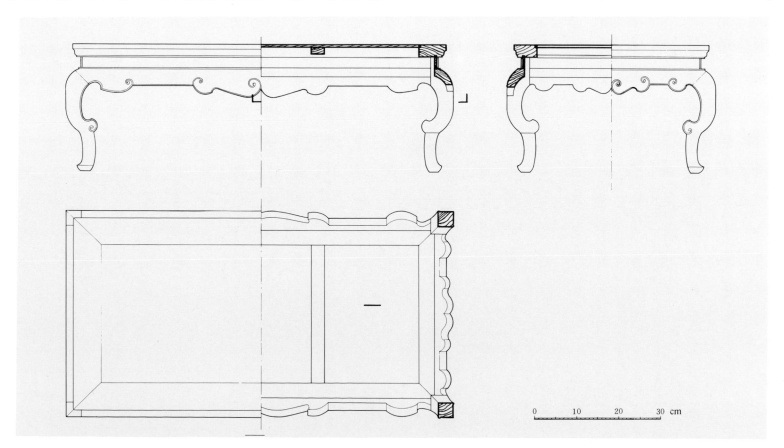

65 Ming dynasty *huanghuali* wood waisted wide *kang* table with cabriole legs
Height 30 cm, top 88 cm × 46 cm
① Side view

Mrs Chen Mengjia Collection

①

66 Ming dynasty *huanghuali* wood high-waisted wide *kang* table
Height 27.5 cm, top 105 cm × 72.5 cm
① One corner of *kang* table
Beijing Timber Factory Collection

①

67 Qing dynasty black lacquer narrow *kang* table
Height 37.2 cm, top 129 cm × 34.5 cm
① Side view

Wang Shixiang Collection

67

0   10   20   30   40 cm

68 Qing dynasty *zitan* wood waistless narrow *kang* table
Height 32.5 cm, top 99 cm × 35 cm
The Summer Palace

68

69 Qing dynasty *zitan* wood narrow *kang* table with recessed legs and elongated bridle joints
Height 32.3 cm, top 93 cm × 32 cm

The Summer Palace

70 Ming dynasty *jichi* wood narrow *kang* table with outward-curving side legs and everted flanges
Height 32.5 cm, top 130 cm × 32.5 cm
① Openwork cloud motifs on apron-head spandrels

Mrs Chen Mengjia Collection

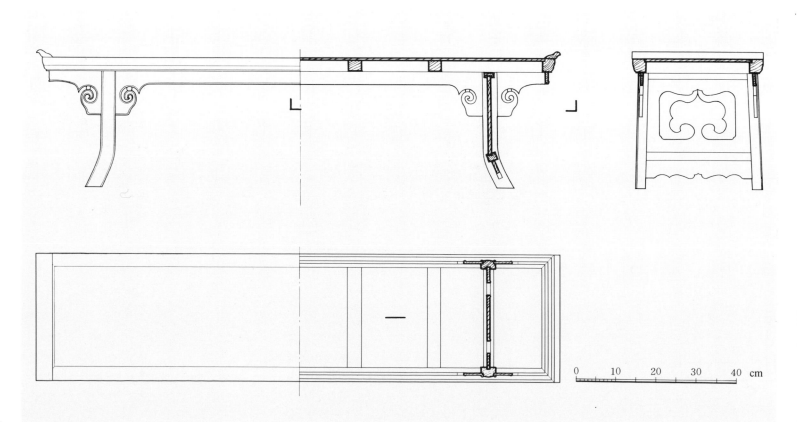

71

①

71 Qing dynasty *jichi* wood large narrow three-drawer *kang* table with recessed legs

Height 48 cm, top 191 cm × 48.5 cm

① Side view showing inset panel with cloud design

Wang Shixiang Collection

①

72 Ming dynasty *huanghuali* **wood three-legged incense stand**
Height 89.3 cm, diameter of top 43.3 cm
① Apron with curling tendril design
Wang Shixiang Collection

72

①

73 Ming dynasty *tieli* wood high-waisted five-legged incense stand
Height 89 cm, diameter of top 61 cm, diameter of shoulder 67 cm
① Ornamental panel with begonia-shaped opening
Wang Shixiang Collection

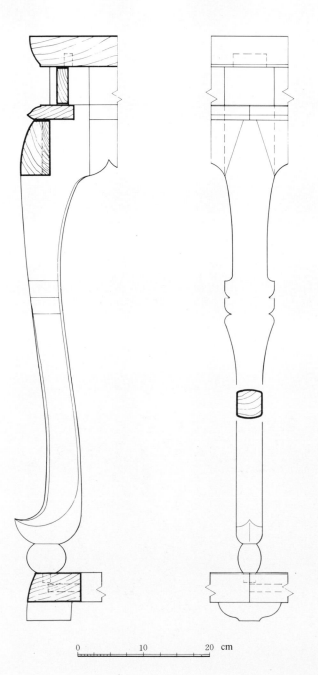

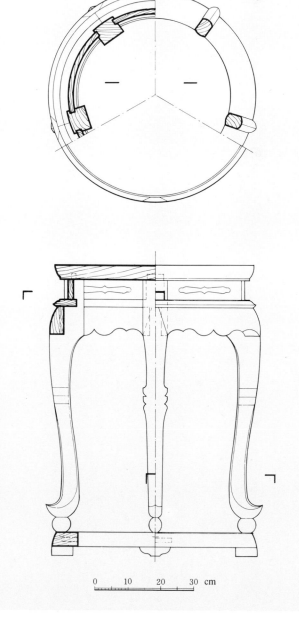

0   10   20 cm

0   10   20   30 cm

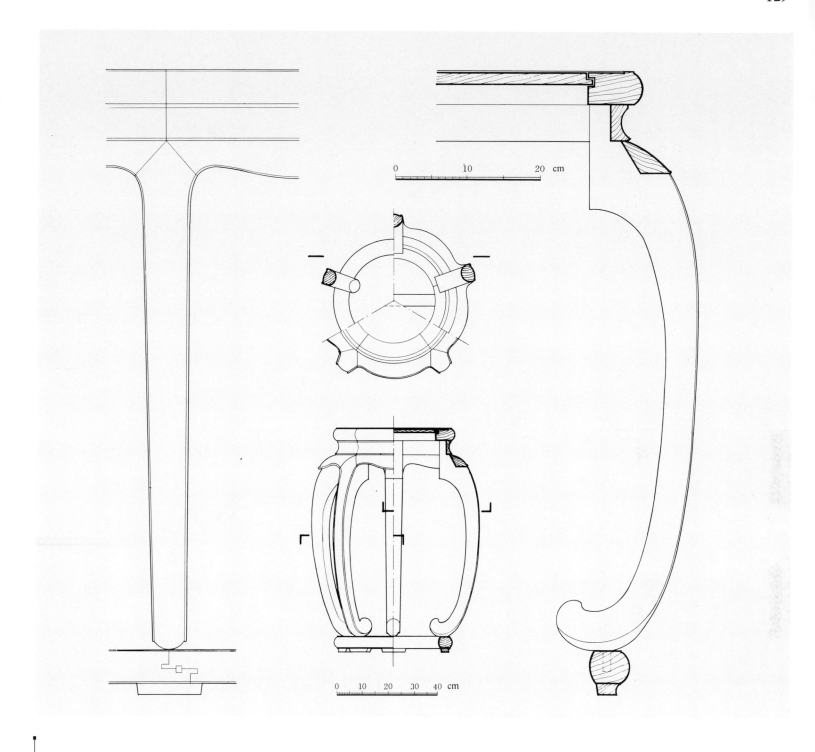

**74 Ming dynasty *huanghuali* wood incense stand
with five inward-turning legs**

Height 85.5 cm, diameter of top 47.2 cm

Mrs Chen Mengjia Collection

75

**75 Ming dynasty *huanghuali* wood
four-legged octagonal incense stand**
Height 103 cm, top 50.5 cm × 37.2 cm
Wang Shixiang Collection

①

76

**76 Ming dynasty *huanghuali* wood
high-waisted incense stand with six
legs**
Height 73 cm, top 50.5 cm × 39.2 cm
① High waist with two registers

The Palace Museum

77

**77 Ming dynasty *huanghuali* wood wine table with
elongated bridle joints**
Height 76 cm, top 57 cm × 79 cm
Mrs Chen Mengjia Collection

78 Ming dynasty *huanghuali* wood wine table with elongated bridle joints

Height 81 cm, top 110 cm × 55 cm

① Openwork cloud motifs on apron-head spandrels

Beijing Hardwood Furniture Factory Collection

**79 Ming dynasty *tieli* wood wine table
with inserted shoulder joints**
Height 72 cm, top 94.7 cm × 50 cm
Wang Shixiang Collection

80

①

80 Ming dynasty *huanghuali* wood wine table with inserted shoulder joints

Height 83 cm, top 106 cm × 54 cm
① Top view showing green marble slab

Beijing Hardwood Furniture Factory
Collection

81

81 Qing dynasty *hong* wood waistless half table with straight leg-encircling stretcher and latticework
Height 82 cm, top 97 cm × 63 cm
Beijing Hardwood Furniture Factory Collection

**82 Qing dynasty southern cypress waistless half table
with straight stretchers and pillar-shaped struts**
Height 84.5 cm, top 98.5 cm × 67 cm
Wang Shixiang Collection

83 Ming dynasty *huanghuali* wood waisted bracket-shaped half table
Height 87 cm, top 98.5 cm × 64.3 cm
① One corner of table

The Summer Palace

84 Ming dynasty *huanghuali* wood waisted half table in the form of a low table with extended legs
Height 87 cm, top 104 cm × 64.2 cm
① One corner of table
② Apron carved with phoenixes facing the sun
③ Side view of top portion of table

Wang Shixiang Collection

84

① ② ③

**85 Ming dynasty *huanghuali* wood waistless square
table with humpbacked stretchers and decorative
struts**
Height 80 cm, top 93.2 cm × 93.2 cm
Mrs Chen Mengjia Collection

85

86

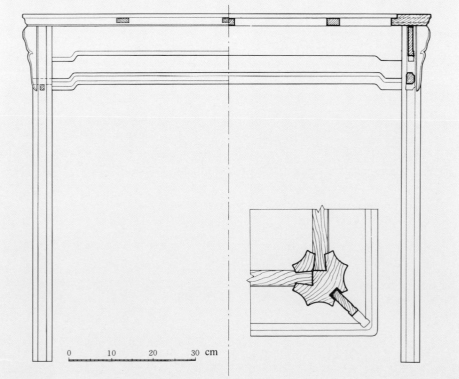

86 Ming dynasty *huanghuali* wood square table with three spandrels to one leg and humpbacked stretchers
Height 83 cm, top 98 cm × 98 cm
Zhang An Collection

87 Ming dynasty *huanghuali* wood small square table with three spandrels to one leg and humpbacked stretchers
Height 81 cm, top 82 cm × 82 cm
① One corner of table

Wang Shixiang Collection

①

87

88

**88 Ming dynasty *huanghuali* wood square table
with three spandrels to one leg and humpbacked
stretchers with decorative struts**
Height 85.5 cm, top 89 cm × 89 cm
① Spandrels, humpback of stretcher and
decorative strut

Wang Shixiang Collection

①

89

① One corner of table

89 Ming dynasty *huanghuali* wood waistless square table with apron and spandrels made by joining the straight
Height 84 cm, top 102.5 cm × 103.8 cm
① One corner of table
The Palace Museum

90 Ming dynasty *huanghuali* wood waisted large square table with protruding top
Height 89.2 cm, top 128 cm × 128 cm
Wang Shixiang Collection

90

91

①

91 Qing dynasty *huanghuali* wood waisted square table in the form of a low table with extended legs
Height 86.5 cm, top 93.5 cm × 91.2 cm
① Relief carving at end of apron and openwork carving at end of stretcher

The Palace Museum

92

92 **Ming dynasty *tieli* wood waistless narrow rectangular table with oval openings on the solid board legs**
Height 87 cm, top 191.5 cm × 50 cm
Mrs Chen Mengjia Collection

93 **Qing dynasty *zitan* wood waistless narrow rectangular table with corner legs, leg-encircling humpbacked stretcher and pillar-shaped struts**
Height 83.5 cm, top 106 cm × 35.5 cm
The Summer Palace

①

94 Ming dynasty *huanghuali* wood waistless narrow rectangular table with corner legs and humpbacked stretchers

Height 87 cm, top 112 cm × 54.5 cm

① Relief and openwork carving on apron-head spandrel

Beijing Hardwood Furniture Factory Collection

95

**95 Qing dynasty *zitan* wood narrow rectangular
table with corner legs and a cusped apron**
Height 83.5 cm, top 105 cm × 35 cm
The Summer Palace

① Side view of top portion of table

**96 Qing dynasty *zitan* wood narrow rectangular
table with corner legs and with three spandrels
to one leg**
Height 82 cm, top 105 cm × 36.5 cm
① Side view of top portion of table

The Palace Museum

97 Ming dynasty *huanghuali* wood straight-form narrow rectangular table with corner legs and everted flanges

Height 86 cm, top 112.5 cm × 48.5 cm

① Drawers slightly open

Beijing Hardwood Furniture Factory Collection

98 Ming dynasty *huanghuali* wood narrow rectangular table with corner legs and giant's arm braces
Height 78.5 cm, top 98 cm × 48 cm
Mrs Chen Mengjia Collection

**99 Ming dynasty *huanghuali* wood high-waisted
narrow rectangular table with corner legs**
Height 80 cm, top 98.5 cm × 48.5 cm
Beijing Hardwood Furniture Factory Collection

100

①

100 **Ming dynasty *huanghuali* wood table with recessed legs, elongated bridle joints, and everted flanges**

Height 86.2 cm, top 126.2 cm × 39.7 cm

① Elongated bridle joint
② Side view

Wang Shixiang Collection

②

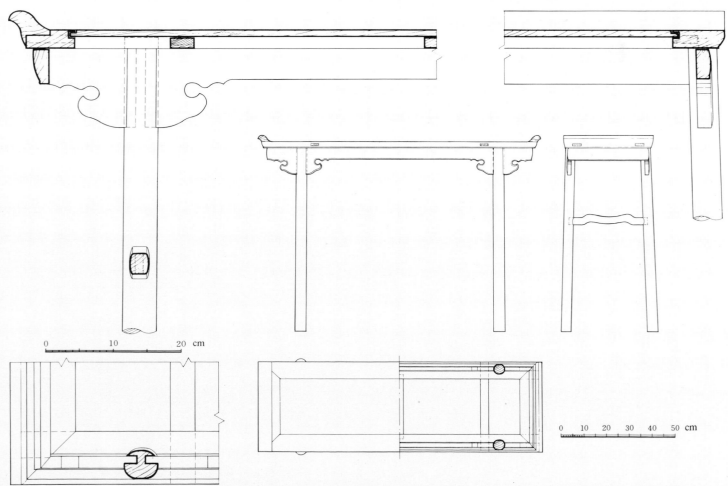

101

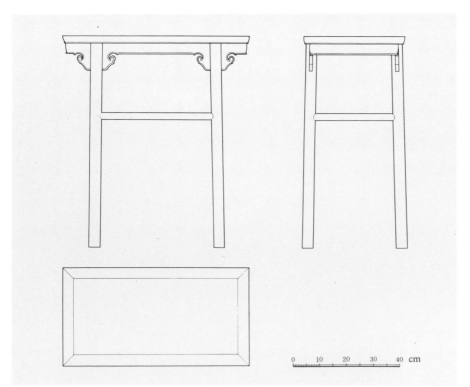

101 Ming dynasty *huanghuali* wood small flat-top narrow table with recessed legs, elongated bridle joints and a shelf
Height 81 cm, top 71.2 cm × 37.7 cm
Mrs Chen Mengjia Collection

0   10   20   30   40 cm

**102 Ming dynasty *jichi* wood flat-top narrow table
with recessed legs, elongated bridle joints and
straight rods**
Height 79.5 cm, top 87 cm × 43 cm
① Side view
Wang Shixiang Collection

103

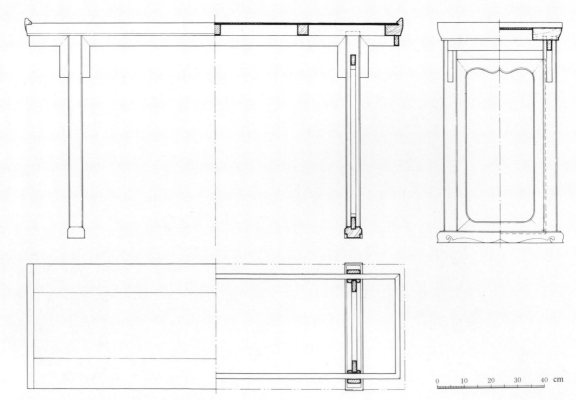

①

**103 Ming dynasty *huanghuali* wood
table with recessed legs, everted
flanges and elongated bridle joints**
Height 83 cm, top 141 cm × 47 cm
① Side view
② Top view showing grain of wood and
floating panel inserted into groove
under everted flanges

Wang Shixiang Collection

②

104

104 Ming dynasty *huanghuali* wood large flat-top narrow table with recessed legs and elongated bridle joints
Height 93 cm, top 350 cm × 62.7 cm
① Table with rectangular stool in Plate 9, showing relative sizes

Wang Shixiang Collection

05

105 Qing dynasty *ju* wood flat-top narrow table with recessed legs, humpbacked stretchers and ornamental struts
Height 83 cm,
top 84.5 cm × 37.5 cm
① Side view

Wang Shixiang Collection

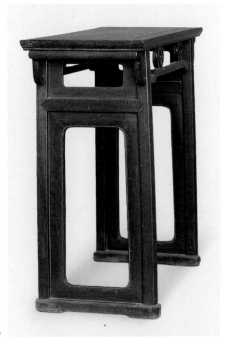

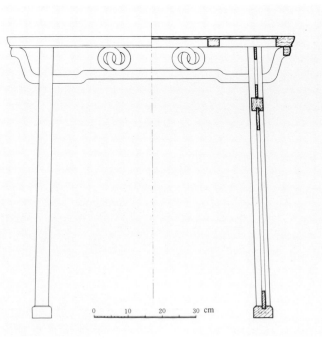

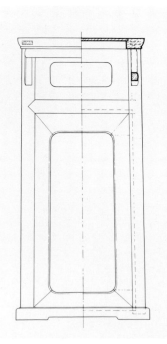

①

106

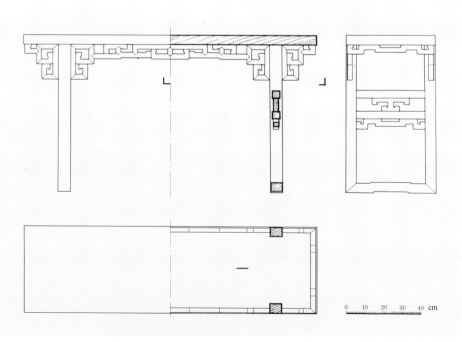

106 Ming dynasty *huanghuali* wood flat-top narrow table with recessed legs, apron made by joining the straight, and floor base stretchers
Height 84.5 cm, top 158 cm × 47.4 cm
① Side view

Mrs Chen Mengjia Collection

①

107 **Ming dynasty** *huanghuali* **wood narrow table with recessed legs, everted flanges and inserted shoulder joints**
Height 87 cm, top 140 cm × 28 cm
① Inserted shoulder joint
Wang Shixiang Collection

①

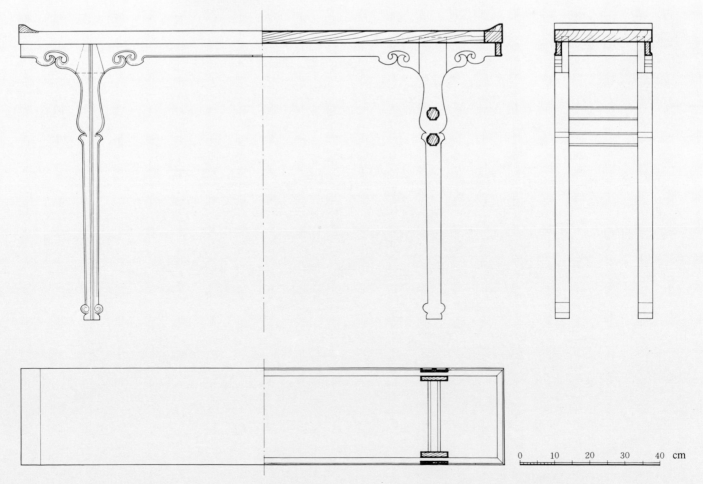

0   10   20   30   40 cm

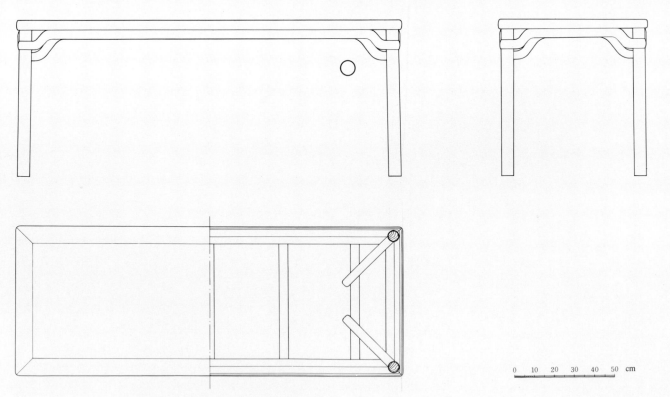

0 10 20 30 40 50 cm

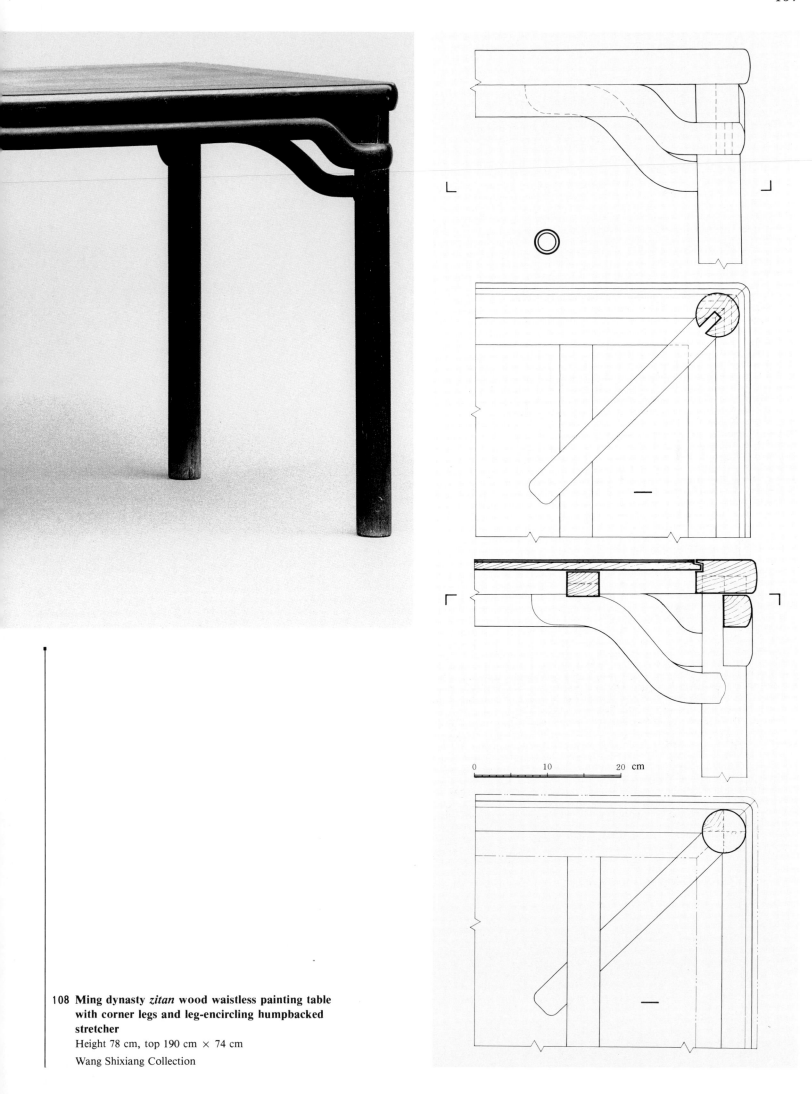

108 Ming dynasty *zitan* wood waistless painting table with corner legs and leg-encircling humpbacked stretcher

Height 78 cm, top 190 cm × 74 cm

Wang Shixiang Collection

0   10   20 cm

109

①

109 Ming dynasty *zitan* wood straight-form painting table with corner legs and relief carving
Height 81.3 cm, top 173.5 cm × 86.5 cm
① Side view
② One corner of table
Zhejiang Provincial Museum

②

①

110 Ming dynasty *zitan* wood waisted painting table
  Height 84 cm, top 171 cm × 74.4 cm,
  largest dimensions 180 cm × 85 cm
① Side view

  The Palace Museum

111 **Ming dynasty** *huanghuali* **wood painting table**
with recessed legs and elongated bridle joints
Height 82.5 cm, top 151 cm × 69 cm
① Elongated bridle joint

Wang Shixiang Collection

①

112

①

②

112 **Ming dynasty *huanghuali* wood small painting
table with recessed legs and elongated bridle
joints**
Height 82 cm, top 107 cm × 70 cm
① Elongated bridle joint
② Marble top
Beijing Timber Factory Collection

13

①

113 **Ming dynasty *huanghuali* wood painting table with recessed legs and elongated bridle joints**
Height 85 cm, top 138 cm × 75.5 cm
① Side view
The Palace Museum

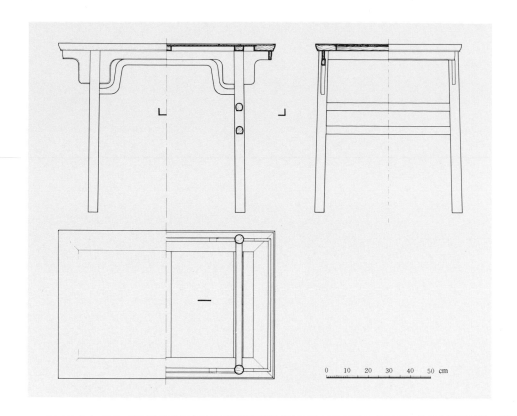

0 10 20 30 40 50 cm

114 **Ming dynasty *huanghuali* wood small
painting table with recessed legs, elongated
bridle joints and humpbacked stretchers**
Height 81.5 cm, top 102 cm × 70.2 cm
Mrs Chen Mengjia Collection

15

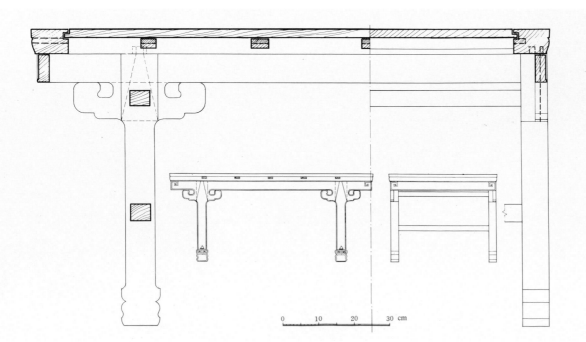

0   10   20   30 cm

①

②

③

115 Ming dynasty *zitan* wood painting table with recessed legs and inserted shoulder joints

Height 83 cm, top 192.8 cm × 102.5 cm

① Table without top and aprons
② Inserted bridle joint
③ Rubbing of Pu Tong's inscription engraved on one of the aprons

Wang Shixiang Collection

116 **Ming dynasty** *huanghuali* **wood trestle painting table**
Overall height 84.5 cm, top 192.2 cm × 69.5 cm × 6 cm thick, stands 36.5 cm × 69.5 cm

Beijing Cultural Relics Store

116

117

①

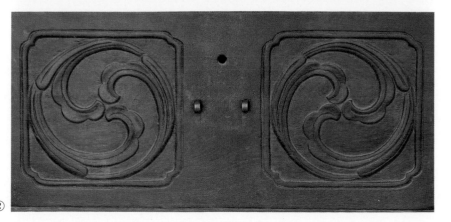

②

117 Ming dynasty *tieli* wood narrow table with four drawers
Height 87 cm, top 174 cm × 51.5 cm
① Floral design on drawer front
② Lucky grass design on drawer front
The Palace Museum

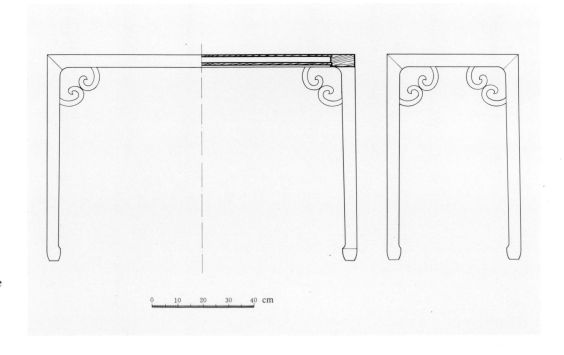

118 Ming dynasty *huanghuali* wood lute table with double-curl spandrels
Height 82 cm, top 120 cm × 51.8 cm
Mrs Chen Mengjia Collection

11

①

**119 Ming dynasty *nan* wood inlaid with *huanghuali*
wood waisted altar table with giant's arm braces**
Height 91 cm, top 152 cm × 82.5 cm
① Leg with elephant design inlaid with *huanghuali* wood
Fayuansi Collection

Beds

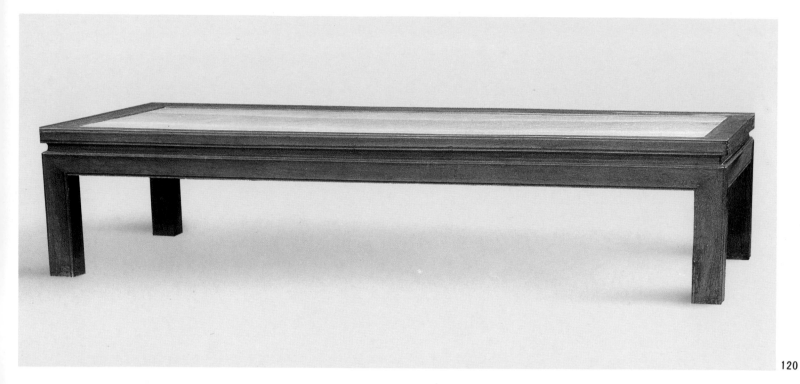

120

21

120 **Ming dynasty *huanghuali* wood waisted straight-leg daybed**
Height 46.4 cm, top 206.5 cm × 80.2 cm
Mrs Chen Mengjia Collection

121 **Ming dynasty *huanghuali* wood six-legged folding daybed**
Height 49 cm, top 208 cm × 155 cm
The Palace Museum

122 Ming dynasty *zitan* wood Luohan bed with solid three-panel screen railings
Height 66 cm, top 197.5 cm × 95.5 cm
Mrs Zhu Guangmu Collection

122

124

**124 Ming dynasty *tieli* wood Luohan bed with *zitan*
wood three-panel screen railings**
Height 83 cm, top 221 cm × 122 cm
① Lattice made by joining the straight
Wang Shixiang Collection

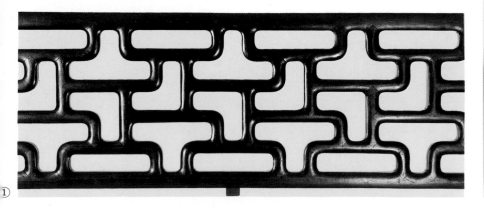

123

123 **Qing dynasty *ju* wood Luohan bed with three-panel screen railings with inset panels**

Height 88 cm, top 200 cm × 92 cm

① Central portion of back panel with hornless dragons and *lingzhi* fungus in high relief

Wang Shixiang Collection

①

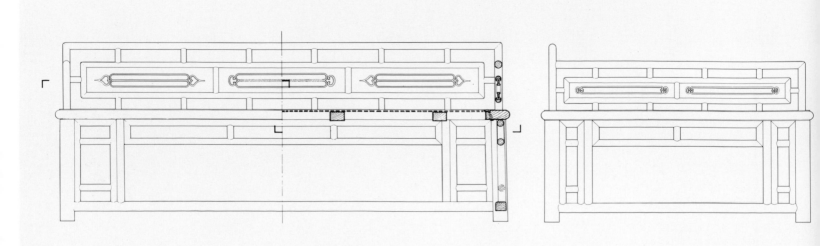

125

125 **Qing dynasty** *zitan* **wood Luohan bed with
three-panel screen railings with inserted panels**
Height 85 cm, top 216 cm × 130 cm
① Ornamental panels

Wang Shixiang Collection

①

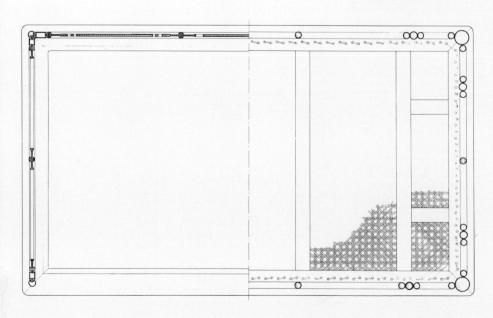

0 10 20 30 40 50 cm

①

126 **Ming dynasty *huanghuali* wood canopy bed with front railings**
Height 231 cm, top 218.5 cm × 147.5 cm
① Side view
The Palace Museum

126

128 Ming dynasty *huanghuali* wood canopy bed with full-moon opening

Height 227 cm, top 247.5 cm × 187.8 cm

① Base of bed with posts and railings
② Base of bed
③ One corner of bed
④ Lattice composed of units of four cloud motifs linked by crosses
⑤ Relief carving of birds and flowers on waist and dragons on apron
⑥ One corner of base of bed

The Palace Museum

①

②

④

⑤

③

⑥

①

②

127 Carved panels of a Ming dynasty *huanghuali* wood canopy bed
Front railings 34.2 cm × 26.2 cm × 2.4 cm thick, side railings 129 cm × 27 cm × 2.4 cm thick
① Side railing carved with openwork hornless dragon design
② Front railing carved with openwork hornless dragon design

Wang Shixiang Collection

129 Ming dynasty *zitan* wood waisted kidney-shaped footstool
Height 17 cm, top 72.5 cm × 36 cm
The Palace Museum

129

Shelves
and
Cabinets

**130 Ming dynasty *huanghuali* wood three-tiered
shelves**
Height 188 cm, shelves 103 cm × 43.6 cm
Mrs Chen Mengjia Collection

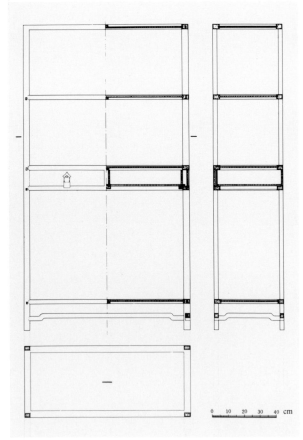

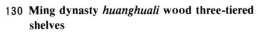

0   10   20   30   40 cm

130

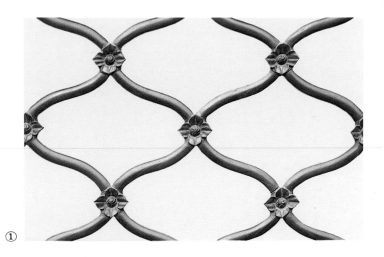

132

①

**132 Ming dynasty *huanghuali*
wood shelves with lattice
back**
Height 168 cm, shelves 107 cm
× 45 cm
① Wavy pattern of lattice back
Mrs Chen Mengjia Collection

131 Ming dynasty *huanghuali* wood shelves with alternating-square-openings lattice railings
Height 177.5 cm, shelves 98 cm × 46 cm
① Lattice above side of top shelf
② Drawer front carved with hornless dragons in relief

Wang Shixiang Collection

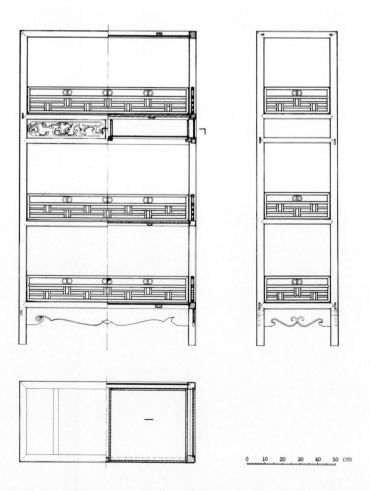

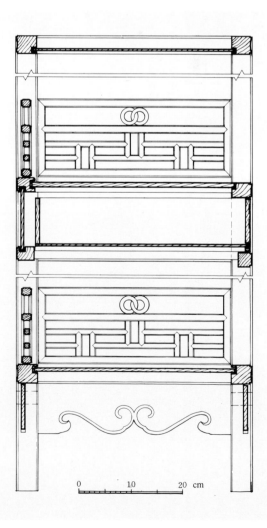

**133 Ming dynasty *zitan* wood shelves
with lattice on three sides made
by joining the straight**
Height 191 cm, shelves 101 cm × 51 cm
The Palace Museum

**134 Ming dynasty *huanghuali* wood shelves
supported by stands**
Height 129 cm, shelves 91 cm × 40 cm
① Shelves supported by two stands
Wang Shixiang Collection

①

135 Ming dynasty *zitan* wood shelves with rods on doors and sides

Overall height 179 cm, shelves 100.3 cm × 48.2 cm × 132 cm high, stand 100.3 cm × 48.2 cm × 47 cm high

① Shelves with one door open

Mrs Chen Mengjia Collection

0 10 20 30 40 cm

136 Ming dynasty *huanghuali* **wood Wanli display cabinet**

Overall height 187 cm, cabinet 113 cm × 55.5 cm × 166 cm high, stand 115 cm × 57.5 cm × 21 cm high

Beijing Cultural Relics Store

138 Ming dynasty *huanghuali* **wood display cabinet with two open shelves**

Height 117 cm, shelves 119 cm × 50 cm

The Palace Museum

①

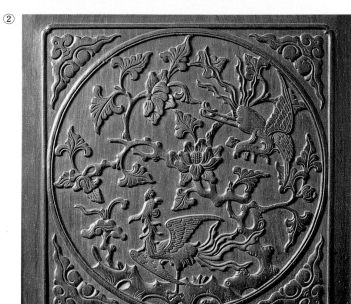

②

137 Ming dynasty *huanghuali* wood carved Wanli display cabinets

Overall height 195.5 cm, 124.8 cm × 55.5 cm × 172 cm high, stand 126.5 cm × 57 cm × 23.5 cm high

① Open shelf

② Top panel of left-hand door and bottom panel of right-hand door, each with design of birds and flowers in relief

Huang Zhou Collection

14

141 Ming dynasty *huanghuali* wood round-corner cabinet
Overall height 130.5 cm, top 77 cm × 41 cm, lowest
part 76 cm × 39.5 cm

Ye Wanfa Collection

142 Ming dynasty *ju* wood round-corner cabinet
Overall height 167 cm, top 94 cm × 49 cm, lowest
part 95 cm × 50 cm

Wang Shixiang Collection

143 Ming dynasty *tieli* wood round-corner cabinet with doors and five horizontal members
Overall height 187.5 cm, top 98 cm × 52 cm, lowest part 97 cm × 51 cm
Beijing Cultural Relics Bureau

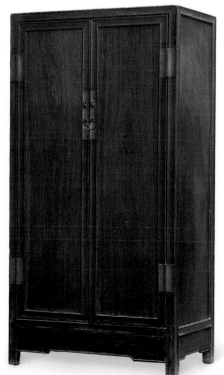

145

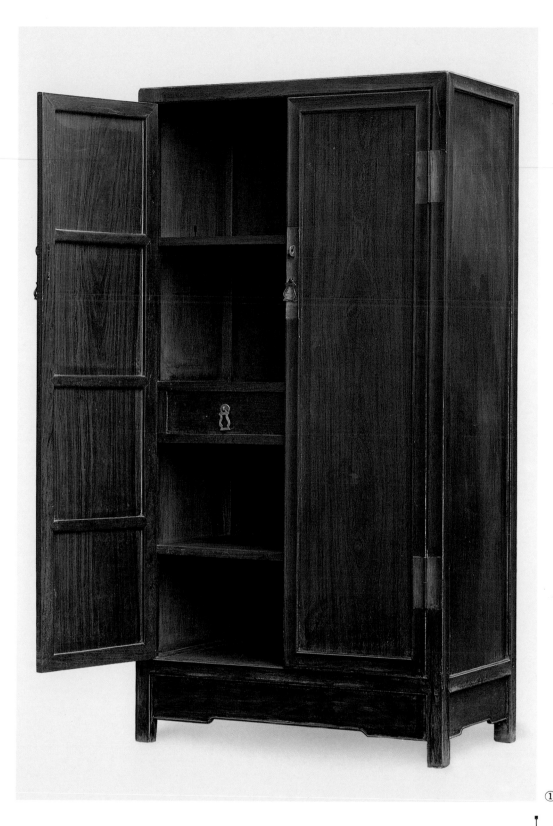

①

145 Qing dynasty *huanghuali* wood square-corner cabinet
Height 161 cm, top 82.5 cm × 47 cm
① Cabinet with one door open
Beijing Cultural Relics Bureau

216

44

① Cabinet with one door open

144 Ming dynasty *huanghuali* wood variation of a round-corner cabinet

Height 175.5 cm, dimensions 106 cm × 53 cm

① Cabinet with one door open

Wang Shixiang Collection

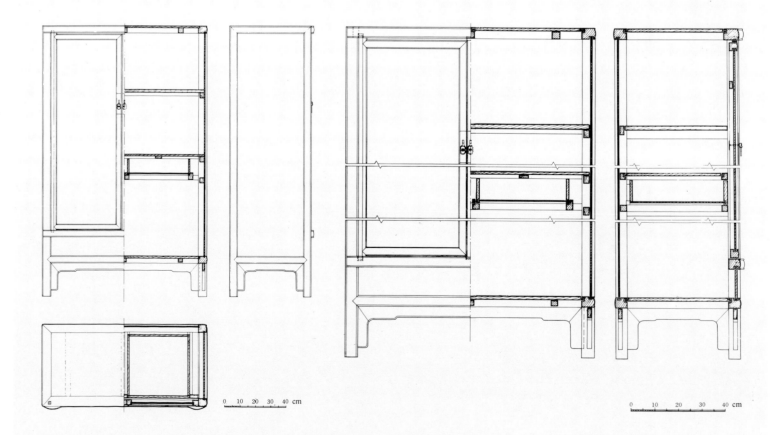

**146 Ming dynasty *huanghuali* wood
doors with four-cloud motif from
a square-corner cabinet**
Each door: height 168 cm,
width 47 cm, thickness 5 cm
① Design composed of four cloud motifs
surrounding a coiled dragon, glued to
a panel

Beijing Hardwood Furniture Factory
Collection

①

**148 Ming dynasty *huanghuali* wood
small compound wardrobe in four
parts**
Overall height 162 cm, lower part 69 cm
× 37.5 cm × 125 cm high, upper part
69 cm × 37.5 cm × 37 cm high

Beijing Hardwood Furniture Factory
Collection

①

②

147 Ming dynasty *huanghuali* wood square-corner cabinet

Height 192 cm, top 123.5 cm × 78.5 cm
① Portion of back with fine crack patterns
② Side view

Tianjin Cultural Relics Store

**149 Qing dynasty *huanghuali* wood large
compound wardrobe in four parts with one-
hundred-precious-material inlay**
Overall height 279 cm, lower part 187.5 cm
× 72.5 cm × 195 cm high, upper part 187.5 cm
× 72.5 cm × 84 cm high
① Front view
② One-hundred-precious-material inlay
③ One-hundred-precious-material inlay and face plate

The Palace Museum

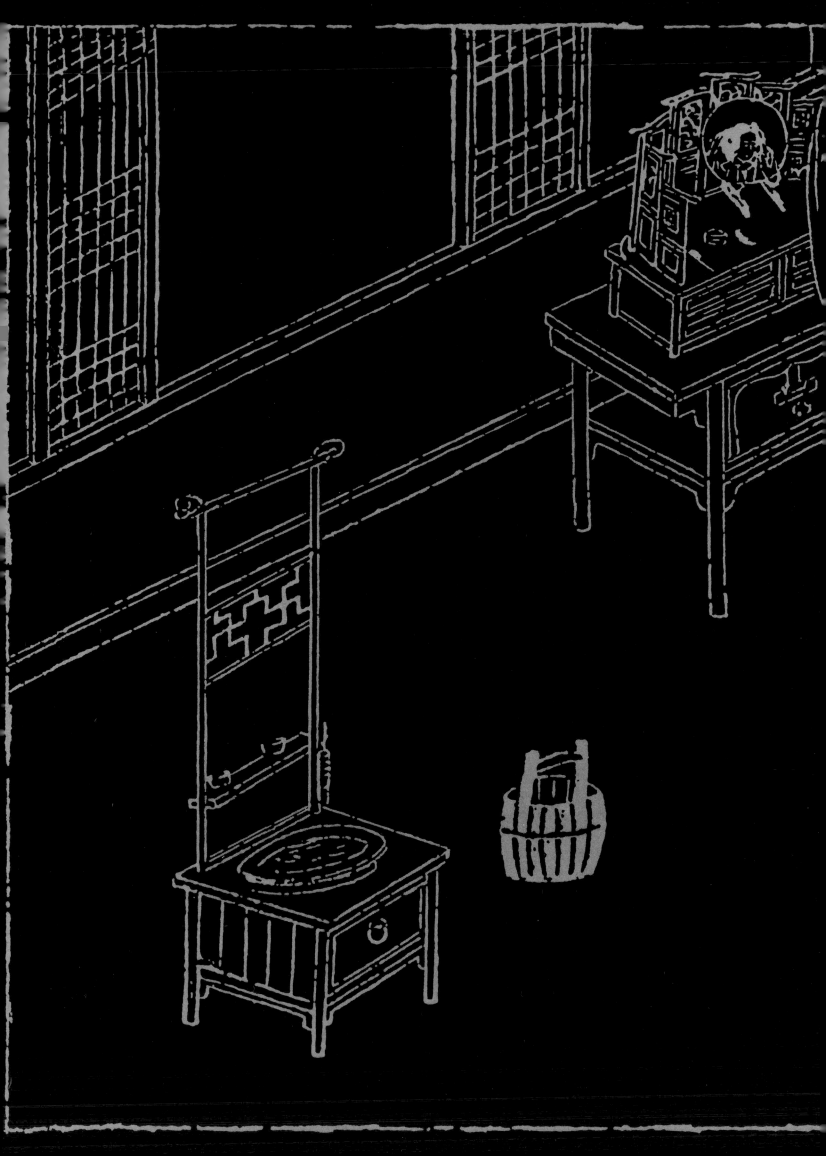

Miscellaneous

①

②

**150 Ming dynasty *huanghuali* wood
screen set in a stand with
removable panel**
Height 245.5 cm, base 150 cm × 78 cm
① Front view of stand
② Side view of stand

The Palace Museum

51

①

②

151 Ming dynasty *huanghuali* wood small screen set in a stand

Height 70.5 cm, base 73.5 cm × 39.5 cm

① Side view of stand
② One corner of frame of screen

Wang Shixiang Collection

152 Ming dynasty *huanghuali* wood small screen set in a stand with removable panel
Height 36.5 cm, base 38 cm × 15 cm
① Side view of stand

Wang Shixiang Collection

153 Ming dynasty *tieli* wood coffer
Height 85 cm, top 98 cm × 47 cm
Wang Shixiang Collection

154

①

**154 Ming dynasty *huanghuali* wood
two-drawer coffer with hornless
dragon designs**
Height 89.5 cm, top 112 cm × 59 cm
① Drawer front carved with hornless
dragons in relief

Wang Shixiang Collection

155

①

②

155 Ming dynasty *huanghuali* wood two-drawer coffer with dragon designs
Height 90 cm, top 160 cm × ·52 cm
① Dragon and flaming pearl carved on portion of front panel of hidden compartment
② Drawer front

Beijing Hardwood Furniture Factory Collection

**156 Ming dynasty *huanghuali* wood
three-drawer coffer**
Height 90.5 cm, top 177.5 cm × 56.8 cm
Tianjin Museum of History

157 Ming dynasty *huanghuali* wood small chest
 Height 18.7 cm, top 42 cm × 24 cm
 Wang Shixiang Collection

①

158

**158 Ming dynasty *huanghuali* wood medicine chest
in the shape of a square-corner cabinet**
Height 46 cm, top 38 cm × 27.5 cm
① Medicine chest with one door open

Beijing Hardwood Furniture Factory Collection

159

**159 Ming dynasty *huanghuali* wood medicine chest
in the shape of a picnic box**
Height 77 cm, chest 69 cm × 41.5 cm,
base 78 cm × 45 cm
① Medicine chest with one door open

Beijing Hardwood Furniture Factory Collection

160 Ming dynasty *huanghuali* wood picnic box
Height 21.3 cm, top 36 cm × 20 cm
① Picnic box with top tier and lid removed

Wang Shixiang Collection

160

161 Ming dynasty *jichi* wood desk tray
Height 15.4 cm, top 35.4 cm × 35.4 cm
Wang Shixiang Collection

165

①

165 Ming dynasty *huanghuali* wood dressing case

Height 37 cm, top 35 cm × 23.5 cm

① Dressing case with lid and two doors open

Beijing Hardwood Furniture Factory Collection

162

162 Ming dynasty *huanghuali* wood folding mirror platform

Height of folding panel when raised 60 cm, when level 25.5 cm, platform 49 cm × 49 cm

① Right segment of top register
② Folding panel
③ Mirror platform with doors open

Wang Shixiang Collection

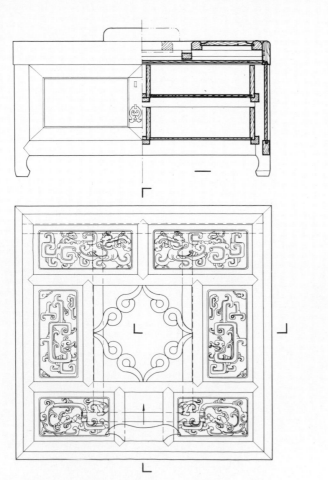

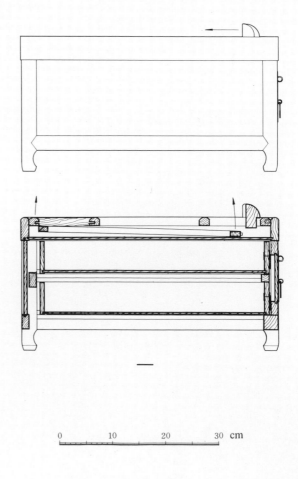

0   10   20   30 cm

②

①

③

**163 Ming dynasty *huanghuali* wood throne-type
mirror platform**
Height 52 cm, top 43 cm × 28 cm
① Side view
② Back view
Wang Shixiang Collection

①

②

**164 Qing dynasty *huanghuali* wood mirror platform
with five-panel screen**
Height 72 cm, top 55.5 cm × 36.5 cm
① Dragon head in the round
② Top of central panel

Beijing Hardwood Furniture Factory Collection

**166 Ming dynasty *huanghuali* wood
clothes rack with phoenix designs**
Height 168.5 cm, base 176 cm × 47.5 cm
① Ornamental panel with openwork
phoenix design
② Top rail and hanging spandrel
③ Side view of lower portion of rack

Wang Shixiang Collection

167 Ming dynasty *huanghuali* wood central panel of a clothes rack

Lattice panel 144.5 cm × 29.4 cm

① Coiled phoenix
② Spandrel
③ Portion of panel

Wang Shixiang Collection

①

②

168 Ming dynasty *huanghuali* **wood six-legged folding washbasin stand**

Height 66.2 cm, diameter 50 cm

① Stand collapsed
② Up-and-down lotus at top of one leg
③ Stand with bronze basin

Wang Shixiang Collection

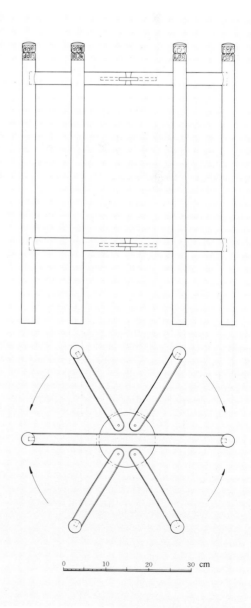

0 10 20 30 cm

169 Ming dynasty *huanghuali* wood washbasin stand with towel rack
Overall height 168 cm, diameter of rack 58.5 cm
① Top rail and hanging spandrel
② Central panel
Mrs Chen Mengjia Collection

①

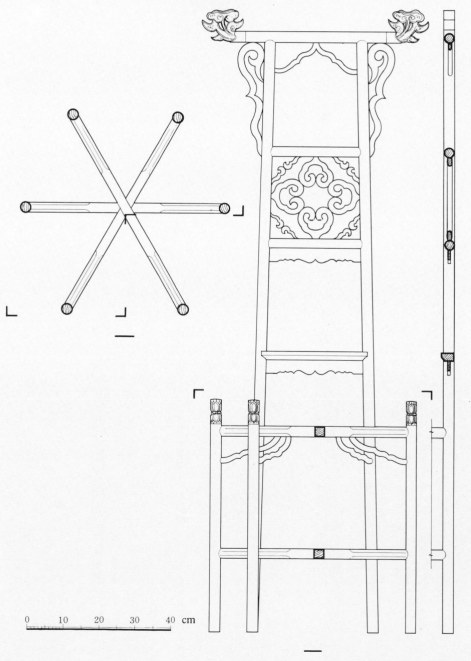

②

0 10 20 30 40 cm

①

②

170 Ming dynasty *huanghuali* wood decorated washbasin stand with towel rack

Overall height 176 cm, diameter of rack 60 cm

① Dragon head in the round at end of top rail

② Central panel carved with openwork design of boy riding a *qilin*

Wang Shixiang Collection

①

171 Qing dynasty *huanghuali* wood washbasin stand with towel rack with one-hundred-precious-material inlay
Overall height 201.5 cm, height of front legs 74.5 cm, diameter of rack 71 cm
① Central panel with scene of tribute bearers with one-hundred-precious-material inlay

The Palace Museum

171

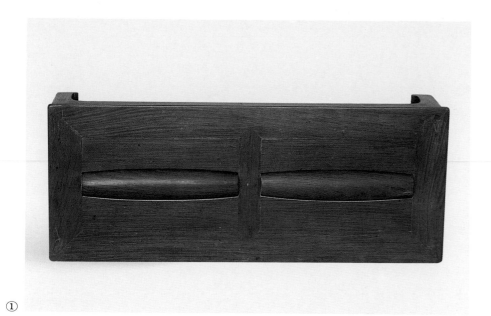

①

②

172 Ming dynasty *huanghuali* wood roller stool
Height 21 cm, top 77 cm × 31.2 cm
① Top view
② Bottom view

Wang Shixiang Collection

172

①

173 Qing dynasty *hong* wood sugar-cane squeezer
Height 27 cm, top 29 cm × 11 cm
① One end of squeezer

Wang Shixiang Collection

174

174 Qing dynasty *zuo* **wood bench- shaped pillow**
Height 9.8 cm, top 20.8 cm × 7.5 cm
Wang Shixiang Collection

175

①

175 Qing dynasty *zitan* wood miniature table with recessed legs and everted flanges
Height 9.5 cm, top 19.6 cm × 4.8 cm
① Miniature table placed on large table of similar form, showing relative sizes

Wang Shixiang Collection

Notes on the Plates

262

1 **Interior view of Shufangzhai 漱芳齋, the Palace Museum**
In this room a number of pieces of Ming and Qing furniture are on display. In the centre there is a small Ming dynasty *huanghuali* wood painting table with recessed legs (Pl. 113) flanked by two drum stools (Pl. 27), the group forming an appropriate spot for playing chess. The *zitan* wood rose chairs placed in a row along the north windows were made in the early Qing dynasty. The tea tables and trestle table date from the mid Qing dynasty.

2 **Interior view of Shufangzhai, the Palace Museum**
Shufangzhai is known for its small stage, on which there is small Ming *huanghuali* wood painting table with recessed legs (Pl. 113).

3 **Interior view of Chuxiugong 儲秀宮, the Palace Museum**
Chuxiugong was one of the six small western residential palaces within the Imperial Palace. Washbasin stands (Pl. 171), both in the palace and in a commoner's dwelling, were always used in the bedroom.

4 **West Hall of Paiyundian 排雲殿, Zixiaoge 紫霄閣, the Summer Palace**
While most of the pieces of furniture in Paiyundian date from the Qing dynasty, the half table (Pl. 83) and the two chairs (one of which is shown in Plate 49) are very good Ming dynasty pieces.

5 **Corner of Huang Zhou's 黃胄 studio**
A pair of Wanli cabinets (Pl. 137) is appropriately placed together along an entire wall, and antiques are displayed on the open shelves. Huang Zhou is a contemporary painter renowned for his paintings of donkeys and figures.

6 **Corner of Wang Shixiang's 王世襄 studio**
In the centre is the large Ming dynasty *zitan* wood painting table (Pl. 115) which once belonged to Song Muzhong 宋牧仲, and beneath it is a Qing dynasty *zitan* wood footstool with mother-of-pearl inlay (Pl. 60). On the right we see a large narrow Qing dynasty *jichi* wood three-drawer *kang* table with recessed legs (Pl. 71). On the left is placed a Ming dynasty *zitan* wood southern official's hat armchair with a medallion carved with a peony design on its splat (Pl. 50). In front of this a Ming dynasty *tieli* wood high-waisted incense stand (Pl. 73) supports the head of a Liao dynasty (907-1125) iron bodhisattva. Between the windows there is a gently smiling stone Buddha of the Northern Wei dynasty, dated AD 528.

7 Ming dynasty *huanghuali* wood lute table, incense stand and square stool

These three pieces all date from the Ming dynasty and are made of *huanghuali* wood, but the lute table has undergone alteration. One of the antique lutes has an inscription stating that it was in the collection of Tang Yifen 湯貽汾 (1778-1853), a famous calligrapher, poet and lute player. It was made in the Yuan dynasty by Zhu Zhiyuan 朱致遠 , one of the most famous Yuan lute makers. The other lute, made in the Ming dynasty and in the form of a banana leaf, was in the collection of Xi Baochen 錫寶臣 , the famous Manchu lute player, connoisseur and collector who was active in the first quarter of the 20th century.

The incense stand is illustrated in Plate 75 and the square stool in Plate 19.

8 Ming dynasty *huanghuali* wood table with recessed legs and everted flanges, incense stand, and rectangular stool

These are all Ming dynasty pieces made of *huanghuali* wood (Pls 103, 72 and 9). The table with recessed legs and everted flanges is ideal for studying a long handscroll. The partially unrolled handscroll on the table is a painting of plum blossoms by Qian Zai 錢載 (1708-93).

9 Ming dynasty *huanghuali* wood waistless rectangular stool

Height 51 cm, dimensions of seat 51.5 cm × 41 cm; one of a pair

This type of stool, with straight legs and straight stretchers, was already a standard form in Song times and was further developed during the Ming dynasty. The structural resemblances of furniture pieces to wooden buildings are clearly visible in the legs which are straight without horse-hoof feet, are rounded on the outside and square on the inside in cross-section, and which have a quite pronounced splay and aprons between them. The rather massive members, simple mouldings and good proportions display the spirit of Ming dynasty furniture. It is an excellent piece, outstanding among many of the same form.

Originally the stool had a fine rattan seat, which, when the piece appeared on the market about 1950, was already in very bad condition. Although the northern craftsman who replaced the seat could find only a rather coarse rattan, he commendably retained the saddle-like transverse braces. Formerly, whenever the furniture shops in Lu Ban Guan 魯班館 obtained a piece with a torn soft mat seat, their restorers would cut deeper into the inside edge of the frame, replace the curved transverse brace with a straight one, and place the mat on a piece of wood to form the seat. The replacement of a soft seat with a hard seat can hardly be described as repair; rather, it is a violation of the stool.

10 Ming dynasty *huanghuali* wood waistless small square stool

Height 26 cm, dimensions of seat 28 cm × 28 cm; one of a pair

Compared to the preceding example (Pl. 9) this stool is much smaller, but the massiveness of its members gives it a charmingly naïve appearance. It is a rare piece and in the past decades I have not seen any similar to this pair. Such furniture was not used in the main hall but only in bedrooms.

The stool originally had a hard seat, as the *huanghuali* wood floating panel is flush with the frame and there are no traces of holes underneath.

11 Ming dynasty *huanghuali* wood rectangular stool and small square stool

This illustration shows how the rectangular stool (Pl. 9) and the small square stool (Pl. 10) are quite different in size but very much alike in spirit.

12 Ming dynasty *huanghuali* wood waistless square stool with humpbacked leg-encircling stretcher and pillar-shaped struts

Height 51 cm, dimensions of seat 52.5 cm × 52.5 cm

Since the humpbacked stretcher protrudes beyond the surface of the legs as if made of a flexible material, cabinetmakers call it a leg-encircling stretcher. This technique is thought to be adopted from bamboo furniture. Echoing the stretcher, the frame of the top also encircles the legs, but its double round moulding is made from two pieces of wood placed one on top of the other. The lower piece is called a frame-thickening insert. This technique gives the stool a pleasing appearance, while the economic use of wood prevents it from being too heavy.

The original soft cane seat has been replaced by a hard mat seat.

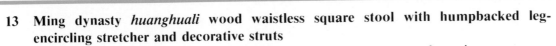

13 Ming dynasty *huanghuali* wood waistless square stool with humpbacked leg-encircling stretcher and decorative struts

Height 46.5 cm, dimensions of seat 50.5 cm × 50.4 cm; one of a pair

The construction of this stool is the same as that in Plate 12, the only difference being that double interlocking circles are used instead of pillar-shaped struts.

14 Qing dynasty *zitan* wood waistless square stool with base stretchers

Overall height 47 cm, dimensions of seat 52.5 cm × 52.5 cm, height of bronze foot 5.5 cm

The round members, humpbacked stretchers with pillar-shaped struts, and base stretchers are all in the Ming style. However, the ice-plate edge moulding has beading which suggests a later date for the stool.

Before seeing this stool I already owned a pair of identical *hong* wood stools which for some inexplicable reason were 5 or 6 centimetres lower than ordinary stools and had a square hole drilled in the base of each leg. Seeing this stool which still had two of its original bronze feet, I at last understood that my own stools must also once have had bronze feet. The feet are about 5.5 centimetres high and consist of bronze cylinders filled with wood, with square mortises in the centre into which fit the bronze tenons of the leg. Such bronze feet prevent the legs from rotting and make the stools the height of an ordinary seat.

The stool has a soft mat seat with a curved brace at each of the four corners of the frame connecting the tenon-bearing and mortise-bearing frame members, instead of long curved braces joining only the tenon-bearing frame members. Under the frame of the seat there are long grooves along the four sides; within these holes have been drilled. After the seat was woven, the grooves were filled with long pieces of wood to hide the knots of the cane and palm-fibre strings. This is a refined method of construction. All these features indicate that the stool was made in the first half of the 18th century.

In his *Chinese Furniture, Hardwood Examples of the Ming and Early Ch'ing Dynasties*, the American author R.H. Ellsworth illustrates in Plate 105 a similar stool made of *jichi* wood. He calls it a litter-bearing stool, inferring that the square holes in the bottom of the legs were used to attach the stool to the base of a sedan chair. Actually this is conjecture. He dates the piece to the 16th century which is too early.

15 Ming dynasty *huanghuali* wood waisted rectangular stool with humpbacked stretchers

Height 50 cm, dimensions of seat 48.5 cm × 42.5 cm; one of a pair

Waisted furniture is usually made up of square members and has horse-hoof feet. Its origins can be traced to the box-construction bed and the Buddhist pedestal.

The waist and apron of this stool are fashioned from a single piece of wood. Typical of the Ming dynasty are the beading of the apron flowing continuously into that of the leg and the well-defined bevel of the horse-hoof foot. Since the humpbacked stretcher is set back a little from the front edge of the leg, the simple straight shoulder joint is used, rather than the more complex double-mitre joint.

16 Ming dynasty *huanghuali* wood waisted rectangular stool with crossed stretchers

Height 48.5 cm, dimensions of seat 55.2 cm × 46.3 cm

Each apron of this stool has three groups of cloud motifs and beading along the edges which continues down the legs to the tips of the horse-hoof feet. The horse-hoof feet are rather short and fat, sturdy and powerful in feeling. Instead of the usual stretcher on four sides, two diagonal stretchers are used. The motif in the centre of each leg echoes those on the aprons, hides the join of the stretcher and leg, and enlarges the leg sufficiently to prevent its being weakened by the mortise for the stretcher. Crossed stretchers occur frequently on washbasin stands but are rather rare on stools.

The original soft cane seat has been replaced by a hard mat seat.

17 Ming dynasty *huanghuali* wood waisted rectangular stool with cabriole legs and humpbacked stretchers

Height 51 cm, dimensions of seat 51 cm × 42 cm

Furniture legs of this form are called cabriole legs in the Qing Dynasty Regulations. The inner contour of apron and legs is derived from the ornamental openings with cusped upper edges of the box construction, intercepted here by a humpbacked stretcher. The individual members are fairly slender and the whole piece has a feeling of lightness and grace.

18 Ming dynasty *huanghuali* wood waisted square stool with cabriole legs and giant's arm braces

Height 52 cm, dimensions of seat 55.5 cm × 55.5 cm

This piece is similar to the stool in Plate 17 in that it has cabriole legs, but the curves are more pronounced. Giant's arm braces are used instead of humpbacked stretchers with the result that the space between apron and legs is unaffected. On account of the giant's arm brace, the upper inside surface of the leg is flattened. The brace is joined to the leg with a hook-and-plug tenon joint and, at its top, meets a curved transverse brace.

19 Ming dynasty *huanghuali* wood waisted square stool with cabriole legs, humpbacked stretchers and pillar-shaped struts

Height 54 cm, dimensions of seat 48 cm × 47.7 cm; one of a pair

This stool resembles the stool in Plate 17 except that its members are larger and there is a curling tendril design on the apron. The greatest difference is that there are two pillar-shaped struts on each side. These are not important for the construction, being merely a superfluous addition spoiling the flow of the lines. Thus in my article "Ming shi jiaju de pin yu bing", I cite this piece as an example of the second defect, redundancy. Such an example shows that not every piece of Ming *huanghuali* wood furniture is necessarily successful.

20 Ming dynasty *zitan* wood waisted square stool with convex aprons and bulging legs ending in horse-hoof feet

Height 52 cm, dimensions of seat 57 cm × 57 cm; one of a set of four

This is a common form of waisted furniture with convex apron and bulging legs ending in horse-hoof feet. The connections between aprons and legs are strengthened with spandrels.

A slightly recessed *zitan* wood board is used for the floating panel of the seat. Since there are no traces of holes on the underside of the frame, the hard seat must be original.

21 Ming dynasty *huanghuali* wood waisted large square stool with convex aprons and bulging legs ending in horse-hoof feet

Height 55 cm, dimensions of seat 64 cm × 64 cm; one of a pair

This stool is similar to that in Plate 20 but more decorative. There is beading along the edge of the apron and foot which terminates in a cloud motif. Instead of separate spandrels, under the apron there is an openwork subsidiary apron attached to the spandrels so as to form an arch. The size of the stool is impressive, and the materials and workmanship are excellent. Although the stool is more ornate than that in Plate 20, it may be earlier in date. The original cane seat has been replaced by a hard mat seat.

22 Ming dynasty *huanghuali* wood small painting table and two waisted large stools

The table (Pl. 112) and the stools, one of which is illustrated in Plate 21, are shown in the Beijing Timber Factory.

23 Qing dynasty *hong* wood waisted square stool with base stretchers

Height 52 cm, dimensions of seat 54.5 cm × 54.5 cm; one of a pair

The flush floating *hong* wood panel is the original hard seat. The apron with a gently curving lower edge is earlier than that with a more angular profile or that carved with a spiral design. Thus the piece may be dated to the first half of the Qing dynasty.

24 Ming dynasty *huanghuali* wood waisted square stool with humpbacked stretchers and continuous floor stretcher

Height 52 cm, dimensions of seat 53 cm × 53 cm; one of a pair

The continuous floor stretcher is a replacement. The lower part of the legs curves only slightly inwards in a manner very different from that of Qing dynasty square stools with a continuous floor stretcher. The stool is highly decorated. The aprons are carved with a design of curling tendrils with confronting dragons on either side; animal faces adorn the corners of the shoulders, and dragon-like motifs are carved at the ends of the humpbacked stretchers. This is a late Ming piece.

25 Qing dynasty waisted round stool with porcelain seat

Height 49 cm, diameter of seat 41 cm; one of a set of eight

This stool is made of a soft wood of yellowish hue with a fine texture and even grain. Although it is certainly not *nan*, camphor or *ju* wood, further study is necessary to determine exactly what the wood is. This stool is one of a set of eight, four of which are in the Palace Museum and four in the Summer Palace. It is not known when those in the Summer Palace were painted black, concealing the grain, as shown in our illustration. The seat is made of Kangxi blue-and-white porcelain with a medallion of hornless dragons and *lingzhi* fungus in the centre surrounded by a wide plain white border which highlights the lively design. Since the porcelain was specially made for the stool, the stool must also date from the Kangxi reign (1662-1722).

26 Ming dynasty *huanghuali* wood eight-legged round stool
Height 49 cm, diameter of seat 38 cm, diameter of widest part 45 cm
This stool is closely related to the drum stool but because it has neither the round openings
nor the bosses of the Ming-style drum stool, I call it a round stool. Its form is rather simple,
its eight curved legs with split mouldings meeting the round seat at the top and the continuous
floor stretcher at the bottom. Originally there were small feet beneath the continuous floor
stretcher.

27 Qing dynasty *zitan* wood drum stool with five openings
Height 52 cm, diameter of seat 28 cm
The upper and lower string mouldings and round bosses are typical of Ming and early Qing
drum stools. The earlier rounded drum stools gradually became more slender during this
period, and thus this stool can be dated to the early Qing dynasty.

28 Qing dynasty *zitan* wood drum stool with five openings
Height 48 cm, diameter of seat 34 cm, diameter of widest part 42 cm; one of a pair
Although this stool is more robust than that in Plate 27 and may at first glance appear to be
earlier, the smaller, more closely spaced bosses as well as the burl wood floating panel with
raised centre suggest a later date. It cannot be earlier than the early Qing dynasty.

29 Qing dynasty *zitan* wood drum stool with straight rods
Height 47 cm, diameter of seat 29 cm; one of a pair
The design of the stool's body reflects the influence of windows with vertical rods; there are
no round openings. The stool resembles a birdcage, neat and airy, and has a pleasing shape.
The craftsman seems to have tried to make use of every available piece of wood, fashioning
the slatted body with twenty-four long pieces while making the top and bottom with short
pieces. Thus he was able to create the stool without using any large pieces of wood.

30 Qing dynasty *huanghuali* wood folding stool
Height 43 cm, dimensions of level seat and frame 47.5 cm × 39.5 cm
Made from eight straight rods, this is a basic folding stool. It was possibly made as late as the
mid Qing dynasty but it is almost identical with the one depicted in "Collating the Texts",
generally considered to be a Northern Song copy of a Tang dynasty painting. Today folding
stools are still being made according to the original construction. Thus one can see that this
kind of stool was common everywhere for more than one thousand years.

31   Ming dynasty *huanghuali* wood folding stool with footrest

Height 49.5 cm, dimensions of level seat and frame 55.7 cm × 41.4 cm
The horizontals at the top and bottom are squared. The legs are round, but are squared at their point of meeting for strength. The front of the seat members is carved with low-relief curling tendril designs while the top of the footrest is decorated with bronze ornaments. At each end of the top of the footrest is a tenon which fits into a mortise in the legs. Thus when the stool is folded the footrest can be turned upwards or removed to facilitate carrying. The seat of woven silk is a recent replacement. Among the few Ming dynasty folding stools still extant, this one is of fine workmanship and in good condition.

32   Qing dynasty *huanghuali* wood upward-folding stool

Height 49 cm, dimensions of seat 56 cm × 49 cm
Unlike the previous two examples, the seat of this stool is not made from woven material but consists of two rectangular slatted frames. At the centre two bronze rings connect these frames with another vertical frame. When the stool is unfolded the vertical frame rests at the juncture of the legs, creating a strong, stable seat. This is a special type of folding stool in which the seat is raised rather than lowered when folded. Because the slats of the seat are shallower than the frame, the frame fits between them when the chair is folded. In the last several decades I have seen only this one piece of this type. The carved decoration indicates that it is a Qing dynasty piece.

33   Qing dynasty *ju* wood small bench with elongated bridle joints

Height 40 cm, dimensions of seat 49.5 cm × 15 cm
The top of this bench with recessed legs is made from a single thick piece of wood. Its markedly splayed legs are joined to the aprons by elongated bridle joints. The mouldings and apron-head spandrels have a pleasing simplicity. The absence of aprons on the short sides of the bench imparts to it an antique flavour as most examples of tables with recessed legs depicted in Song and Yuan dynasty paintings are without aprons on the sides. This piece was used in a household in southern China where the style of furniture and utensils tended to remain unchanged for several hundred years. In the dating of furniture, it is best whenever possible to go the place where a piece was produced and visit the household in which it was used to learn its history, rather than rely solely on the appearance of the piece.

34   Qing dynasty *zuo* wood waistless two-seater bench with humpbacked stretchers and pillar-shaped struts

Height 39 cm, dimensions of seat 83 cm × 31 cm
This bench follows the basic form with humpbacked stretchers and pillar-shaped struts. The seat, instead of being made of woven rattan, is made of bamboo slats, a common practice for ordinary benches in the south. This type of bench, both large and small, is commonly seen in the south; it is called a spring bench. In the north such a bench would be called a two-seater bench; only very large ones whose sizes approach those of small couches are known as spring benches. *Zuo* wood is an easily identifiable oak wood which is semi-hard, of a yellowish-brown colour, and with grain lines a few centimetres long and pointed at both ends.

35 Ming dynasty *huanghuali* wood waisted two-seater bench with humpbacked stretchers
Height 49 cm, dimensions of seat 102 cm × 42 cm
This piece is a typical waisted bench with square members, straight legs, horse-hoof feet, and humpbacked stretchers. Compared to the preceding example, the wood is of better quality, and its dimensions are larger; it is altogether a more standard two-seater bench than those used in a common household. The original seat has been replaced by a hard mat seat.

36 Qing dynasty *ju* wood small lamp-hanger chair
Overall height 83.5 cm, dimensions of seat 43 cm × 37 cm, height of seat 37 cm; one of a pair
This chair is from an ordinary home in the Taihu District of Suzhou. The seat is more than 10 centimetres lower than is usual for a lamp-hanger chair. Its simple form and rather large members give it a naïve appearance. Since it is low, an arched-shaped apron is not used; instead a single straight piece of wood is fashioned into apron and spandrels. The original soft cane seat is still in good condition, although it is frayed in a few places. The owner told me that for many years it was covered with a cushion; otherwise the cane seat would have worn out long ago.

37 Ming dynasty *huanghuali* wood large lamp-hanger chair
Height 117 cm, dimensions of seat 57.5 cm × 41.5 cm; one of a pair
This chair is rather large for a lamp-hanger chair. The stepped stretchers are lowest in front, higher at the sides, and highest at the back. This design was adopted in order to avoid having the mortises close together, which would have weakened the chair's structure. The other method of changing the level of a chair's base stretchers is to make the front and back ones low and the side ones higher (Pl. 36). The centre of the apron is very slightly lowered in a subtle convex curve rather than cusped, giving a pliant grace to the chair.

38 Ming dynasty *huanghuali* wood square table and large lamp-hanger chairs
Arranged here are a square table (Pl. 85) and two lamp-hanger chairs, one of which is shown in Plate 37. Similar arrangements are depicted in Ming and Qing dynasty paintings and woodblock illustrations.

39 Qing dynasty *hong* wood small side chair
Height 85 cm, dimensions of seat 48 cm × 44 cm; one of a pair
This form of chair has been called the ox head type perhaps on account of its top rail. I have seen three or four pairs of exactly this form but of different dimensions, which shows that it is a standard type made in sets. They date from early to mid Qing, or even later.

40 Ming dynasty *huanghuali* wood carved side chair

Height 99.5 cm, dimensions of seat 62.5 cm × 42 cm

The back of this piece is of superb workmanship, its combination of rich motifs and complex design rendering it extremely rare. Since the cursive form of the character *shou* 壽 (longevity) is similar to that on carved lacquers of the Jiajing period (1522-66), the back of the chair can be dated to mid Ming. However, there is still some disagreement as to whether or not the upper and lower portions came originally from the same chair. The lower part, with its undecorated straight waistless form, resembles a large rectangular stool and is not harmonious with the back. Moreover, the manner of joining the back to the seat is not correct. For these reasons some suspect that the back might have belonged originally to a folding chair. None the less, this chair is a remarkable piece worthy of further study.

41 Ming dynasty *huanghuali* wood rose chair

Height 85.5 cm, dimensions of seat 56 cm × 43.2 cm; one of a pair

The back of this chair has an arch-shaped apron supported by a stretcher with pillar-shaped struts. This is the basic and most common form of the rose chair.

42 Ming dynasty *huanghuali* wood rose chair

Height 69 cm, dimensions of seat 58 cm × 45 cm; one of a pair

The top rail and armrests have indented corners. The arched apron carved with angular spirals is supported by a humpbacked stretcher; the struts below are in the form of openwork *lingzhi* fungus rather than pillar-shaped. Arched aprons are also found under the armrests. The apron of the seat has a curling tendril design. In this example the basic form of the rose chair (Pl. 41) has been embellished in several places.

43 Ming dynasty *huanghuali* wood rose chair with openwork carving

Height 87 cm, dimensions of seat 61 cm × 46 cm; one of a pair

Among our three rose chairs this one has the most elaborately carved decoration. A panel has been inserted in the back with openwork carving of six hornless dragons supporting a *shou* 壽 character (longevity). Below the arm stretchers the struts are in the form of coiled hornless dragons. Beneath the seat there are decorated arched aprons on three sides. By comparing our three examples it can be seen how Ming cabinetmakers gradually succumbed to increasingly elaborate decoration.

44 Ming dynasty *tieli* wood official's hat armchair with four protruding ends
Height 116 cm, dimensions of seat 74 cm × 60.5 cm; one of a pair
The top rail and arms of this official's hat armchair are straight. The side posts are also straight but have an upward taper. Only the gooseneck front posts, which are made from the same piece of wood as the legs, curve forward. Beneath the seat there is a humpbacked stretcher and between them pillar-shaped struts. Far from being dull and monotonous, the chair has lasting appeal because of its simple construction and perfect proportions. It has the original hardwood seat.

45 Ming dynasty *huanghuali* wood official's hat armchair with four protruding ends
Height 120.4 cm, dimensions of seat 55.5 cm × 43.4 cm; one of a pair
The top rail, armrests, front posts and side posts of this chair are all curved. It has an arched apron instead of a humpbacked stretcher and pillar-shaped struts. This, rather than the preceding example, represents the standard form of a Ming dynasty official's hat armchair with four protruding ends.

46 Ming dynasty *huanghuali* wood official's hat armchair with four protruding ends
Height 119.5 cm, dimensions of seat 58.5 cm × 47 cm; one of a pair
On the splat there is a low-relief design composed of a cloud surrounded by confronting dragons, which is typical of the Ming dynasty both in its motifs and in the fine quality of the carving. The unusual effect of this chair lies not in its ornamentation but in the slenderness and sweeping curves of its members. As such members can only be made from thick and large pieces of wood, the craftsman could easily have produced a much sturdier piece. However, he chose not to do so, and spared neither material nor labour in the creation of this particularly slender and elegant chair.

47 Ming dynasty *huanghuali* wood low-back southern official's hat armchair
Height 82 cm, dimensions of seat 59 cm × 47 cm; one of a pair
Beijing craftsmen call an official's hat armchair with no protruding ends a southern official's hat armchair. This low-back chair bears some resemblance to a rose chair but differs from it in that the members curve and are not all at right angles to each other. The back has three rods and appears to be a simplified form of the comb-back chair.

48   Ming dynasty *huanghuali* wood high-back southern official's hat armchair
Height 119.5 cm, dimensions of seat 57.5 cm × 44.2 cm; one of a pair
This high-back southern official's hat armchair is a more common Ming dynasty form than the preceding low-back example. Its material is excellent and its craftsmanship superb. The low-relief hornless dragon motif is especially praiseworthy for the liveliness of its form, the fluidity of its carving, the smoothness of its curves and the strength of its lines. There is no doubt that it is the work of a highly skilled craftsman and is of a quality rarely found in Ming dynasty furniture.

49   Ming dynasty *huanghuali* wood southern official's hat armchair with high arms
Height 93.2 cm, dimensions of seat 56 cm × 47.5 cm; one of a set of four
The top panel of the three-part splat has a recessed ground inset with a rectangular jade plaque carved in openwork with a dragon design. Close study reveals that the jade came from a belt and was not carved specifically for the chair. The centre piece of the splat has a flush *huanghuali* wood panel, and the recessed lower panel has a curling tendril design and a large opening. The fact that the top and lower panels of the splat are recessed while the central one is flush with the frame indicates that it is designed to be leant against. The gooseneck front posts are set back from the front edge and are not in one piece with the legs. There are no side posts. The backs of the armrests are very high, not far below the top rail, and so the form is quite close to that of the armchair with curved rest. Also rather unusual are the straight lines of the arched aprons on all four sides beneath the seat.

This chair is one of a set of four which were for a long time in the Summer Palace. Since the chairs' original very finely woven cane seats were covered by brocade cushions, they have survived intact. These pieces of Ming furniture are not only of great artistic value but are also in good condition.

50   Ming dynasty *zitan* wood fan-shaped southern official's hat armchair
Height 108.5 cm, dimensions of seat: width of front 75.8 cm, width of back 61 cm, depth 60.5 cm; one of a set of four
The four legs of the chair have an outward splay. The seat is about 15 centimetres wider at the front than at the back. The convex curve along the front edge of the seat is echoed by the concave curve of the back edge, and mirrored by the bow of the top rail. The only decoration is a low-relief peony medallion, which resembles those on early Ming carved red lacquer ware. Beneath the seat on three sides there are arch-shaped aprons with lowered centre and rather plump beading. The tenons of the stretchers are not only exposed but even protrude a little, thus increasing the strength of the chair but without spoiling its form. Such a feature is most unusual and perhaps points to an early technique derived from wooden architecture. This is one of a set of four armchairs which, because of their size, are quite rare among Ming dynasty *zitan* wood furniture. Their form is spacious yet dignified, their craftsmanship of superior quality. Not only are they among the finest *zitan* wood pieces, but they are also among the very few that can be dated to the early Ming.

51 Qing dynasty *ju* wood small lamp-hanger chair and Ming dynasty *zitan* wood southern official's hat armchair

In this juxtaposition of the chairs illustrated in Plates 36 and 50, the reader can compare their dimensions as well as the style of furniture used by the commoner with that used in courtly circles.

52 Ming dynasty *ju* wood low southern official's hat armchair

Overall height 77 cm, dimensions of seat 71 cm × 58 cm, height of seat 31.5 cm

The top rail has a considerable backward curve and small spandrels where it meets the back posts. The gooseneck front posts, which are not in one piece with the front legs, also have small spandrels where they join the armrests. The legs are straight and on four sides there is an apron with no curves.

The seat is about 20 centimetres lower than usual, and if a soft cushion were added the chair would be like a modern one. There are very few low seats from Ming and Qing times. Those which have recently appeared on the market have all been made by shortening the legs of a higher chair. This chair, however, is original and may have been a meditation chair in a Buddhist temple. The user would have sat crossed-legged on it.

The large rectangular panel on the splat was most carefully planned to match perfectly the proportions of the chair. If a medallion had been used, it would not have filled the comparatively wide splat. The design, carved in relief on a smoothed ground, is a variant of the phoenix motif, in a style reminiscent of designs on Song archaistic bronzes.

53 Ming dynasty *huanghuali* wood hexagonal southern official's hat armchair

Overall height 83 cm, dimensions of seat 78 cm × 55 cm, height of seat 49 cm; one of a set of four

This is a hexagonal variation of the southern official's hat armchair. All the members above the seat — top rail, arms, back posts, double side posts, front posts — have mouldings. The legs have mouldings along their outer edge and are flat on the other three sides. Along the edge of the seat there is a double convex moulding with flat edges while the base stretchers have split mouldings. These mouldings all help to give the piece a unified appearance. The splat is divided into three panels inset into grooves in the frame, composed of verticals and horizontals with double convex mouldings. In the bottom panel is a cloud-shaped brightening-the-feet opening (a fanciful term denoting the opening at the bottom of chair splats). The central panel is plain, and in the lower half of the top panel is an elongated and flamelike openwork cloud motif.

This chair is far superior to other hexagonal chairs that I have seen. Although it is a variation of the southern official's hat armchair, it has a freshness and a naturalness unsullied by any trace of artificiality.

54 Ming dynasty *huanghuali* wood armchair with curved rest

Height 93 cm, dimensions of seat 54.5 cm × 43 cm

This armchair with curved rest is fairly plain and its form is a common one. However, the carving of the medallion on the splat is by no means ordinary. Not only is the dragon especially strong and animated but its diaper ground is also quite rare. Examples of such a motif in furniture carving that I have seen can be counted on the fingers of one hand.

55　Ming dynasty *huanghuali* wood armchair with curved rest and openwork splat
Height 107 cm, dimensions of seat 60.7 cm × 48.7 cm; one of a pair

The armchair's curved rest, which is slightly flattened at the back, is constructed of three joined pieces of wood. On the splat there is an ornamental opening with cusped upper edge containing an openwork carving of a *qilin*, his tongue darting from a gaping mouth, his mane rigidly upright, and the surrounding flames flickering. From the configuration of the animal and the style of the carving, it is quite certain that the piece dates from no later than mid Ming times. The upper part of the splat is embellished with two pieces of wood with curling tendril patterns which are actually spandrels. These spandrels are not out of place as others are found on either side of the back posts and where the arms and front posts meet. There is a brightening-the-feet opening on the lower part of the splat. Such openings usually appear on the bottom of three-part splats and it is rare to find one, as in this example, at the bottom of a single-panel splat. There are vigorously curved arch-shaped aprons beneath the seat. I rate this armchair as having the highest artistic merit of all the Ming dynasty armchairs with curved rests that I have seen.

56　Qing dynasty *zitan* wood waisted armchair with curved rest and floor stretcher
Overall height 99 cm, dimensions of seat 63 cm × 50 cm, height of seat 49 cm; one of a set of four

In most Ming dynasty chairs the front and back legs pass through the seat and are made of the same piece of wood as the respective front and back posts. This is a practical method of construction which strengthens the chair, and is precisely the reason why very few Ming dynasty chairs are waisted. If there is a waist it is difficult for the leg to pass through the seat and it is necessary to use one piece of wood for the leg and another for the post, which is impractical. By the mid Qing dynasty waisted chairs were more common than in earlier periods, reflecting the greater value placed on appearance than on construction from that time onwards. Our four armchairs with curved rests not only have waists but also floor stretchers. They are most likely imperial pieces from the early 18th century.

The detailing of this chair is quite unusual. The top panel of the segmented splat has openwork carving in the form of a variant of the curled tendril design; the central section consists of a burl wood panel flush with the frame; the lowest panel has a cloud-shaped brightening-the-feet opening. Where the splat joins the seat and the armrest there are four large openwork spandrels, which render the chair more decorative when viewed from the front. The ends of the arms and bottoms of the legs are carved with curling tendrils, which is an unusual feature. The original finely woven cane seat is still in good condition. The conscious striving after effect, evident in both the form and the decoration of the chair, does not detract from the excellence of its material and workmanship, nor from its importance as a representative piece of its period.

57　Yuan dynasty *huanghuali* wood folding armchair with curved rest
Height 94.8 cm, dimensions of seat when level 69.5 cm × 53 cm

The curved rest of this chair is constructed of five joined pieces of wood. The splat has a relief motif of a cloud surrounded by confronting dragons, quite similar to that on the chair in Plate 46. The joints of the members are reinforced with iron, into which silver lotus scrolls have been hammered; the iron is partially rusted. Judging from the texture of the wood and metal mounting, I rank this as the earliest folding chair that I have seen. My good friend Chen Mengjia 陳夢家, who owned this chair for many years, believed that it was made in the Yuan dynasty.

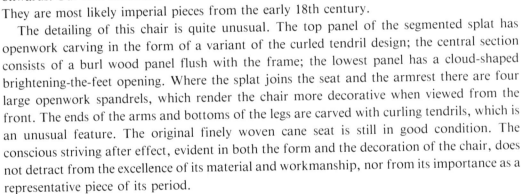

58 Ming dynasty *huanghuali* wood folding armchair with curved rest
Height 112 cm, dimensions of seat when level 70 cm × 46.5 cm; one of a pair

The top panel of the three-part splat has an openwork medallion depicting a hornless dragon. The openwork rectangular panel in the centre is carved with a design composed of a *qilin*, a gourd, *lingzhi* fungus and fantastic rocks. The motifs in these openwork designs are jumbled together and lifeless. The brightening-the-feet opening on the bottom panel has beading and a curling tendril pattern. Although this chair is similar in form to that in Plate 57, the thickness of its members and the fact that the metal mounts are of bronze rather than of iron decorated with silver suggest a mid or late Ming date.

59 Ming dynasty *zitan* wood waisted throne with continuous floor stretcher
Height 109 cm, dimensions of seat 98 cm × 78 cm

Three pieces of wood were used to make the back and sides, but they are fashioned in such a way as to give the impression that seven pieces of wood were used. The entire chair, except for the seat and waist, is completely carved with lotuses and rushes so that no ground is visible. The carving, rounded and with no ridges, resembles that of carved lacquer of the late Yuan and early Ming dynasty. The flowers and leaves, depicted from different angles, and the intertwining branches and stems fit well into the shape of the throne. The throne is unquestionably the work of a master craftsman. In front of it is a lotus-shaped footstool with the same decorative design; it is also very well made.

60 Qing dynasty *zitan* wood waisted footstool with mother-of-pearl inlay, damaged
Height 11.5 cm, dimensions of top 117 cm × 38 cm

Since this footstool originally belonged with a throne, it is placed here.

    The footstool is waisted and once had a continuous floor stretcher which is now lost. The decoration, in the form of three hornless dragon medallions in rather thick mother-of-pearl inlaid on the surface of the stool, is spacious and archaistic in feeling. This inlay is entirely different from the mother-of-pearl inlay on mid to late Qing furniture in material, design and workmanship.

61 Qing dynasty *huanghuali* wood bamboo-style waistless square *kang* table
Height 24 cm, dimensions of top 80.5 cm × 80.5 cm

This *kang* table is derived from the basic form with straight stretchers and pillar-shaped struts. At the corners curving pieces resembling bamboo stems connect the feet and top. The top moulding is a variation of split moulding with the top segment narrower than the lower one. It has a high water-stopping moulding with grooves beneath, into which are fitted the edges of the floating panel. Thus the panel covers the frame of the top and looks very neat when viewed from above. All members have a bamboo joint design and the bottom of the legs imitates the root of the bamboo stem. These are all rather unusual features and make this piece a most pleasing imitation of bamboo furniture.

62 Qing dynasty *huanghuali* wood waisted wide *kang* table with openwork aprons
Height 31.8 cm, dimensions of top 99.5 cm × 67 cm

The form of this piece is typical of waisted wide *kang* tables, but the aprons (which in this type of table are usually solid) have in the centre pierced angular spiral designs. Where the aprons and legs meet there are openwork angular spiral spandrels. Thus the appearance of the standard wide *kang* table is transformed. This *kang* table can be dated to the first half of the Qing dynasty.

63 Ming dynasty *huanghuali* wood waisted wide *kang* table with unmitred joint of apron and legs
Height 29.5 cm, dimensions of top 108 cm × 69 cm

This is an example of a type of waisted wide *kang* table in which the apron joins the legs in a vertical line rather than at a 45° angle. This feature also occurs on most high tables whose shoulder is carved in the form of an animal's head. Thus it is clear that this type of joint is used to avoid interfering with the design of the animal's head. On some of these examples, on which there is an animal's head at the shoulder, the legs terminate in a claw-and-ball foot.

64 Ming dynasty *huanghuali* wood waisted wide *kang* table with convex apron and bulging legs ending in horse-hoof feet
Height 29 cm, dimensions of top 84 cm × 52 cm

This wide *kang* table is a very exaggerated example of the type with convex apron and bulging legs ending in horse-hoof feet. Both the outward and inward curves of the legs are pronounced and the feet end in a ball-like shape. The apron is elaborately decorated, the luxuriant lotuses and confronting limbed dragons which are carved in relief on a recessed ground fitting well into the space defined by the curving lower edge of the apron. The decoration gives a feeling of sumptuousness to the *kang* table.

65 Ming dynasty *huanghuali* wood waisted wide *kang* table with cabriole legs
Height 30 cm, dimensions of top 88 cm × 46 cm

The cabriole legs of this table are unique. They are shaped in such a way that it looks as though four extra legs have been added to a *kang* table with convex apron and bulging legs ending in horse-hoof feet. The form of this table is most unusual and ingenious, but not very practical since the curved section of wood is only about 5 centimetres thick and thus liable to split, as has already happened in one leg where the vertical grain is too short.

66 Ming dynasty *huanghuali* wood high-waisted wide *kang* table
Height 27.5 cm, dimensions of top 105 cm × 72.5 cm

This is a high-waisted piece with a very thick stepped apron moulding. The upper part of the leg is exposed and the lower part is a cabriole leg ending in a ball. The long waist fits into grooves in the frame of the top, the stepped apron moulding, and the upper part of the leg. Except for the top and its moulded edge, the stepped apron moulding, and the lower part of the leg, the surface is covered with carved designs. Although the decoration is elaborate, it is still in Ming dynasty style and is very different from the crowded and incoherent designs of mid Qing times. There are animal heads at the shoulders which necessitated an unmitred joint of apron and leg. The four corners of the top are reinforced with cloud-shaped bronze mounts.

67 Qing dynasty black lacquer narrow *kang* table
Height 37.2 cm, dimensions of top 129 cm × 34.5 cm

This narrow table is made of three thick pieces of wood lacquered black, the colour resembling ebony and the surface having ox hair crack patterns. It has neither carved nor painted decoration. The two side legs are as wide as the table, and their openings, resembling the cross-section of a roof tile and rather archaic in feeling, are large enough for a hand to be inserted in them. Each leg has been made from a board about 6 centimetres thick from which the inner surface of the upper portion and the outer surface of the lower portion have been cut away, so that each leg terminates in an outward-curling scroll. The rounded edges and absence of angularity give the table a solid and stable appearance. It appears to have been specially designed by a scholar rather than by an ordinary craftsman. The texture of the lacquer indicates that it was made in the Qing dynasty.

68 Qing dynasty *zitan* wood waistless narrow *kang* table
Height 32.5 cm, dimensions of top 99 cm × 35 cm

The upper surface of the humpbacked stretcher has a groove into which the apron and spandrels fit, so that there is no opening between stretcher and table top. This construction, which evolved from the type with three spandrels to one leg and a humpbacked stretcher, is frequently found on small narrow *kang* tables. If it is used on high tables, some space should be left between stretcher and apron (as in the example in Plate 114) in order to avoid too heavy a feeling.

69 Qing dynasty *zitan* wood narrow *kang* table with recessed legs and elongated bridle joints
Height 32.3 cm, dimensions of top 93 cm × 32 cm

This narrow *kang* table with recessed legs has standard elongated bridle joints and typical cloud motif apron-head spandrels. Although the table is basically in Ming style, the form of the apron-head spandrels and the manner in which the fairly high beading rises from a flat surface give the piece a rather late feeling and suggest an early Qing date.

70 Ming dynasty *jichi* wood narrow *kang* table with outward-curving side legs and everted flanges
Height 32.5 cm, dimensions of top 130 cm × 32.5 cm

One is immediately attracted by this table's outward-curving side legs, which create a beautiful silhouette as well as increase the sense of stability. The table is further enlivened by the downward-turning openwork cloud motifs on the apron-head spandrels and upward-soaring cloud motifs on the inset panels on the side legs.

The spandrel's cloud pattern is connected to the apron by a bead, which, despite its small size, is important since it helps to prevent the cloud from breaking.

71 Qing dynasty *jichi* wood large narrow three-drawer *kang* table with recessed legs
Height 48 cm, dimensions of top 191 cm × 48.5 cm

This is a large version of the narrow *kang* table with drawers. As well as being placed on a *kang* it can be put on the floor and used as a large bench. On the inset side panels there is an upturned cloud design enclosed by a square of beading, which is a typical Ming dynasty furniture motif. However, the style of the decoration on the front apron, consisting of cloud scrolls and a moulding raised fairly high above a flat surface, is rather later and suggests a Qing dynasty date for the *kang* table.

The original *jichi* wood floating panel split some years ago; it was replaced by a solid piece of *tieli* wood in about 1955.

72 **Ming dynasty _huanghuali_ wood three-legged incense stand**
Height 89.3 cm, diameter of top 43.3 cm

The top of the stand has a frame formed of four curved pieces of wood grooved to hold the floating panel. The edge of the frame has an ice-plate edge moulding. The lower edge of the flat waist is joined to an apron with a curling tendril design carved in relief. The cabriole legs curve outwards at the shoulders and have inserted shoulder joints connecting them with the aprons. Beneath the aprons the long slender legs curve inwards and then gently outwards again. In Ming dynasty novels and the Qing Dynasty Regulations they are called dragonfly legs. Tenons at the bottom of the feet penetrate a continuous floor stretcher standing on three small feet. The three spaces between the legs are bordered at the top by the cusped edges of the apron, thereby creating the effect of three ornamental openings. Although this stand is somewhat decorative, it none the less can be considered a basic example of a Ming dynasty three-legged incense stand.

73 **Ming dynasty _tieli_ wood high-waisted five-legged incense stand**
Height 89 cm, diameter of top 61 cm, diameter of shoulder 67 cm

A single board 5.5 centimetres thick is used to make the top of this stand; there is no frame. The upper parts of the legs are exposed at the waist, resembling pillar-shaped struts. They are grooved on both sides to hold the small ornamental panels with begonia-shaped openings. There are two reasons for the great thickness of the flat stepped apron moulding beneath the waist. First, it has to harmonize with the proportions of the ice-plate edge moulding of the top board. With the waist it creates a form resembling a Buddhist pedestal. Second, it has to be thick enough to contain the grooves holding the small decorated panels. This is a thrice-attached piece in which the apron, stepped apron moulding, and waist are made from three separate pieces of wood. Each leg stands on a ball, with a tenon penetrating the continuous floor stretcher, which is also large and heavy.

The members of this stand are thick and large, imbuing it with an archaic awkwardness. It was most probably a temple stand which could hold, besides an incense burner, a bronze chime or other ritual objects. It is quite different in feeling from the other incense stands shown.

74 **Ming dynasty _huanghuali_ wood incense stand with five inward-turning legs**
Height 85.5 cm, diameter of top 47.2 cm

Beneath the slightly concave waist of this stand an inserted shoulder joint is used to connect the apron and legs. Unlike the rounded surfaces on the shoulders and legs of pieces with convex apron and bulging legs, the surfaces on these parts are flat and outlined by a beading which is quite striking. The legs curve outwards from the shoulders, inwards towards the bottom, and rest on a continuous floor stretcher. This incense stand resembles a large quince in shape and is very different from the usual type with three cabriole legs. Originally on the inner side of each leg there was a giant's arm brace, as evidenced by the filled mortises. I myself feel that these braces were unnecessary and without them the lines of the stand are much neater. Perhaps this is why the braces were not replaced.

75 Ming dynasty *huanghuali* wood four-legged octagonal incense stand
Height 103 cm, dimensions of octagonal top 50.5 cm × 37.2 cm

This is not a standard form of incense stand. One would expect the octagonal top to be made from a thick rectangular piece of wood cut off at the four corners, but it has a frame and floating panel. The waist and apron are made from a single piece of wood. The edge of the apron is scalloped. The rectangular continuous floor stretcher, curving slightly inwards at each side, stands on four small feet. Cabriole legs, with a discreet curve, are attached to the four corners of the stretcher. Since the stand is over 10 centimetres higher than normal, it is more slender and elegant. Its form is rather novel, and I have not seen another stand like it.

76 Ming dynasty *huanghuali* wood high-waisted incense stand with six legs
Height 73 cm, dimensions of foliated hexagonal top 50.5 cm × 39.2 cm

The foliated top resembles a lotus leaf. Above the double-layered stepped apron moulding there is a very high waist, consisting of two registers of ornamental panels. The upper panels have pierced cloud designs, while the lower ones have rectangular openings with stepped corners. The apron covers the tops of the legs like a cloud collar and thus the joint is not an inserted shoulder joint. The sweeping curve of the leg terminates in a flower-leaf motif standing on a ball made from the same piece of wood. The ball tenons into the base. Hardwood examples of this type are very rare. However, I have seen several similarly shaped lacquered wood pieces, such as the lacquered example inlaid with mother-of-pearl illustrated in Plate 236 of Lee Yu-kuan's *Oriental Lacquer Art*.

77 Ming dynasty *huanghuali* wood wine table with elongated bridle joints
Height 76 cm, dimensions of top 57 cm × 79 cm

Small rectangular recessed-leg tables such as this had been used for serving food and drink since the Five Dynasties period and the Song dynasty, as may be seen in the painting "The Night Revels of Han Xizai 韓熙載夜宴圖". Beijing craftsmen clearly differentiate between corner-leg tables (*zhuo* 桌) and recessed-leg tables (*an* 案). One exception is this type which, despite having recessed legs, is none the less called a *jiuzhuo* 酒桌, a *zhuo* for serving wine; we have no alternative but to follow their terminology.

This piece has a burl wood floating panel, round legs, an undecorated apron, and double stretchers along the sides. It is of the basic wine table form.

78   Ming dynasty *huanghuali* wood wine table with elongated bridle joints
Height 81 cm, dimensions of top 110 cm × 55 cm

This table has more decoration than the preceding example. The apron and apron-head spandrels are ornamented with beading along the edge and openwork cloud designs. The front and back surfaces of the legs are convex and each leg has beading along all four edges. These are unusual features as most table legs are flat and without beading on the inside. The beading down the centre of the legs is of the type graphically described as one-incense-stick.

79   Ming dynasty *tieli* wood wine table with inserted shoulder joints
Height 72 cm, dimensions of top 94.7 cm × 50 cm

The black lacquer floating panel of the table top is surrounded by a water-stopping moulding. The flowing line of the apron's cusped edge continues down to the foot, and along the centre of each leg there is two-incense-stick beading. Just below the mid point of each leg there is a leaf-like motif protruding slightly on both sides. At the base of the legs there is a cloud motif, now partially decayed. Since the wood of this table is very old and its form rather early, it can be dated to the mid Ming or even earlier.

80   Ming dynasty *huanghuali* wood wine table with inserted shoulder joints
Height 83 cm, dimensions of top 106 cm × 54 cm

This table, like the preceding one, has inserted shoulder joints but since the apron is very thin these joints are short, which inevitably reduces the stability of the table. Unlike most inserted shoulder joints, which are decorated on the apron-head spandrel, here there are openwork leaf scrolls at the sides of the apron. The top of the table is an elegantly muted green marble slab, the provenance of which has yet to be determined.

81   Qing dynasty *hong* wood waistless half table with straight leg-encircling stretcher and latticework
Height 82 cm, dimensions of top 97 cm × 63 cm

Between the straight leg-encircling stretcher and the frame of the top there is a lattice consisting of renditions of the character *shan* 山 oriented alternately upright and upside down. For the sake of symmetry, the lattice has five characters at the front and at the back, and three at the sides. The table is made of dark *hong* wood, which was a popular furniture wood during the Qing dynasty. However, as the shape of the table suggests a pre-Qing date, the *hong* wood, when seen from a distance, could be mistaken for *zitan* wood.

82   Qing dynasty southern cypress waistless half table with straight stretchers and pillar-shaped struts
Height 84.5 cm, dimensions of top 98.5 cm × 67 cm

Tables with straight stretchers and pillar-shaped struts are common, but in this piece the struts are joined to the apron rather than to the frame of the top, a treatment which is rather unusual. All the aprons and stretchers have split mouldings. The upper part of the table is indented about the thickness of a finger and thus it appears to have a waist, but in reality it is waistless because the four legs divide the indentation. Southern cypress, which is yellowish and has little grain, resembles boxwood and is likewise quite highly valued. The top of the table is made from birch wood, which is cracked in places.

83 Ming dynasty *huanghuali* wood waisted bracket-shaped half table

Height 87 cm, dimensions of top 98.5 cm × 64.3 cm

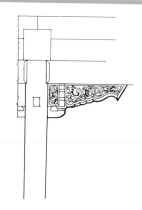

From each leg project two spandrels in the form of a dragon's head. Immediately one is reminded of the brackets of Ming and Qing dynasty architecture and once again we see the close relationship between architecture and furniture.

This half table is made from *huanghuali* wood but has been painted black in imitation of *zitan* wood. This was because *zitan* was highly valued in mid and late Qing, and some pieces made of *huanghuali* or *huali* wood were painted a darker colour so that they could pass for *zitan*.

84 Ming dynasty *huanghuali* wood waisted half table in the form of a low table with extended legs

Height 87 cm, dimensions of top 104 cm × 64.2 cm

Visually this table can be divided into an upper and a lower part. The upper part bears a close resemblance to a waisted, square-membered, wide *kang* table with cabriole legs. The lower part is similar to waistless round-leg furniture. The bottom of the leg is bulbous like the stone base of a pillar. I have also seen waistless square tables with legs and feet fashioned in exactly the same manner. Although the leg appears to have been made from two pieces of wood, it is actually a single piece. This form is not limited to half tables but may also be found on square tables (Pl. 91). I have asked many craftsmen for the name of this type, but to no avail. Thus I tentatively call it a low table with extended legs. The origins of this particular form of furniture can be explained by the principles governing furniture design which are discussed in Chapter III.

The scalloped waist of this half table resembles the edge of a lotus leaf. The front aprons are carved with a pair of phoenixes facing the sun and bands of clouds, which are similar to the motifs found on Ming dynasty brocades. The side aprons, ornamented with floral sprays and birds, resemble designs on Wanli period polychrome porcelains. Beneath the aprons there are dragon-shaped spandrels and giant's arm braces carved with *lingzhi* fungus. Although the decoration is elaborate, it does not burden the half table; on the contrary the piece is elegant from whichever side it is viewed.

85 Ming dynasty *huanghuali* wood waistless square table with humpbacked stretchers and decorative struts

Height 80 cm, dimensions of top 93.2 cm × 93.2 cm

This table, with humpbacked stretchers, decorative struts, and round legs without horse-hoof feet, is the basic form of waistless table. Even more common are pieces with pillar-shaped struts instead of decorative struts. Since pillar-shaped struts are usually higher than decorative struts, tables having such struts have less leg room than this one.

86 Ming dynasty *huanghuali* wood square table of the type with three spandrels to one leg and humpbacked stretchers

Height 83 cm, dimensions of top 98 cm × 98 cm

This type derives its name from the fact that each leg joins the apron-head spandrels of two long aprons and a corner spandrel, and that there is a humpbacked stretcher below. However, unlike the tables in Plates 87 and 88, this is not a standard example of the type, because the top of the table does not protrude much beyond the legs and thus the corner spandrels are very small.

Another special feature of this table is its powerful mouldings. The legs have eight concave mouldings with sharp ridges extending along their entire length. The relatively narrow aprons have leather-strip mouldings while sword-ridge mouldings are used on the humpbacked stretchers. All these imbue the table with a sense of sharpness.

87 Ming dynasty *huanghuali* wood small square table of the type with three spandrels to one leg and humpbacked stretchers

Height 81 cm, dimensions of top 82 cm × 82 cm

This square table is about 10 centimetres smaller on each side than the ordinary Eight Immortals table and so craftsmen call it a Six Immortals table. Since there is a considerable splay to the legs, they are well recessed at the top, and thus the corner spandrels are large. A frame-thickening insert is added beneath the frame of the top. The purpose of this is to increase the height of the ice-plate edge and cover part of the apron, giving a greater sense of depth. The table is undecorated except for the beading along the edges of the two outward-facing sides of the square legs. It may be considered a basic form of the type with three spandrels to one leg and humpbacked stretchers. It has a marble top which is not original.

88 Ming dynasty *huanghuali* wood square table of the type with three spandrels to one leg and humpbacked stretchers with decorative struts

Height 85.5 cm, dimensions of top 89 cm × 89 cm

The legs have mouldings which render them melon-like when seen in section and there are rounded undulations with sharp corners on the humpbacked stretchers. Curling tendril designs ornament the spandrels and there are cloud-patterned decorative struts. These elegant motifs embellish the dignified form of the table, which can be considered the mature form of the type with three spandrels to one leg and a humpbacked stretcher. Since I have seen at least four almost identical Ming dynasty tables, this is evidently a standard Ming form.

89 Ming dynasty *huanghuali* wood waistless square table with apron and spandrels made by joining the straight

Height 84 cm, dimensions of top 102.5 cm × 103.8 cm

The aprons and spandrels are made of straight pieces of different sizes joined to form lattice patterns. Separate tenons are used to connect them with the legs and top on all four sides of the table. Actually this form is derived from the type with humpbacked stretchers and pillar-shaped struts. The difference is that here the humpbacked stretcher and pillar-shaped struts form a complete separate unit, with long horizontal and vertical members meeting the frame of the top and the legs. This is very different from the manner in which humpbacked stretchers and struts meet the adjoining members at only a few points.

90 Ming dynasty *huanghuali* wood waisted large square table with protruding top
Height 89.2 cm, dimensions of top 128 cm × 128 cm
Since the frame of the top extends considerably beyond the four legs on all sides, it is called a protruding top. It occurs not only on square tables, but also on other types such as a *zitan* wood painting table in the Palace Museum.

All the surfaces of this table have concave mouldings and the apron and waist are made from a single piece of wood. In order to make the waist more visible, part of the underside of the frame of the top has been cut back, the aim being the opposite of adding a frame-thickening insert to the table of the type with three spandrels to one leg and a humpbacked stretcher. The narrow long frame of the apron has been made by joining the straight, while each of the curved spandrels below has been carved from a single piece of wood, resulting in an appearance similar to that of a humpbacked stretcher.

This table, with dimensions much greater than those of an Eight Immortals table, is the largest square table I have ever seen. The floating panel is recessed, rather than flush with the frame; most probably the original top was made of marble. The replacement of stone slabs with wood panels is quite common.

91 Qing dynasty *huanghuali* wood waisted square table in the form of a low table with extended legs
Height 86.5 cm, dimensions of top 93.5 cm × 91.2 cm
The form of this table is basically the same as the half table with giant's arm braces (Pl. 84). However, instead of spandrels there are humpbacked stretchers between the legs. At the corners of the humpback the craftsman has made use of the wood that is usually cut away to carve openwork plum branches, which are reminiscent of the carving on the *zitan* wood armchair with curved rest (Pl. 56). When one compares the flowers carved in relief on the aprons of this table with those on the half table (Pl. 84), it is clear that this is a later piece, and should be ascribed to the early Qing dynasty.

92 Ming dynasty *tieli* wood waistless narrow rectangular table with oval openings on the solid board legs
Height 87 cm, dimensions of top 191.5 cm × 50 cm
This waistless narrow rectangular table is fashioned from three boards about 5 centimetres thick joined at right angles with hidden tenons and rounded at the corners. The sides have oval openings and a scroll termination made of a separate piece of wood. The only mouldings are the concave ones along the long sides. The piece has a dignified archaic appearance.

93 Qing dynasty *zitan* wood waistless narrow rectangular table with corner legs, leg-encircling humpbacked stretcher and pillar-shaped struts
Height 83.5 cm, dimensions of top 106 cm × 35.5 cm
Although this is a very well made Ming-style waistless narrow rectangular table with corner legs, upon close inspection it is obvious that it was made in the Qing dynasty because of a certain studied restraint. It is one of several dozen *zitan* wood small side tables and narrow *kang* tables to be found in the Palace Museum and the Summer Palace. Probably they were all made for the Imperial Palace in the early Qing dynasty. Documentary proof of this may some day come to light in the archives of the imperial household.

94 **Ming dynasty *huanghuali* wood waistless narrow rectangular table with corner legs and humpbacked stretchers**

Height 87 cm, dimensions of top 112 cm × 54.5 cm

This table is decorated with low-relief and openwork carving on the apron-head spandrels. The motif is similar to that in the medallion on the splat of the chairs in Plates 46 and 57, except that the leg divides it down the centre, and the two cloud-like loops are cleverly linked to the beading of the apron. This is an example of how a standard motif may be freely rearranged.

95 **Qing dynasty *zitan* wood narrow rectangular table with corner legs and a cusped apron**

Height 83.5 cm, dimensions of top 105 cm × 35 cm

The aprons of Ming dynasty tables and the seats of stools and chairs often have cusped edges. As a result the openings framed by legs and apron resemble the ornamental openings of the box-construction bed. But here only the upper edge is cusped. From the many pieces of *zitan* wood furniture in the imperial household, it is clear that early Qing craftsmen attempted to produce variations on Ming furniture forms. Some of these, as for example the table in Plate 96, are quite successful, while others such as this are less so.

96 **Qing dynasty *zitan* wood narrow rectangular table with corner legs and with three spandrels to one leg**

Height 82 cm, dimensions of top 105 cm × 36.5 cm

This piece is also from the Qing dynasty Imperial Palace. In form it is a hybrid of two types, that with humpbacked stretchers and pillar-shaped struts and that with three spandrels to one leg and humpbacked stretchers. Most narrow rectangular tables with corner legs have little splay, but here the legs are so splayed that they are recessed enough at the top for corner spandrels. Usually the spandrels in the type with three spandrels to one leg are solid; however in this example the spandrels are hollow and framed by rods. Thus the Ming style has become lighter and more airy in appearance, as well as more stable in construction. This is one of the successful Qing transformations of Ming prototypes.

97 **Ming dynasty *huanghuali* wood straight-form narrow rectangular table with corner legs and everted flanges**

Height 86 cm, dimensions of top 112.5 cm × 48.5 cm

Everted flanges often appear on narrow rectangular tables with recessed legs, but rarely on narrow rectangular tables with corner legs. However, this example has small everted flanges. There are also three small shallow hidden drawers, a feature of Qing dynasty pieces of this type but seldom of Ming pieces. Ming dynasty narrow tables with drawers are of a quite different type. This table breaks some of the conventions and can only be considered as a variation of the narrow rectangular table. I have not seen another example like it.

98 Ming dynasty *huanghuali* wood narrow rectangular table with corner legs and giant's arm braces

Height 78.5 cm, dimensions of top 98 cm × 48 cm

Although the top of this table protrudes slightly to form a barely noticeable waist, the general appearance still places it in the straight-form category. It has high horse-hoof feet but, because of their cross-section, the legs are none the less called carpenter's-square legs. Since there are no stretchers, the giant's arm braces are very large and low. These features are all rather rare and I have not yet found a similar piece.

99 Ming dynasty *huanghuali* wood high-waisted narrow rectangular table with corner legs

Height 80 cm, dimensions of top 98.5 cm × 48.5 cm

Although the upper parts of the legs of this table are not exposed, it is still known as a high-waisted type. Beneath the apron the cusped opening is similar to the ornamental openings in box-contruction beds. In the middle of the leg there is a relief foliage design. The carpenter's-square legs terminate in horse-hoof feet each with a pair of pointed tips. These are all vestiges of the box-construction bed and help us to trace the origins of waisted furniture with corner legs.

At the end of the apron where the curve flows downwards to form a point, the wood, being very thin and having a very short, straight grain, could easily split. In order to strengthen and protect the fragile tip, a half-moon-shaped piece of wood has been left along the inside of the edge of the apron where it is not visible. This is an example of a cabinetmaker's understanding of the nature of wood, and of his practical solution to the problem of having to choose between decorative effect and structural strength.

100 Ming dynasty *huanghuali* wood table with recessed legs, elongated bridle joints, and everted flanges

Height 86.2 cm, dimensions of top 126.2 cm × 39.7 cm

At first glance this table with four recessed legs, everted flanges, and only one stretcher on each side appears relatively simple. However, close scrutiny of the details reveals some rather special techniques. The straight apron is unusually thick, the front surfaces are not flat but higher at the middle and slope gently towards the sides, and there is an incised line along the edge. All these give the piece a certain roundness. Since the apron is so thick it cannot be completely inserted into the mortise of the leg, and thus it is partially inserted into the leg and partially encircles the front of the leg. Therefore the appearance of the joint is very different from that of an ordinary elongated bridle joint. The side stretchers are not straight but curved like a bridge. All these features point to a skilful craftsman.

At one time this table was painted black and I myself cleaned it to restore the original colour. In the process I discovered that the floating panel is made from *tieli* wood rather than *huanghuali* wood. It was painted black to conceal this and to simulate *zitan* wood at a time when *zitan* which is dark, sometimes almost black, was highly valued.

101 Ming dynasty *huanghuali* wood small flat-top narrow table with recessed legs, elongated bridle joints and a shelf

Height 81 cm, dimensions of top 71.2 cm × 37.7 cm

About 30 centimetres below the top of this small flat-top narrow table with recessed legs, four stretchers are mortised and tenoned into the leg. A groove was made along the inner edge of each stretcher to hold the floating panel which forms the shelf. Such a shelf is usually found only on small tables and rarely on a table of this size, for two reasons. First, the mortises and tenons, all being at the same level, have to be small; consequently the shelf is not strong and cannot hold much. Second, a person seated at a large table would have no space for his legs if there were a shelf, whereas the problem would not arise with a small table as it would not be the kind of table at which a person would sit. Therefore, shelves are found only in small tables, and examples are few.

102 Ming dynasty *jichi* wood flat-top narrow table with recessed legs, elongated bridle joints and straight rods

Height 79.5 cm, dimensions of top 87 cm × 43 cm

This strikingly simple flat-top narrow table with recessed legs has side floor stretchers with three straight rods above. It retains the flavour of the Sui and Tang table with vertical railing and appears to be a simplified version of the Tang dynasty eighteen-legged narrow waistless table now preserved in the Shosoin in Japan. This kind of construction was prevalent in pre-Song times, as may be seen in Dunhuang wall paintings, but few pieces were made during the Ming dynasty.

103 Ming dynasty *huanghuali* wood table with recessed legs, everted flanges and elongated bridle joints

Height 83 cm, dimensions of top 141 cm × 47 cm

This table with recessed legs has plain apron-head spandrels with short, square, sharply cut corners. The side floor stretcher has carved cloud motifs. Above is a four-sided inner frame and an ornamental opening with cusped upper edge. Such openings are usually surmounted by a side stretcher but it has been omitted from this piece. The top has very wide tenon-bearing frame members. The mortise-bearing frame members and everted flanges are made from a single piece of wood. An unusual feature is the groove under the everted flange into which the floating panel is inserted. The tenon-bearing frame members are tenoned, thus concealing the mortise-bearing frame member. The *huanghuali* wood of the floating panel is exceptionally beautiful, the grain resembling a rushing mountain torrent with here and there a devil's face. It is possible that the craftsman, having acquired such a superb long piece of wood, was unwilling to cut it, and so adopted the groove construction under the everted flange.

104 Ming dynasty *huanghuali* wood large flat-top narrow table with recessed legs and elongated bridle joints

Height 93 cm, dimensions of top 350 cm × 62.7 cm

Ming dynasty *huanghuali* wood large tables with recessed legs of over 3 metres in length are rare, and rarer still if both the material and workmanship are fine. Therefore, this table has been well known in Beijing for many years and is considered an exceptional piece.

Although the top has a frame, the floating panel is made of one piece of wood which is as lustrous and smooth as jade. The apron and spandrels have a leather-strip moulding which turns smoothly and with great vitality into a design of abutting curls. Between each pair of frontward-curving legs there is a base stretcher with a rounded corner and a four-sided inner frame above. This frame is formed of four thick pieces of wood carved into cloud motifs at the corners, and at the centre of the bottom member. In most examples there is a narrow plain apron with small spandrels beneath the base stretcher. However, this piece has a heavy round stretcher made of a single piece of wood. The table is so large that a simple strip stretcher would neither harmonize with the proportions nor provide sufficient support.

105 Qing dynasty *ju* wood flat-top narrow table with recessed legs, humpbacked stretchers and ornamental struts

Height 83 cm, dimensions of top 84.5 cm × 37.5 cm

This small table with recessed legs has humpbacked stretchers with struts in the form of double interlocking circles. Beyond each leg and under each protruding end is a hollow spandrel. On each side of the table, between the side stretcher and the side floor stretcher, is fitted a round-cornered rectangular inner frame. The side stretchers are surmounted by an ornamental panel with a rectangular opening. All these features show that the craftsman broke with convention, cleverly combining elements from various types without giving the impression of striving after novel effects. It is therefore a successful design.

Since the table is less than one metre long, its strength is not seriously affected by the fact that neither the elongated bridle joint nor the inserted shoulder joint is used. A small defect in the design is that the four legs are a little too narrow. If they were just one centimetre wider, the proportions of the table would be more satisfactory.

106 Ming dynasty *huanghuali* wood flat-top narrow table with recessed legs, apron made by joining the straight, and floor base stretchers

Height 84.5 cm, dimensions of top 158 cm × 47.4 cm

Both the construction and the form of this table are unusual. It appears to have an elongated bridle joint, but in fact the leg is attached to the top with a double-mitred tenon. The lattice apron is made by joining the straight, and it is attached to the legs by planted tenons. The base stretcher rests on the ground and meets the legs in a mitred joint. This is contrary to the usual practice of attaching a base stretcher to the leg by an unmitred joint. I have made inquiries of many craftsmen but have been unable to ascertain the name for this construction, so I have called it the floor base stretcher. The so-called solid-piece-of-jade top board is thick and has a mortise-bearing frame member on each end to conceal the unattractive end grains. The legs and the apron's members are relatively large and the joints neat and tight fitting. This compensates to a certain extent for the defect of not using the logical elongated bridle joint construction. The whole piece has a neat and regular appearance and a feeling of solidity.

107 Ming dynasty *huanghuali* wood narrow table with recessed legs, everted flanges and inserted shoulder joints

Height 87 cm, dimensions of top 140 cm × 28 cm

The solid-piece-of-jade top is 3.5 centimetres thick. The everted flanges and mortise-bearing frame members are made of a single piece of wood. There is beading along the aprons and legs and two-incense-stick beading down the middle of each leg. Flanking the inserted shoulder joints on the apron are two openwork cloud motifs, thoughtfully designed so that they tilt slightly and have small points along their bottom edge. If these had been made horizontal or without the points, the whole table would be robbed of much of its character. A short distance below the shoulder the leg swells to form a floral silhouette at the exact spot where there are mortises for the tenons of the two side stretchers. At the base of the leg there is another cloud motif, of a kind often seen in furniture depicted in Southern Song paintings.

108 Ming dynasty *zitan* wood waistless painting table with corner legs and leg-encircling humpbacked stretcher

Height 78 cm, dimensions of top 190 cm × 74 cm

This table is different from the usual form which has humpbacked stretchers with pillar-shaped or decorative struts. Here the stretcher is thicker and meets the top of the table, so that there is no space for struts. It is a simpler, purer form. To compensate for the loss of stability due to the fact that the point where the stretcher joins the leg is higher than normal, a giant's arm brace has been added.

What makes this table particularly rare is the original Ming dynasty black lacquer flush floating panel which is still in good condition. Its subtly shimmering surface, dark as ebony, has random crack patterns and a natural patina. This lacquer panel matches the dark *zitan* wood, the one enhancing the other.

109 Ming dynasty *zitan* wood straight-form painting table with corner legs and relief carving

Height 81.3 cm, dimensions of top 173.5 cm × 86.5 cm

Although this table is covered with smooth, rounded relief carving of archaistic hornless dragons it is still grouped with the straight-form examples. Since the middle of the legs resembles a carpenter's square in cross-section, its form is clearly derived from the box-construction bed. I have not seen another *zitan* wood straight-form painting table with similar carving.

This important table belonged to the famous early 20th-century collector Zhu Yi'an 朱翼盦, who bought it from Jia Tengyun 賈騰雲, owner of the Rongxingxiang Antique Shop 榮興祥古玩店 south of Dongsi Pailou 東四牌樓 in Beijing. It was sold to Jia by the Manchu scholar Foniyinbu 佛尼音布 (*zi* Hefu 鶴伏, *hao* Heding 荷汀), who acquired it from a certain Zhu 朱, a Chinese who was made a Manchu bannerman. Zhu was a descendant of the Duke of Cheng 成國公 of the Ming dynasty. Thus, this is an important piece of *zitan* wood furniture whose pedigree can be traced back to the Ming dynasty.

110 Ming dynasty *zitan* wood waisted painting table

Height 84 cm, dimensions of top 171 cm × 74.4 cm, largest dimensions 180 cm × 85 cm

The legs of this painting table curve outwards and then in. However, because this curve does not begin just at the four corners and the four legs do not terminate in horse-hoof feet, the table does not belong to the type with a convex apron and bulging legs ending in horse-hoof feet. The legs are connected by a horizontal member which projects upwards in the centre in a cloud motif composed of *lingzhi* fungus. Thus the form, bearing some resemblance to the narrow waistless table, is unique among painting tables.

Except for the top, the entire surface of the table is richly decorated with smoothly rounded high-relief carvings of *lingzhi* fungus, small and large ones freely intermingled. There are similarities between this carving and that found on the lotus throne (Pl. 59) and on the *zitan* wood painting table (Pl. 109).

At the beginning of the century this table was sold by the Huang 黃 family, Muslim candlemakers in Beijing's Ox Street, to Guo Jing'an 郭靜安, owner of the Tianhezhai 天和齋 antique shop. Guo sold it to Guan Mianjun 關冕鈞, a famous collector and compiler of the painting catalogue *Sanqiuge shu hua lu* 三秋閣書畫錄. At that time the well-known collector Guo Baochang 郭葆昌 greatly coveted the table, but Guan refused to part with it. Guo had a copy made, which is nothing like the original because it was impossible to find large enough pieces of *zitan* wood. Now both the original and the copy are in the Palace Museum.

111   Ming dynasty *huanghuali* wood painting table with recessed legs and elongated bridle joints

Height 82.5 cm, dimensions of top 151 cm × 69 cm

This is a standard Ming dynasty painting table with recessed legs and elongated bridle joints. The apron-head spandrels in the form of cloud motifs are commonly seen. What makes the table unusual is that all its members are made from especially large pieces of wood, thus giving the piece an archaic and dignified style.

112   Ming dynasty *huanghuali* wood small painting table with recessed legs and elongated bridle joints

Height 82 cm, dimensions of top 107 cm × 70 cm

This piece is close to the standard form of small painting table with recessed legs and elongated bridle joints. What makes it special are the beautifully carved addorsed phoenixes on the apron-head spandrels. Derived from archaic jades, the phoenixes give a new vitality to an ancient motif. A rare feature of the table is the marble top whose pattern suggests rugged mountain ranges and dense forests, giving the impression of a splashed ink landscape painting.

113   Ming dynasty *huanghuali* wood painting table with recessed legs and elongated bridle joints

Height 85 cm, dimensions of top 138 cm × 75.5 cm

The base stretchers distinguish this table from the two preceding examples. There are many ways in which the space above such stretchers may be treated. For instance there may be a four-sided inner frame, an openwork inset panel, or a lattice formed of straight members. Here the inner frame is formed of four rounded members meeting in abutting spirals at the corners. This unusual method of treating the space produces a light and airy feeling.

114   Ming dynasty *huanghuali* wood small painting table with recessed legs, elongated bridle joints and humpbacked stretchers

Height 81.5 cm, dimensions of top 102 cm × 70.2 cm

The very small size of this painting table prompts some to call it a half table. However, a half table serves as a surface on which to place things and a painting table is for writing and painting. Since the very high humpbacked stretcher of this table leaves plenty of leg space, it must have been used as a painting table. The apron is so low that when combined with the stretcher their height equals that of an ordinary apron. Thus the proportions of the piece are most pleasing.

115 Ming dynasty *zitan* wood painting table with recessed legs and inserted shoulder joints

Height 83 cm, dimensions of top 192.8 cm × 102.5 cm

This table is not highly decorated, having only an ice-plate edge moulding along the bottom of the top frame, beading along the apron and legs, and an ornament on the feet. On account of the great length and width of the table and the massiveness of its members, it was constructed in such a way that it may be taken apart. The eleven component parts in the order of their assembly are: (1 and 2) two side pieces each consisting of two legs connected by two stretchers; (3-6) four spandrels in the form of double cloud heads; (7 and 8) two long aprons; (9) top; and (10 and 11) two short side aprons. In the upper part of each leg there is a slot with a tenon on each side. Below the front tenon the wood is cut into a double mitre, resembling shoulders. First the spandrels and then the aprons are inserted into the slots in the legs so that the three members form a flush surface. At this point the table is already a stand with four legs. The heavy top is then put on this stand, the two tenons on the leg fitting into mortises on the long tenon-bearing frame member of the table top. The two side aprons are put in place and the table is complete.

Since the width of each leg is about 10 centimetres, the shoulders are almost 20 centimetres long, thus making the joint of leg, spandrel and apron very stable. This is a solution to the problem of constructing large, heavy tables. The cloud-head spandrels are not only decorative but also play an important part in supporting the heavy top and strengthening the joint.

On one of the aprons there is engraved the following inscription by Prince Pu Tong 溥侗 dated in correspondence to 1907:

Formerly Zhang Shuwei 張叔未 [Zhang Tingji 張廷濟, 1768-1848] had in his possession a table that once belonged to Xiang Molin 項墨林 [the famous Ming dynasty collector Xiang Yuanbian 項元汴, 1525-90] and a *zitan* chair that once belonged to Zhou Gongxia 周公瑕 [the calligrapher and painter Zhou Tianqiu 周天球, 1514-95]. Zhang composed poems and had them engraved on the table and chair; the poems can be found in his collected works, *Qingyige ji* 清儀閣集 . This painting table I acquired from the Song 宋 family of Shangqiu 商丘 [in Henan Province]. Originally it belonged to Xipi 西陂 . It is bequeathed by former scholars and is still in good condition; it should be treasured just like Xiang Molin's table and Zhou Gongxia's chair. I caress it and dust it with loving care, secretly delighted to be destined to own it. Therefore I write a few sentences to express my respect for the former scholars. Inscribed by Xiyuan 西園 , Lazy Tong 侗, on an autumn day in the year *ding wei* [1907].

Xipi is the *hao* of the famous collector and connoisseur Song Luo 宋犖 (1634-1713), who lived from the late Ming to the early Qing dynasty. His father, Song Chuan 宋權 , and his grandfather, Song Xun 宋纁 , were both prominent Ming dynasty officials. This table is designed with such an archaic simplicity that it must have been an heirloom piece in Song Luo's family. Since late Qing times it has been considered the foremost *zitan* wood painting table.

116 Ming dynasty *huanghuali* wood trestle painting table

Overall height 84.5 cm, dimensions of top 192.2 cm × 69.5 cm × 6 cm thick, dimensions of stands 36.5 cm × 69.5 cm

Since this table consists of two rectangular stands supporting a framed floating panel, craftsmen call it a board and stand desk. The two stands are made of square members. The rather low flat horse-hoof feet are supported by a continuous floor stretcher, somewhat resembling rectangular incense stands. In the middle of each stand is a shallow drawer, the spaces above and below which have no inner frame. The top of the table, consisting of a frame with a tongued-and-grooved panel, is as wide as the greatest depth of the stands. The undecorated table has sharp corners and crisp lines. It belongs to the category of straight-form furniture.

In 1950 this painting table was sold by Zhang Huofu 張護福 , who had a shop in Lu Ban Guan 魯班館 in Beijing, and it was repaired by the famous craftsman Shi Hui 石惠 . Zhang told me that the table first appeared in the morning market at Haidian 海淀 . At that time the top board was about 2.5 metres long, but Zhang was afraid it was too large to sell and so cut off about half a metre. It is most unfortunate that such a large table should have been mutilated.

117 Ming dynasty *tieli* wood narrow table with four drawers
Height 87 cm, dimensions of top 174 cm × 51.5 cm

This table differs from the ordinary table with corner legs and drawers in having an apron and small spandrels on the outer edges of the legs, causing the piece to resemble a coffer without the hidden storage (see Pls 153-6). Two of the four drawers are ornamented with floral sprays and two with lucky grass motifs. Although the workmanship is not particularly good, there is a simplicity and a rustic quality to the table which make it a fine example of provincial furniture.

118 Ming dynasty *huanghuali* wood lute table with double-curl spandrels
Height 82 cm, dimensions of top 120 cm × 51.8 cm

The top board of this table has a hollow centre which is a sound box. Inside there are bronze springs which produce a humming sound when the table is struck. Thus the table was made specifically as a lute table. Some say the table's structure can enhance the sound of the lute. However, the famous lute player Guan Pinghu 管平湖 believes that the springs interfere with the sound of the lute, impairing rather than improving it, and that it was made by a dilettante who did not know any better. This straight-form table has abutting-curl spandrels, one of which is missing.

119 Ming dynasty *nan* wood inlaid with *huanghuali* wood waisted altar table with giant's arm braces
Height 91 cm, dimensions of top 152 cm × 82.5 cm

The form of this table, whose red lacquered top is concave on the four sides and indented at the corners, is rather rare. The sides of the frame, waist and cabriole legs are inlaid with *huanghuali* wood in various patterns, such as angular spirals and triangles. The shape of the four legs simulates those on bronze *ding* 鼎 and they are inlaid with an elephant design. The whole table is most elaborate and much labour was expended in creating its form and decoration, which suggest that it was an altar table rather than one used in the hall of a private house.

120 Ming dynasty *huanghuali* wood waisted straight-leg daybed
Height 46.4 cm, dimensions of top 206.5 cm × 80.2 cm

Since this daybed is less than one metre wide, it is a single bed. Unlike the majority of waisted furniture, it does not have horse-hoof feet. There are Ming dynasty tables and stools which are similarly waisted, without horse-hoof feet and composed of square members with concave mouldings. The reason why these do not accord with the principles governing traditional furniture forms is not because of the concave mouldings but because of the squareness of the members. Since the legs are square and of uniform cross-section, it would be most difficult to make horse-hoof feet.

121 Ming dynasty *huanghuali* wood six-legged folding daybed

Height 49 cm, dimensions 208 cm × 155 cm

The tenon-bearing frame members of this daybed have been cut at the middle and joined with an iron hinge so that the bed can be folded. Silver designs have been hammered into the iron. The two middle legs have inserted shoulder joints and are connected by a stretcher to form an H-shaped stand. When the bed is unfolded the tenons on top of the legs fit into mortises in the apron. When folded, the H-shaped stand can be removed and the four corner legs folded into the cavity between the aprons. The details of construction are shown in the accompanying illustrations.

The bed has a waist, cabriole legs and outward-curving horse-hoof feet. On the aprons and legs there are relief designs of curling tendrils, flowers, birds and animals. The designs are rather common, but the construction of the bed is very unusual. Perhaps the construction of this daybed has some connection with the folding beds in Yongjia 永嘉 (in Zhejiang Province) and the eastern part of Guangdong, mentioned by the Ming dynasty author Wen Zhenheng 文震亨 in *Zhangwu zhi* 長物志 (*Notes on My Belongings*), *juan* 6, p. 36.

122 Ming dynasty *zitan* wood Luohan bed with solid three-panel screen railings

Height 66 cm, dimensions of top 197.5 cm × 95.5 cm

This Luohan single bed is made entirely of *zitan* wood. Three thick undecorated boards form the railings. The back panel has a narrow strip of wood added along the bottom, because the form of a Luohan bed demands that the back panel be higher than the side panels. It is extremely difficult to find such a large piece of *zitan* wood, and for this reason we should be satisfied with the way in which the requirement is met. The frame of the seat has a simple ice-plate edge moulding. The legs are round and solid and extend straight to the ground. Around the four sides there is a leg-encircling humpbacked stretcher with pillar-shaped struts. Both the construction and the decoration of this bed are extremely simple, and it is visually so satisfying that it will never cease to please. It is an excellent example of Ming dynasty furniture.

123 Qing dynasty *ju* wood Luohan bed with three-panel screen railings with inset panels

Height 88 cm, dimensions of top 200 cm × 92 cm

As the back railing of this bed is higher at the centre it appears to be a five-panel screen. However, the back is a single piece and therefore it is a three-panel screen. The inset panels are carved with high-relief hornless dragons and *lingzhi* fungus. Since such high relief can only be made from a thick board, we know that the craftsman was concerned with achieving the proper decorative effect rather than saving material. Both the subject matter and the style of carving are typically Ming. Also typical of Ming style are the making of apron and waist from a single piece of wood, the convexity of the apron, and the strong legs ending in powerful horse-hoof feet. However, the previous owner of this piece, a resident of Dongting Dongshan 洞庭東山 on the shore of Lake Tai 太湖 (in Jiangsu Province), believed that the bed was made in the Qing dynasty.

124 Ming dynasty *tieli* wood Luohan bed with *zitan* wood three-panel screen railings

Height 83 cm, dimensions of top 221 cm × 122 cm

This bed has a waist, convex apron, and bulging legs ending in horse-hoof feet. The carpenter's-square lattice railings are made by joining the straight. This kind of lattice is found on balustrades depicted in the Northern Wei (535-56) caves at Yungang, and this is further evidence of the connection between architecture and furniture.

To make a bed with convex apron and bulging legs ending in horse-hoof feet requires large pieces of wood. The difficulty of finding *zitan* wood of such a size may explain why two kinds of hardwood are used here, although there is also the possibility that the bed and the railings of this piece were reassembled from two different beds.

125 Qing dynasty *zitan* wood Luohan bed with three-panel screen railings with inserted panels

Height 85 cm, dimensions of top 216 cm × 130 cm

This bed is waistless and has base stretchers. On the front of the bed, 23 centimetres to the sides of the legs there are straight vertical rods. The spaces between these and the legs are inserted with a frame. Between the two vertical rods there is another frame resembling the canopy lattice around the top of a canopy bed. These vertical rods and inserted frames are all quite slender and recessed, so that there is enough space for the base stretcher to be used for resting the feet in the absence of a footstool. The construction of the four round legs of the bed is similar to that of most armchairs, with legs and posts made from a single piece of wood which passes through the frame of the seat and meets the top rail of arms and back in a hidden mitred tenon joint. The three railings can be compared to a southern official's hat armchair, with the highest horizontal member of the back similar to the top rail of the chair and those along the sides equivalent to the arms of the chair. As in an armchair the back top rail mitres into the back posts and the side top rails mitre into the front posts and double-mitre into the back posts. In the middle of each railing an ornamental panel is connected by short struts to the frame members and the seat. The ornamental panels have openings resembling the so-called fire-cracker-shaped openings, as well as a small opening at each end. I have seen this kind of opening on a *ju* wood Luohan bed belonging to the Yan 嚴 family of Dongting Dongshan on the shore of Lake Tai in Jiangsu Province. Thus we have reason to believe that this bed was made in the same district.

The workmanship of the bed is extremely fine and its appearance elegant. However, in the ornamental panel of the back railing there is a twisted rope pattern which I find somewhat common and lacking in refinement. The general appearance of the bed bears some resemblance to the one illustrated in the Yuan dynasty woodblock edition of *Shi lin guang ji* 事林廣記 (*Extensive Record of the Forest of Facts*) by the Song writer Chen Yuanjin 陳元靚 (Yuan edition reprinted in *Gugong zhoukan* 故宮周刊, no. 358, p. 4). The resemblance demonstrates that the form of this bed is derived from a much older prototype.

The main members of the bed are made of *zitan* wood. The inner frames and the ornamental panels in the railings are fashioned from a softer golden-hued wood which contrasts in a most pleasing manner with the *zitan* wood. I have asked several old craftsmen about this wood and none can tell me its exact name; a botanist may be able to identify it.

126 Ming dynasty *huanghuali* wood canopy bed with front railings

Height 231 cm, dimensions of top 218.5 cm × 147.5 cm

As all canopy beds with front railings have six posts they are also known as six-post beds. The *wan* 卍 motif lattice of the two square front railings, as well as the side and back railings, is made by joining the straight. The canopy lattice is made from openwork ornamented panels.

This is one of the more elaborately decorated types of canopy bed. A much simpler example, also with a *wan*-motif lattice, is illustrated in the Wanli edition of *Lu Ban jing jiangjia jing*.

127 Carved panels of a Ming dynasty *huanghuali* wood canopy bed

Dimensions of front railings 34.2 cm × 26.2 cm × 2.4 cm thick, dimensions of side railings 129 cm × 27 cm × 2.4 cm thick

In the 1950s I bought these pieces from a family in Tongzhou 通州 (about 20 kilometres east of Beijing). From the dimensions of the pieces we know that they are the front and side railings of a canopy bed. The double-faced openwork carving has a seeming effortlessness and an evident mastery of technique that identify the panels as from the Ming dynasty.

Tongzhou (present-day Tong Xian) is at the end of a canal along which hardwood furniture of southern manufacture was transported to the north on boats whose principal cargo was rice. Consequently one used to find a great deal of *huanghuali* wood furniture in Tongzhou. By the middle of this century only a few incomplete examples remained.

128 Ming dynasty *huanghuali* wood canopy bed with full-moon opening

Height 227 cm, dimensions of top 247.5 cm × 187.8 cm

The full-moon opening is surrounded by three lattice panels, two at the lower sides and a top piece. These, the side and back railings, and the canopy lattice are all made by joining the straight and assembling the curved. The design is composed of units of four cloud motifs, the units linked by crosses. Although the design is complex, it does not appear too fussy because one is struck by the rhythmic pattern and the overall effect of order that prevails over such an extensive surface.

The high-waisted base has pillar-shaped struts and panels ornamented with flowers and birds in low relief. The apron is carved with curling limbed dragons and floral scrolls. On the apron beneath the canopy lattice, clouds and cranes are carved.

This large and sumptuous canopy bed, with its great variety of decorative techniques and motifs, has a rich and noble beauty. It was presented to the Palace Museum by the antique dealer Xia 夏, who bought it in Shanxi, most likely from an old merchant family which traded with the south. The bed was probably made in the Suzhou district. The original *huanghuali* wood right back post has been replaced by one made of *ju* wood, which is indigenous to Suzhou, and thus supports my belief that the bed was manufactured there.

129 Ming dynasty *zitan* wood waisted kidney-shaped footstool
Height 17 cm, dimensions of top 72.5 cm × 36 cm; one of a pair
Originally Ming dynasty Luohan and canopy bedsteads all had matching footstools, most of which have been separated from their beds. This piece, with kidney-shaped top, convex apron and bulging legs ending in horse-hoof feet, is a variation of the standard form. We place it here to complete the section on beds.

130 Ming dynasty *huanghuali* wood three-tiered shelves
Height 188 cm, dimensions of shelves 103 cm × 43.6 cm
This is an example of three-tiered open shelves. It represents the most basic form of shelves to which two drawers have been added.

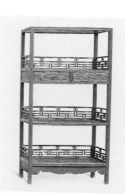

131 Ming dynasty *huanghuali* wood shelves with alternating-square-openings lattice railings
Height 177.5 cm, dimensions of shelves 98 cm × 46 cm; one of a pair
The shelves are made from square members with concave mouldings with indented edges. Beneath the top shelf there are two hidden drawers whose fronts are carved with hornless dragons in relief. The animated design is not interrupted by pulls or handles. On three sides there are railings composed of vertical and horizontal members in a variation of the alternating-square-openings lattice. Between the two uppermost horizontal members are decorative struts in the form of double interlocking circles. Beneath the lowest shelf the deep apron is carved with the dividing-the-heart motif and cloud design. The good proportions and the tasteful decoration endow the shelves with a lightness and a beauty that are quite outstanding.

132 Ming dynasty *huanghuali* wood shelves with lattice back
Height 168 cm, dimensions of shelves 107 cm × 45 cm
This piece has two shelves, and there are two drawers beneath the upper shelf. The openings on the front and sides are ornamented with cusped upper edges. Since the frames of the upper ornamental openings do not extend all the way down to the top shelf, it is possible that originally there was a small railing here. The back has a removable openwork panel secured by loose tenons. In its repeated design, the open areas represent the quatrefoil blossom of the date tree, and its outline is defined by four slightly S-shaped pieces of wood which form a wave-like pattern, similar to the lattice illustrated in *Yuan ye* 園冶 (*The Art of the Garden*), Figure 46.

For a long time there was some argument about whether the back panel was original or a replacement. However, the illustration in *Yuan ye* at least proves that this kind of lattice existed in Ming times.

133 Ming dynasty *zitan* wood shelves with lattice on three sides made by joining the straight

Height 191 cm, dimensions of shelves 101 cm × 51 cm

The three shelves are all made of *zitan* wood and only the strip in the centre of the back is *huanghuali* wood. The lattice pattern, evolved from the so-called windmill pattern, is very regular despite the fact that it is slanted. As is the case with the preceding piece, there is an argument about whether the lattice is original or a replacement. Those who consider it a replacement say that the lattice is not exactly symmetrical, and since it was not wide enough an extra *huanghuali* wood board was added to make it fit. It is certain, however, that in Ming times there were shelves with lattice on three sides.

134 Ming dynasty *huanghuali* wood shelves supported by stands

Height 129 cm, dimensions of shelves 91 cm × 40 cm

The two rectangular stands are now missing.

The shelves, which have no legs, were originally supported by two stands, and are thus a variation of the standard form. The entire piece is composed of square members with concave mouldings. There are three shelves, and under the middle shelf are two drawers, each having a floating panel with raised centre and a bronze pull. The back consists of two frames with inserted panels. On the front, the upper corners all have cloud-head design spandrels with concave surfaces. At the sides there are four-sided inner frames with beaded edges.

The rectangular stands also had square members with concave surfaces and at the bottom four small feet made of the same piece of wood as the legs. The top of the stands had beading along all but the inner edge. The shelves were placed within this beading and were therefore very stable. Thus the dimensions of the bottom of the shelves were one beading smaller than those of the two stands. The two stands were lost sometime during the Cultural Revolution and now can only be seen in this old photograph.

135 Ming dynasty *zitan* wood shelves with rods on doors and sides

Overall height 179 cm, dimensions of shelves 100.3 cm × 48.2 cm × 132 cm high, dimensions of stand 100.3 cm × 48.2 cm × 47 cm high; one of a pair

Although this de luxe piece was especially made for holding books and antiques, Beijing craftsmen still call it by the colloquial term vexing the cat. It is constructed in two parts, the lower one being a stand. The upper part has three shelves, a solid wood back, and two wood hinged doors consisting of rods which form a ridged surface and are divided vertically into three sections by flat rectangular frames. The stand has two drawers with an open shelf beneath. Under the shelf there is an apron with small, plain spandrels. The whole piece is made of the best quality *zitan* wood, except for the back, shelves, and insides of the drawers which are made from *tieli* wood. It is very neat with rounded surfaces. In thirty years of looking in the more than ten furniture stores in Lu Ban Guan 魯班館, I have never come across a piece similar to this pair.

136 Ming dynasty *huanghuali* wood Wanli display cabinet
Overall height 187 cm, dimensions of cabinet 113 cm × 55.5 cm × 166 cm high,
dimensions of stand 115 cm × 57.5 cm × 21 cm high
This Wanli display cabinet has a solid back and arch-shaped inner frame with a simple
angular spiral design. It rests on a low railing carved with hornless dragons in relief. The rest
of the cabinet is plain except for carving on the apron of the separate stand which echoes that
of the top. It is close to the basic form of a Wanli display cabinet.

137 Pair of Ming dynasty *huanghuali* wood carved Wanli display cabinets
Overall height 195.5 cm, dimensions of cabinet 124.8 cm × 55.5 cm × 172 cm high,
dimensions of stand 126.5 cm × 57 cm × 23.5 cm high
These display cabinets have solid backs and on the other three sides arch-shaped inner frames
carved with *shou* 壽 (longevity) characters and hornless dragons. Each door is divided into
two panels by a short horizontal frame member and has a floating panel with raised centre
and lowered edges on the outside. The square upper panel with indented corners is decorated
with a medallion carved with peonies and phoenixes, the corner areas filled with cloud motifs.
The slightly rectangular lower panel is ornamented with peonies and birds. A curling tendril
design decorates the apron of the stand. Inside each cabinet there is a shelf with two drawers.
These elaborate Wanli display cabinets are the most richly decorated ones I have seen.

138 Ming dynasty *huanghuali* wood display cabinet with two open shelves
Height 117 cm, dimensions of shelves 119 cm × 50 cm
The cabinet has two display shelves open at the back and arch-shaped inner frames on the
other three sides. Unlike the preceding example, the three drawers are placed outside the
doors. Inside the cabinet there is a shelf with two pierced knobs affixed to the front edges.
When the doors are closed, these pierced knobs will protrude beyond the tenon-bearing frame
members and face plates so that a lock can be passed through them. On pieces with this type
of pierced knob, all other metalwork ornaments on the doors are flush with the surface. In
other words, a groove the shape and thickness of the metal is made in the surface of the wood
and into this the metal is inserted and nailed, so that the surfaces are flush.

The panels of this cabinet are flush, not recessed as in the preceding example, and
following the usual practice the metalwork ornaments are also flush. I believe that this was
done by the craftsman to give the piece a neat and unified appearance.

139 Ming dynasty *jichi* wood round-corner *kang* cabinet
Height 64 cm, dimensions of top 65.5 cm × 39.5 cm; one of a pair
Since in north China this kind of small round-corner cabinet is often placed on a *kang*, it is known as a *kang* cabinet. On large round-corner cabinets the top board is often recessed, but here it is flush. This is a practical consideration because often all kinds of objects are placed on top of such low cabinets.

140 Ming dynasty *huanghuali* wood shelves with lattice back and *jichi* wood round-corner *kang* cabinet
The juxtaposition of these two pieces clearly shows that the *kang* cabinet (Pl. 139) is less than half the height of the shelves with openwork lattice back (Pl. 132).

141 Ming dynasty *huanghuali* wood round-corner cabinet
Overall height 130.5 cm, dimensions of cabinet top 77 cm × 41 cm, dimensions of lowest part 76 cm × 39.5 cm
This plain cabinet with a central removable stile and no hidden compartment is relatively close to the standard form of the medium-sized round-corner cabinet. Round-corner cabinets have splayed legs and in most examples the width of the cabinet's cap is equal to the amount of the splay. However, in some pieces such as this, the cap is slightly wider, so that when two such cabinets are placed side by side, the caps would touch while there would still be a small space between the legs at the bottom. In other examples the cap is a little smaller than the amount of the splay (Pl. 142), so that when the two pieces in a pair are placed adjacent to each other, the legs meet but there is a small space between the tops. The cap protrudes in order to allow space for the door pivot mortises as well as for aesthetic reasons. One can easily imagine that if a cabinet is larger at the bottom than at the top and has no cap, it will not look well when standing by itself, and will be even more unsightly when placed in a pair.

142 Ming dynasty *ju* wood round-corner cabinet
Overall height 167 cm, dimensions of cabinet top 94 cm × 49 cm, dimensions of lowest part 95 cm × 50 cm
This cabinet has a central removable stile and a hidden compartment. The inside has a drawer frame with two drawers and is lacquered dark red. The workmanship of the entire cabinet, including the lacquering and the metalwork ornaments, is identical to that of Ming dynasty *huanghuali* wood round-corner cabinets. The original apron was lost and the present one was done following the design of the side aprons. The manner in which the centre of the apron is slightly indented can be found on *huanghuali* wood cabinets such as that in Plate 144.

The cabinet came from the village of Shiqiao 石橋村 , Dongting Dongshan, on the shore of Lake Tai near Suzhou; it was the native village of the Ming official Wang Ao 王鏊 (1450-1524) who served as Grand Secretary from 1506 to 1509. Local peasants call the cabinet a book cabinet, and tell me that in the old days this kind of furniture could only be found in the homes of scholar-officials.

143 Ming dynasty *tieli* wood round-corner cabinet with doors and five horizontal members

Overall height 187.5 cm, dimensions of cabinet top 98 cm × 52 cm, dimensions of lowest part 97 cm × 51 cm

The doors of this cabinet each have four panels. Three of these are made of birch, with four-sided inner frames glued on top, so that only the centre of the birch panel is visible. Portions of the inner frames have already fallen off. There is a hidden compartment with the outside of its front panel divided into three by two struts.

Dividing doors into panels provides an opportunity to make new types of decoration. However, since the round-corner cabinet is typically splayed, it is best to make each door from a single piece of wood. Even better is to make both doors from one board by cutting it down the middle so that their grains are symmetrical. This is just one example of a round-corner cabinet with segmented doors.

144 Ming dynasty *huanghuali* wood variation of a round-corner cabinet

Height 175.5 cm, dimensions 106 cm × 53 cm; one of a pair

This one-part square-corner cabinet is a variation of the round-corner cabinet. The back of the top lacks a cap but has three square members meeting at one corner mortise-and-tenon joint, a feature which appears in square-corner cabinets. At each end of the front of the top there are two crescent-moon shaped protuberances which create space for the door pivot mortises and somewhat resemble a cap. Thus, when viewed from the front the cabinets seem to be rather like round-corner cabinets. The doors and sides of the cabinets appear to have been cut from the same piece of wood, which was not quite wide enough, and so a narrow strip had to be added along the side of each board. This pair of Ming dynasty cabinets is well made from fine materials, as well as being of a rare form.

145 Qing dynasty *huanghuali* wood square-corner cabinet

Height 161 cm, dimensions 82.5 cm × 47 cm

This cabinet has neither a central removable stile nor a hidden compartment. All frame members have concave mouldings. The straight, deep apron with rather sharp beading has a rigid angularity that suggests a date around the mid Qing dynasty.

146 Ming dynasty *huanghuali* wood doors with four-cloud motif from a square-corner cabinet

Each door: height 168 cm, width 47 cm, thickness 5 cm

The square-corner cabinet is in poor condition and should be repaired. However, since its doors are intact and are rather special, they are included here.

Although the lattice, like that on Luohan beds and clothes racks, is made by assembling the curved, there is a difference in these doors because there is a board at the back. The doors consist of a frame with a board which is recessed to a depth equal to the thickness of the decoration. The decoration, consisting of four-cloud motifs surrounding a circular hornless dragon design, is glued on to a panel. It is unlike the lattice work of beds and clothes racks in which the separate pieces are joined by small tenons. This is a simpler technique but has the disadvantage that the glue is likely to lose its adhesive quality over a long period and pieces may consequently fall off.

The carefully planned design consists of three columns of the motif flanked by half columns. In the central column the dragon heads are frontal, while in the side columns they face inwards, the thoughtful decorative scheme creating an appealing effect. The contrast of the meticulously decorated doors to the plainness of the rest of the cabinet is especially pleasing.

147 Ming dynasty *huanghuali* wood square-corner cabinet

Height 192 cm, dimensions 123.5 cm × 78.5 cm; one of a pair

This is a comparatively rare large square-corner cabinet. The frame members all have convex mouldings edged with beading. The front and side aprons have cusped edges. These features frequently appear on round-corner cabinets but seldom on square-corner ones. On the back of the cabinet, cloth has been pasted and covered with black lacquer, which has fine crack patterns. The piece looks imposing and its details are smooth and rounded. Consequently, whether viewed from near or far it has an antique air. When compared with the square-corner cabinet with concave mouldings (Pl. 145), the difference in date is obvious.

148 Ming dynasty *huanghuali* wood small compound wardrobe in four parts

Overall height 162 cm, dimensions of lower part 69 cm × 37.5 cm × 125 cm high, dimensions of upper part 69 cm × 37.5 cm × 37 cm high; one of a pair

This is a relatively small example of the compound wardrobe in four parts which can also be used on a *kang*. Although this piece with its veneered frame is not of the highest quality, it is a good illustration of this particular type of furniture.

149 **Qing dynasty *huanghuali* wood large compound wardrobe in four parts with one-hundred-precious-material inlay**
Overall height 279 cm, dimensions of lower part 187.5 cm × 72.5 cm × 195 cm high, dimensions of upper part 187.5 cm × 72.5 cm × 84 cm high
At the side of each door there is a removable outer panel joined to the cabinet by loose tenons. It is considerably wider than ordinary compound wardrobes in four parts and Beijing craftsmen call it a court costume cabinet as court costumes can be placed inside without being folded.

The cabinet is a straight-form piece so that the surface is appropriate for inlaying with one hundred precious materials. The theme of the decoration is that of foreigners bringing tributes of exotic products and animals such as lions and elephants. The inlay, made of soapstone of various colours and mother-of-pearl, is less valuable than the one-hundred-precious-material inlay on the washbasin stand with towel rack (Pl. 171). Furthermore, this wardrobe uses *huanghuali* wood veneer and so is not a piece of quality. In every period, one may find pieces of good material and workmanship as well as others which are of inferior quality despite their glittering appearance. Our inlaid washbasin stand and this inlaid compound wardrobe are examples of these respective grades.

150 **Ming dynasty *huanghuali* wood screen set in a stand with removable panel**
Height 245.5 cm, dimensions of base 150 cm × 78 cm; one of a pair
Two pieces of thick wood are carved into shoe-feet with embracing drums. On top of each there is a post flanked by standing spandrels. It resembles the one illustrated in *Lu Ban jing jiangjia jing* in that between the posts there are two stretchers joined and divided into two parts by a central strut, with openwork panels between them. Beneath the lower stretcher there is a slanted apron with relief carving of hornless dragons. A large panel is inserted into grooves on the inner sides of the posts. The panel has an outer and inner frame, with the spaces between filled with small panels decorated with openwork carvings of hornless dragons. Although the piece is about 2.5 metres high, it has a light and airy appearance. The glass oil painting of court ladies in the central panel is obviously a later addition from the Qianlong period or slightly later. The ancestry of this kind of screen can be traced to Southern Song prototypes, such as the one depicted in one of the hanging scrolls of "Eighteen Scholars 十八學士圖 " in the National Palace Museum, Taiwan.

151 **Ming dynasty *huanghuali* wood small screen set in a stand**
Height 70.5 cm, dimensions of base 73.5 cm × 39.5 cm
This small screen was designed to be used on a table, but it is modelled after large pieces. It resembles a Ming dynasty white marble screening wall in the Forbidden City's Jingrengong 景仁宮. Like the marble screen, its frame is divided into three panels along the top and bottom, and two panels on the sides. But unlike the marble screen whose stand has three-dimensional seated dragons, this stand has a shoe-foot with cloud ends, flower-patterned embracing drums, and standing spandrels. Although this type of construction complies with the Qing Regulations, we believe that it was also used in Ming times. Originally the screen had a central panel of Dali marble which was broken into fragments and had to be removed.

152 **Ming dynasty *huanghuali* wood small screen set in a stand with removable panel**
Height 36.5 cm, dimensions of base 38 cm × 15 cm
The frame of the panel has concave mouldings but the two posts and stretcher have flat surfaces with indented-corner mouldings. This use of two kinds of moulding in a single piece is rather unusual and very successful. The screen is much simpler than the two preceding screens (Pls 150 and 151). There are no ornamental openwork panels and one apron replaces the slanted aprons on both sides. There is still a shoe-foot but the embracing drums are smaller and closer together, and the standing spandrels less complex. Since the screen is so small its members must all be simplified, and by comparing it with the larger models we can see exactly how this was done.

153 Ming dynasty *tieli* wood coffer
Height 85 cm, dimensions of top 98 cm × 47 cm

This piece was used in an ordinary household. It is quite plain and there are exposed tenons on the tenon-bearing frame member of the top and the front of the drawer. Under the hidden compartment there is a humpbacked stretcher instead of the usual apron. The cabinetmaker has used very thick boards, especially for the two side walls of the hidden compartment. Both the exposed tenons and the thickness of the boards suggest that he was more concerned with strength than aesthetics.

154 Ming dynasty *huanghuali* wood two-drawer coffer with hornless dragon designs
Height 89.5 cm, dimensions of top 112 cm × 59 cm

The entire front surface of this two-drawer coffer is carved with hornless dragon designs, except for the apron which is carved with a lotus scroll. This kind of hornless dragon design is in some ways similar to the curling limbed dragon in that it can be curled in any way to fit the available space. The front panels of the drawers and hidden compartment have raised centres which make the ornament stand out vividly. The motifs on the drawers are downward-curling cloud heads with empty centres, designed in such a way as to accommodate the metal face plate. The two are so well matched that there is no doubt that the metalwork is original. Most coffers have round metal face plates but these plates are an unusual and fine example of the long rectangular type.

155 Ming dynasty *huanghuali* wood two-drawer coffer with dragon designs
Height 90 cm, dimensions of top 160 cm × 52 cm

This coffer has everted flanges. Each of the drawer fronts has an arch-shaped inner frame which Beijing craftsmen describe as a country stove opening. Beneath the arch-shaped inner frame there is a square face plate with a handle. The metal tongue can be pulled up behind the inner frame and slid into a groove in the bottom of the tenon-bearing frame member. When thus raised, the hole at the bottom of the tongue will be level with the handle's two knobs, and a lock can be inserted.

On the front panel of the hidden compartment there are relief carvings of two dragons chasing a pearl. Since the dragons have wings, they are called flying dragons by Beijing craftsmen. Such dragons are a popular Ming dynasty motif often seen on blue-and-white porcelain as well as on carved cinnabar lacquer. They are called winged dragons (*ying long* 應龍) in ancient texts, such as *Huainan zi* 淮南子 , and Ban Gu's 班固 essay, "Da bin xi 答賓戲 " ("Reply to Guests").

Beneath the protruding ends there are four hanging spandrels, all decorated with relief carving which is visible when the piece is viewed from the front. The fact that the inside of the back spandrels is decorated is quite unusual.

The hidden compartment seems too deep in proportion to the rest of the piece, so that although the coffer's storage capacity is increased it has a rather clumsy appearance. The curling tendril design on the apron is very fluent, but the dragons and carvings on the arch-shaped inner frames of the drawers are rather coarse and perfunctorily done. This suggests that the coffer is a provincial piece rather than a finely made one used in a wealthy household.

156 Ming dynasty *huanghuali* wood three-drawer coffer
Height 90.5 cm, dimensions of top 177.5 cm × 56.8 cm

This coffer has everted flanges and the drawer fronts have cusped arch-shaped inner frames and round face plates with handles. The entire piece is plain except for the hanging spandrels beneath the protruding ends of the top, which have curved edges echoing the arch-shaped inner frames of the drawers. The front of the hidden compartment is strengthened by a post placed between two panels, a design which would make the coffer stronger than if one long panel had been used.

157 Ming dynasty *huanghuali* wood small chest
Height 18.7 cm, dimensions of top 42 cm × 24 cm

This piece is representative of the basic form of the small chest. It is plain except for the beading along the edge of the lid and the top of the box. The beading is not only for decoration but also serves to strengthen the wood which is thinner where lid and box overlap.

Bronze plates reinforce the four corners and side edges of the chest, and the corners of the lid are decorated with bronze cloud motifs. There is a round face plate and cloud motif hasp. All these metalwork fixtures are flush with the surface of the chest. On each side there is a handle.

158 Ming dynasty *huanghuali* wood medicine chest in the shape of a square-corner cabinet
Height 46 cm, dimensions of top 38 cm × 27.5 cm

This chest resembles a small square-corner cabinet. However, when the doors are opened we find the space entirely filled by drawers, and realize that it is a medicine chest. Of course, a small piece like this can also be used for storing other kinds of small objects. Although it is a functional storage chest, it may be placed as a decorative object on a table.

159 Ming dynasty *huanghuali* wood medicine chest in the shape of a picnic box
Height 77 cm, dimensions of chest 69 cm × 41.5 cm, dimensions of base 78 cm × 45 cm

Behind the two doors of this chest there are eighteen drawers. The entire piece, including the back, and the sides and bottom of the drawers, is made of *huanghuali* wood, and it is therefore quite rare. The chest rests on a base. The sides have standing spandrels and posts extending across the top in the form of a handle. The members are very light and fashioned in the shape of a picnic box, a shape which is merely decorative and not at all functional. All the metalwork is flush with the surface, giving the piece a very neat appearance.

160 Ming dynasty *huanghuali* wood picnic box
Height 21.3 cm, dimensions of top 36 cm × 20 cm

The base of this picnic box consists of a rectangular frame with braces. On each side there are standing spandrels flanking a post which joins a horizontal bar to form the handle. All joints are reinforced with metal. The box is composed of four pieces: two tiers, a tray in the upper tier, and a lid. The edge of each tier is thickened with beading, just as in the small chest (Pl. 157). Holes have been made in the short sides of the lid and the posts, so that a bronze rod can pass through them to hold the lid firmly in place. The box is further secured by the manner in which the bottom tier fits into an indentation in the base, the top tier into an indentation in the bottom tier, so there is no danger of any of the parts slipping out of place.

161 Ming dynasty *jichi* wood desk tray

Height 15.4 cm, dimensions 35.4 cm × 35.4 cm

On the four sides of this square tray there is a lattice railing patterned on the character for a well (*jing* 井), referred to by some Beijing cabinetmakers as a windmill lattice railing. Beneath the railing there are two drawers. The wood, carefully selected for its attractive grain, is extremely handsome. At each corner there is a post extending to the bottom of the piece. Three sides are made from whole thick pieces of wood which tenon into the posts. The tenons are staggered so as not to interfere with those from the adjoining side. This construction of thick wall and post differs from the more usual method which consists of a frame filled in with panels.

162 Ming dynasty *huanghuali* wood folding mirror platform

Height of folding panel when raised 60 cm, height when level 25.5 cm, dimensions of platform 49 cm × 49 cm

On top of the platform and within the frame there is a square folding panel used to support a bronze mirror. It can be folded flat or supported at a 60° angle by another frame at the back. The panel consists of a frame divided into three registers and eight segments. The middle segment in the bottom register has a lotus-leaf support which can be moved up and down in order to fit mirrors of different sizes. The central segment has four spandrels forming a cloud motif with hollow centre, so that the mirror's tassel can pass through it. All the other segments have panels with relief carving of hornless dragons. These designs are emphasized by the use of floating panels with lowered edges on the outside. The platform has two doors which open to reveal three drawers. The low horse-hoof feet are sharp and flat, giving a feeling of great strength. Not only is this piece carefully designed, but the carving is also excellent, and beautifully grained wood has been selected for all the front surfaces. It is an exceptionally fine example of a small piece of furniture.

163 Ming dynasty *huanghuali* wood throne-type mirror platform

Height 52 cm, dimensions 43 cm × 28 cm

The fronts of the five drawers of this mirror platform are decorated with floral sprays carved in relief. Animal designs adorn the sides of the platform and there is a slanted *wan* 卍 motif on the back. The back and arms of the throne-like arrangement on top of the platform have double-faced openwork panels tongued-and-grooved into a frame. The back panel is carved with a pair of phoenixes, whose heads turn back to gaze at each other, and on the sides there are fruit trees. These designs are very lively yet orderly. The humpbacked top rail turns upwards at each end, terminating in a three-dimensional dragon head. The arms are finished in the same manner. At the front inner edge of each armrest there is a spandrel in the shape of a crouching upward-looking hornless dragon. The two dragons focus one's attention on the centre of the platform, where the mirror would have been placed. The original support for the mirror is now missing.

The construction of the mirror platform is quite unique. The four feet are each made from a large square piece of wood about 3 centimetres square in cross-section. At the bottom their thickness is clearly visible. Higher up, three-quarters of the wood has been cut away to form the corner posts of the platform. Higher up still, the square posts are rounded and pass through the platform to become the front and back posts of the throne-shaped top. Thus the three parts — foot, platform posts and chair posts — are made from a single piece of wood. This seems very wasteful since most of the wood has been cut away. Yet this method of construction makes the piece stronger and more stable than if it were made in three pieces. Moreover, it is labour saving. The form and decoration of this piece are earlier than those of the preceding example and so I believe it dates from the mid Ming.

164 Qing dynasty *huanghuali* wood mirror platform with five-panel screen
Height 72 cm, dimensions 55.5 cm × 36.5 cm

The platform has two doors, three drawers, a railing on four sides, and at the back a small five-panel screen with feet fitting into mortises in the platform. The panels are arranged in order of decreasing height with the tallest one in the centre. Each panel is itself divided into three panels. The ends of the top rail of each panel terminate in dragon heads, with the central one having an additional cloud motif. The original support for a bronze mirror in front of the screen is now lost. The carving is meticulously executed and the style of the dragons indicates that it is a Qing dynasty piece. The whole mirror platform is somewhat damaged and in need of repair.

165 Ming dynasty *huanghuali* wood dressing case
Height 37 cm, dimensions of top 35 cm × 23.5 cm

This medium-sized dressing case has a flat top and no decoration, and is representative of the basic form. The thick boards used for the base have curving edges; they give a feeling of stability to the piece.

166 Ming dynasty *huanghuali* wood clothes rack with phoenix designs
Height 168.5 cm, dimensions of base 176 cm × 47.5 cm

Each of the shoe-feet is made from a thick piece of wood to which is attached a post flanked by standing spandrels. Between the shoe-feet and posts are horizontal members which provide stability to the rack as well as space for the storage of shoes and other small objects. The central panel of the clothes rack consists of two stretchers with three exceptionally lovely openwork panels with phoenix design. The top rail has protruding ends carved with twisting flower and leaf patterns. All horizontal members, except the bottom lattice, have spandrels where they meet the vertical members.

Of all the clothes racks that I have seen this is the most beautifully designed and carved, as well as being in the best state of preservation. Although it has been illustrated a number of times in Western publications, it fortunately still remains in China.

167 Ming dynasty *huanghuali* wood central panel of a clothes rack
Dimensions of lattice panel 144.5 cm × 29.4 cm

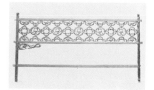

Although this is only the central panel of a clothes rack, it illustrates a type different from the preceding example. The panel is attached to side posts which terminate in lotus buds above, and are connected by a stretcher below. Thus a single unit, composed of vertical and horizontal members, is formed, which tenons into the side posts of the clothes rack. This is unlike the rack in Plate 166 where the horizontal members all tenon directly into the main posts of the rack.

The central panel, made by assembling the curved, has a design consisting of a long-eyed phoenix with curling crest and sharp beading along its backbone alternating with the so-called ice character patterns derived from archaic jade. Unlike the majority of motifs found on Ming dynasty furniture, it is a very ancient design which none the less still looks fresh. Although incomplete, this is still an important piece and merits our attention.

168 Ming dynasty *huanghuali* wood six-legged folding washbasin stand
Height 66.2 cm, diameter 50 cm

The stand is made of round members and the legs, resembling the posts of a balustrade, terminate in up-and-down lotus finials which are very simple yet perfectly capture the essence of the flower. Two of the six legs are fixed in place by a connecting stretcher. The other four legs are joined by short horizontal members. Each of these short horizontals has a mouth-shaped opening in which a hole is drilled and through it passes a nail to fasten it to the round disc fitted into the centre of the stretcher. This construction means that the four legs can be folded and the stand collapsed to a flat shape for easy storage when not in use. Most of the drum stands in temples and on the stage are of the same construction.

The stand supports a lotus-shaped bronze basin, decorated on the interior with a repoussé design of lotus pond and aquatic fowl which in subject matter and treatment is reminiscent of the decoration found on some Ding ware 定窰 porcelain bowls and dishes. On the side there is an inscription saying "Made by the craftsman Yang Shifu 匠人楊世福造 ". The basin can be dated to the Song dynasty (960-1279), or the Liao (916-1125) and Jin (1115-1234); it fits very well with the stand.

169 Ming dynasty *huanghuali* wood washbasin stand with towel rack
Height 168 cm, diameter 58.5 cm

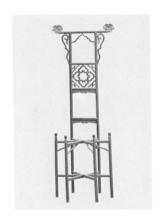

The ends of the top rail of the towel rack are carved with three-dimensional *lingzhi* fungus and the hanging spandrels are formed of round members resembling climbing shoots. The central panel has tendril-motif spandrels at the four corners and in the centre a four-cloud motif, which appears to be made by assembling the curved but is actually cut from a single piece of wood. The whole towel rack has a light and airy feeling and is even more pleasing aesthetically than the highly decorated one in Plate 170. The stand was published in Gustav Ecke's *Chinese Domestic Furniture*; subsequently it was in the collection of Chen Mengjia 陳夢家 and Zhao Luorui 趙蘿蕤 .

170 Ming dynasty *huanghuali* wood decorated washbasin stand with towel rack
Height 176 cm, diameter 60 cm

This washbasin stand has much more decoration than that in Plate 169. Beneath the top rail, which terminates in three-dimensional dragon heads, there is an arch-shaped inner frame. The openwork hanging spandrels are ornamented with curling limbed dragons. The central panel is carved with the auspicious design of a boy riding a unicorn amid trees and rocks. The design is very elaborate, its excesses verging on vulgarity. Most likely this piece was ordered from the shop by a family on the occasion of a daughter's marriage.

171 Qing dynasty *huanghuali* wood washbasin stand with towel rack with one-hundred-precious-material inlay
Overall height 201.5 cm, height of front legs 74.5 cm, diameter 71 cm

The dragon ends of the top rail are each fashioned from a piece of greyish-coloured jade and the washbasin stand is covered with a hornless dragon pattern inlaid in mother-of-pearl. The central panel has a scene of figures in a landscape made from various kinds of precious materials such as ivory, horn, rhinoceros horn, turquoise, high-quality soapstone, agate, gold and silver. One of the figures leads a dancing lion on a leash and others carry precious objects. The theme is that of tribute-bearers from foreign lands. Both the material and the workmanship are far superior to that of the compound wardrobe in four parts (Pl. 149), proving that one-hundred-precious-material inlay can vary a great deal in quality. There are few such elaborate pieces of furniture, even in the Palace Museum.

172 Ming dynasty *huanghuali* wood roller stool

Height 21 cm, dimensions of top 77 cm × 31.2 cm; one of a pair

This waisted stool has inward-turning horse-hoof feet and resembles a small *kang* table. The two panels of the top are separated by a stretcher, and each has a long opening into which a roller is fitted. The roller decreases in diameter towards the sides and is pivoted so that it can rotate. It is similar to a stool illustrated in *Lu Ban jing jiangjia jing*.

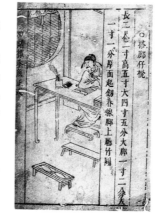

An illustration in Yang Dingjian's 楊定見 Ming dynasty woodblock edition of *Shuihu zhuan* (*Zhongyi shuihu quanzhuan* 忠義水滸全傳 / *The Complete Story of the Loyal Heroes of the Water Margin*, Fig. 56) shows a scene in a main hall where a roller stool is placed beneath a table flanked by two armchairs with curved rests. To use the roller stool a person would sit on an armchair with curved rest and with his two feet he would tread the rollers to improve the circulation of his blood.

173 Qing dynasty *hong* wood sugar-cane squeezer

Height 27 cm, dimensions 29 cm × 11 cm

The sugar-cane squeezer resembles a small bench, but is slanted towards one end with a rounded groove ending in a spout so that the juice can run down into a container. The presser is racket-shaped, with the tip fitting under the stretcher so that it can be used as a lever. Although the piece dates from mid Qing times, its form and decoration preserve features of Ming dynasty furniture.

174 Qing dynasty *zuo* wood bench-shaped pillow

Height 9.8 cm, dimensions of top 20.8 cm × 7.5 cm

The top of this bench dips in the centre and it can be used as a pillow when the top is covered with a padded cotton cushion tied to the legs. People who are accustomed to this kind of pillow say that they cannot fall asleep without one. It can also be used as a wrist rest when a Chinese doctor is feeling the pulse of his patient. The shape of the piece is rather archaic and, since it resembles a much larger bench, is a good example of "seeing the large through the small".

175 Qing dynasty *zitan* wood miniature table with recessed legs and everted flanges

Height 9.5 cm, dimensions of top 19.6 cm × 4.8 cm

The cabinetmaker selected the best *zitan* wood to make this miniature table with recessed legs and everted flanges, elongated bridle joint, plain apron-head spandrels and frontward-curving legs. This piece is a miniature version of a large table with recessed legs, some as long as 250 centimetres, and it embodies all the characteristics of their form. Such a miniature table could serve as an altar table in front of a gilt-bronze statue of Buddha; it could have been a decorative object on a scholar's desk. Having been handled for many generations this miniature table is all the more attractive because its surface is as smooth and lustrous as a piece of black jade. When this, the smallest piece in the book, is placed beside the largest piece in the book, the *huanghuali* wood flat-top narrow table with recessed legs (Pl. 104), their black and reddish-gold colours complement each other and create a most pleasing effect.

Glossary

English terms and their Chinese equivalents

Abutting curls, *liangjuan xiangdi*.
Alcove bedstead, *babuchuang*.
Allover grape pattern, *manmian putao*.
Alternating-square-openings lattice, *pinzi lingge*.
Angular spirals, *huiwen*.
Apron, *yatiao*.
Apron or apron and spandrel made by joining the straight, *cuan yazi*.
Apron and spandrels, *yazi*.
Apron-head spandrel, *yatou*.
Arch-shaped apron, *quankou yazi*.
Arch-shaped inner frame, *quankou*.
Armchair, *fushouyi*.
Armchair with circular rest, *quanyi* or *yuanyi*.
Armchair with four protruding ends, *sichutou guanmaoyi*.
Armrest, *pingji*.
Arms of a chair, *fushou*.
Assembling a mortised-and-tenoned frame with floating panel, *cuanbian dacao zhuangban*.
Assembling the curved, *doucu*.
Assembly, *dou*.

Back of chair or throne, *kaobei*.
Bamboo-shaped, *zhujiewen*.
Bantam, *kuancai*. See also **Coromandel.**
Barbarian seat, *huchuang*.
Base stretcher, *guanjiaocheng*.
Basket back, *kaolaoyang*.
Beading, *dengcaoxian*.
Bed, *chuang*.
Bed railing made by joining the straight, *cuanjie weizi*.
Begonia-shaped, *haitangshi*.
Bench-shaped pillow, *zhendeng*.
Blood *ju* wood, *xieju*.
Board and stand desk, *daban shu'an*.
Book cabinet, *shuchu*.
Book shelf, *shuge* or *shujia*.
Bosses, *guding*.
Box-construction bed, *kunmenchuang*.
Boxwood, *Buxus microphylia*, *huangyang*, and *xiangsimu*, an alternative name for *jichi* wood.
Boy riding a *qilin*, *qilin songzi*.
Bracket, *queti* or *tatou*.

Bracket model, *dougongshi*.
Brightening-the-feet opening, *liangjiao*.
Buddhist pedestal, *xumizuo*.
Bulging leg, *gutui*.
Burl of *nan* wood, *doubainan* or *toubainan*.
Burl wood, *yingmu* or *yingzi*.

Cabinet, *chu* or *gui*.
Cabinet without a central removable stile, *yingjimen*.
Cabinet's cap, *guimao*.
Cabriole leg, *sanwantui*.
Canopy bed, *jiazichuang*.
Canopy bed with front railings, *menweizi jiazichuang*.
Canopy lattice, *guayan*.
Cap, see **Cabinet's cap.**
Carpenter's-square lattice, *quchishi*.
Carpenter's-square lattice railing, *quchi lan'gan*.
Carpenter's-square leg, *waque*.
Carving, *diaoke*.
Central panel of a clothes rack or washbasin stand with towel rack, *zhongpaizi*.
Central panel of a screen set in a stand, *pingxin*.
Central removable stile, *shuan'gan*.
Chair, *yi*.
Changing the level of stretchers, *gancheng*.
Chess table, *qizhuo*.
Chest, *xiang*.
Chicken-wing wood, *jichimu*.
Clothes rack, *yijia*.
Cloud design, *yunwen*.
Cloud-head design, *yuntouwen*.
Cloud-surrounded-by-confronting-dragons motif, *duoyun shuangchiwen*.
Coffer, *menhuchu*.
Collapsible mirror platform, *paizishi jingtai*.
Comb-back chair, *mushubei*.
Complete veneer, *baoxiang*.
Completed part, *shanhuo*.
Compound wardrobe in four parts, *sijiangui* or *dingxiang ligui*.
Concave moulding, *aomian*, *dawa* or *wamian*.
Continuous floor stretcher, *tuoni*.
Continuous flow, *jiaoquan*.
Convex apron and bulging leg ending in a horse-hoof foot, *gutui pengya*.
Convex moulding, *gaimian*, *hunmian* or *tumian*.

Convex surface, see **Convex moulding**.
Corner-leg altar table, *gongzhuo*.
Corner-leg painting table, *huazhuo*.
Corner-leg table, *zhuo*.
Coromandel, *kuancai*. See also **Bantam**.
Court costume cabinet, *chaoyigui*.
Crack patterns, *duanwen*.
Crossed stretchers, *shizicheng*.
Curling limbed dragon, *caolong*.
Curling tendril design, *juancaowen*.
Curved rest of a chair, *yiquan*.
Curved transverse brace, *wandai*.
Cushion, *yinnang*.

Dalbergia hainanensis, *hainantan*.
Dali marble, *dalishi*.
Daybed, *ta*.
Decorative opening, *yumendong*.
Decorative strut, *qiazihua*.
Decorative strut in the form of double interlocking circles, *shuangtaohuan qiazihua*.
Desk tray or **desk treasure tray**, *duchengpan, dushengpan,* or *duzhenpan*.
Devil's face, *guimian*.
Display cabinet, *lianggegui*.
Dividing-the-heart motif, *fenxinhua*.
Door pillars, *mengzhu*.
Door pivot mortise, *jiuwo*.
Door pivot of a round-corner cabinet, *mengzhou*.
Door with five horizontal members, *wumomen*.
Double convex moulding with flat edges, *shuanghunmian ya bianxian*.
Double-faced openwork, *liangmianzuo*.
Decorative strut in the form of double-interlocking circles, *shuangtaohuan qiazihua*.
Double-mitred tenon, *gejiansun*.
Dovetailed groove for the penetrating transverse brace on the back of a floating panel, *daikou*.
Dovetailed tenon, *yindingsun*.
Dragon-and-phoenix joint, see **Tongue-and-groove joint**.
Dragon design, *longwen*.
Dragonfly leg, *qingtingtui*.
Drawer frame, *choutijia*.
Dressing case, *guanpixiang*.
Drum stool, *zuodun* and *gudun*. Also called **embroidery stool**, *xiudun*.

Ebony, *wumu*.
Edge beading, *qibianxian*.
Eight Immortals table, *baxianzhuo*.
Elongated bridle joint, *jiatousun*.
Embracing drums, *baogu*.
Embracing-shoulder tenon, *baojiansun*.
Embroidery stool, *xiudun*.
Endless *wan* motif railing, *wanzi lan'gan*.
Everted flange, *qiaotou*.
Exposed tenon, *mingsun*.
Extension table, *jiezhuo*.

Face plate, *mianye*.
Fan-shaped table, *shanmianzhuo*.
Fire-cracker-shaped opening, *paozhangtong*.
Fish glue, *biaojiao*.
Five joined pieces, *wujie*.
Flat edges of a moulding, *yabianxian*.
Flat-top narrow recessed-leg table, *pingtouan*.
Floating panel, *mianxin*.
Floating panel with lowered edges on the outside, *waishuacao*.
Floating panel with raised centre, *laotang caigu*.
Floor base stretcher, *zhuodi guanjiaocheng*.
Floral sprays, *zhezhihua*.
Flush, *pingzhuang;* also *pingxiang*.
Flush metalwork, *wocao pingxiang*.
Folding chair, *jiaoyi*.
Folding chair with curved rest, *yuanhoubei jiaoyi*.
Folding daybed, *zhedieta*.
Folding mirror platform, *zhedieshi jingtai*.
Folding screen, *weiping*.
Folding side chair, *zhihoubei jiaoyi*.
Folding stool, most commonly *mazha;* also *jiaowu*.
Folding washbasin stand, *zhedieshi mianpenjia*.
Food box, *shige*.
Food cupboard, *qisimao*.
Footrest stretcher, *tajiaocheng*.
Footstool, *jiaota, jiaochuang* or *tachuang*.
Four-cloud motif, *sicuyunwen*.
Four Immortals table, *sixianzhuo*.
Four-post canopy bed, *sizhuchuang*.
Four-sided inner frame, *quankou*.
Frame, *biankuang*.
Frame-thickening inserts, *duobian*.
Front, *kanmian*.
Front of a drawer, *choutilian*.
Frontward-curving legs, *xianglutui*. Also *pietui*.
Full-length mirror, *chuanyijing*.
Full-moon opening, *yueliangmen*.

Giant's arm brace, *bawangcheng*.
Ginkgo wood, *Ginkgo biloba*, *yinxing*.
Gold designs hammered into iron, *jianjin*.
Gooseneck front posts, *ebo*.
Groove, *suncao*.

Half-and-half relief, *bancaodi*.
Half-moon table, *yueyazhuo*.
Half table, *banzhuo*.
Hand-carried box, *tihe*.
Handle, *tihuan*.
Hanger tenon, *guaxiao*.
Hanging spandrel, *guaya*.
Hard seat, *yingti*.
Hasp, *paizi*.
Hexagonal-seat chair, *liufangyi*.
Hidden compartment, *guitang*.
Hidden drawers, *anchouti*.
Hidden storage, *mencang*.
Hidden tenon, *mensun*.

High humpbacked stretcher, *gaogong luoguocheng*.
High table, *gaozhuo*.
High waist, *gaosuoyao*.
Hole-protecting coin, *huyanqian*.
Hong wood, *hongmu*.
Hook-and-plug tenon joint, *gouguadiansun*.
Hornless dragons intertwined with *lingzhi* fungus, *chihu nao lingzhi*.
Horse-hoof edge, *matibian*.
Horse-hoof foot, *mati*.
Hourglass-shaped stool, *quanti*.
Huali wood, *Ormosia henryi*, *huali*. Also *hualü*.
Huanghuali wood, *Dalbergia odorifera*, *huanghuali*. Also *jiangxiang huangtan*.
Humpbacked stretcher, *luoguocheng*.
Humpbacked stretcher with decorative struts, *luoguocheng jia qiazihua*.
Humpbacked stretcher with pillar-shaped struts, *luoguocheng jia ailao*.

Ice-plate edge, *bingpanyan*.
Incense stand, *xiangji*.
Indented box lid, *zikou*.
Indented corner moulding, *wojuexian*.
Inkstone screen, *yanping*.
Inlay, *xiangqian*.
Inner frame, *zikuang*.
Inserted shoulder joint, *chajiansun*.
Inset panel on a recessed-leg table with side panels, *dangban*.
Ivory inlay, *yaqian*.

Jichi wood, *jichimu*.
Join, *cuan*.
Joining the straight, *cuanjie*.
Joining the straight and assembling the curved, *cuan dou*.
Ju wood, *Zelkova schneideriana*, *jumu*.

Kang, *kang*.
Kang cabinets, *kanggui*.

Lamp-hanger chair, *dengguayi*.
Large bed with full-moon opening, *yuedongshi dachuang*.
Large bench, *chundeng*.
Large leaf elm, *dayeyu* or *juyu*.
Large square box carried on a pole, *dafang gangxiang*.
Large tables with ornamental openings on four sides, *kunmen'an*.
Lattice or latticework, *cuan dou*.
Leather-strip moulding, *pitiaoxian*.
Leather-strip moulding and beaded moulding with concave centre, *pitiaoxian jia wa'er*
Leg-encircling, *guotuizuo*.
Leg-encircling stretcher, *guotuicheng*.
Lock knob, *niuhi* or *suobi*.
Lock tongue, *suoxiao*.
Long bench, *changdeng*.

Long narrow bench, *tiaodeng*.
Loose tenon, *huoxiao*.
Lotus leaf support, *heyetuo*.
Low table with extended legs, *aizhuozhantuishi*.
Lower part of a compound wardrobe in four parts, *ligui*.
Lowered centre apron, *watangdu*.
Lowering the surface of the wood, *cai*.
Lowest stretcher on a cabinet, *dicheng*.
Lucky grass, *jixiangcao*.
Luohan bed, *luohanchuang*.
Luohan bed railing lattice made by assembling the curved, *doucu weizi*.
Luohan bed railing lattice made by assembling the curved together with joining the straight, *doucu weizi*.
Luohan bed with five-panel screen, *wupingfengshi luohanchuang*.
Luohan bed with seven-panel screen, *qipingfengshi luohanchuang*.
Luohan bed with three-panel screen, *sanpingfengshi luohanchuang*.
Lute table, *qinzhuo*.

Marble, *dalishi*.
Medallion, *kaiguang*.
Medicine chest, *yaoxiang*.
Medium-sized picnic box, *shige*.
Melon-shaped moulding, *gualengxian*. Also *tiangualeng*.
Metal hinge, *heye*.
Metal pivot, *zhouding*.
Metal pull, *diaopai*.
Metalwork ornaments, *jinshu shijian*.
Mirror box, *jingxiang*.
Mirror platform, *jingtai*.
Mirror stand, *jingjia*.
Mitre, *gejian*.
Mortise and tenon, *sunmao*.
Mortise-and-tenon joint at which three square members meet at one corner, *zongjiaosun*.
Mortise-bearing frame member, *matou*. See also **Short horizontal frame member**.
Mother-of-pearl inlay, *luodianqian* or *qianluodian*.
Moulding, *xianjiao*.

Nan wood, *Phoebe nanmu*, *nanmu*.
Narrow *kang* table, *kangji*.
Narrow recessed-leg *kang* table, *kang'an*.
Narrow rectangular table with corner legs, *tiaozhuo* or *qinzhuo*.
Narrow rectangular table with recessed legs, *tiaoan*.
Narrow table with drawers, *choutizhuo*.
Narrow waistless table, *ji*.
New *huali* wood, *xinhuali*.
New *jichi* wood, *xinjichimu*.
Noodles cabinet, *miantiaogui*.

Official's hat armchair, *guanmaoyi*. See also **Southern official's hat armchair**.
One-drawer coffer, *guisai*.

One-hundred-precious-material inlay, *baibaoqian*.
One-incense-stick beading, *yizhuxiang*.
One-part square-corner cabinet, *yifengshushi*.
Open shelf, *liangge*.
Opening, *touguang*.
Opening with cusped upper edge, *zaohuomen*.
Openwork carving, *toudiao*.
Ornamental openings or medallions with cusped upper edges, *kunmen*.
Ornamental panel, *taohuanban*.
Outer panel, *yusaiban*.
Outward-curving apron, *pengya*.
Outward-curving horse-hoof foot, *waifanmati*.
Ox hair crack pattern, *niumaoduan*.
Ox head side chair, *niutoushiyi*.

Pagoda pattern, *baotawen*.
Pair of phoenixes facing the sun, *shuangfeng chaoyang*.
Panel tongued-and-grooved into a frame, *zhuangban*.
Peg tenon joint, *xiedingsun*.
Penetrating transverse brace, *chuandai*.
Pierced knob, *niutou*.
Pillar-shaped strut, *ailao*.
Pillow screen, *zhenping*.
Platform, *diping*.
Planted tenon, *zaisun*.
Post, *lizhu*.
Protruding end, *diaotou*.
Protruding top, *penmianshi*.
Pseudo thrice attached, *jiasanshang* or *zhenliangshang*.
Pull, *lashou*.

Railing, *lan'gan*.
Railing decorated with carpenter's-square lattice, *quchi lan'gan*.
Railing on Luohan and canopy bed, *chuangweizi*.
Railing on Luohan bed consisting of frames with inset panels, *cuanbian zhuangban weizi*.
Recessed, *laotang*.
Recessed-leg altar table, *gongan*.
Recessed-leg painting table, *huaan*.
Recessed-leg table, *an*.
Recessed-leg table with everted flanges, *qiaotouan*.
Recessed-leg writing table with drawers, *shu'an*.
Rectangular stool, *changfangdeng*.
Relief and openwork carving, *fudiao toudiao jiehe*.
Relief carving, *fudiao*.
Relief carving on diaper ground, *jindi fudiao*.
Relief on smoothed ground, *chandi fudiao*.
Removable-panel screen set in a stand, *chapingshi zuopingfeng*.
Roller stool, *gundeng*.
Rose chair, *meiguiyi*. See also **Writing chair**.
Rosewood, *Pterocarpus indicus*, *qiangweimu*.
Round-corner cabinet, *yuanjiaogui*.
Round stool, *yuandeng*.
Rounding the edges, *daoleng*.
Running horse tenon, *zoumaxiao*.

Sag, *tayao*.
Screen, *pingfeng*.
Screen set in a stand, *zuopingfeng*.
Screen-type mirror platform, *pingfengshi jingtai*.
Scroll termination, *juanshu*.
Scrolling lotus design, *chanzhi lianwen*.
Seat, *yideng*.
Seat railing, *weizi*.
Shadow wood, *yingmu*.
Shelf, *jiage* or *tiban*.
Shelf supported by two separate stands, *jitui jiage*.
Shoe-foot, *dunzi*.
Shoe-foot with cloud ends, flower-patterned embracing drums, and standing spandrel, *ruyiyun baogu quhua zhanya*.
Short horizontal frame member, *matou*.
Short horizontal members on the base of a washbasin stand, *hengguaizi*.
Side chair, *kaobeiyi*.
Side floor stretcher, *tuozi*.
Side of a cabinet, *guibang*.
Side posts of an armchair, *liandaoba* or *lianbanggun*.
Side stretcher, *hengcheng*.
Silver designs hammered into iron, *jianyin*.
Six Immortals table, *liuxianzhuo*.
Six-post canopy bed, *liuzhuchuang*.
Slanted apron, *pishui yazi*.
Slanted *wan* motif, *xiewanzi*.
Slide lock tenon, *zasun*. See also **Running horse tenon**, *zoumaxiao*.
Small chest, *xiaoxiang*.
Smoothed ground of relief carving, *pingdi*.
Soft mat seat of woven cane, *tengti*.
Soft mat seat of cane, palm or silk for stools, chairs and beds, *ruanti*.
Solid board railing, *dubanweizi*.
Solid board top, *dubanmian*.
Solid piece of jade, *yikuaiyu*.
Southern cypress, *nanbai*.
Southern official's hat armchair, *nanguanmaoyi*.
Spandrel, *jiaoya*.
Splayed legs, *cejiao*.
Split moulding, *piliao*.
Square-corner cabinet, *fangjiaogui*.
Square or rectangular frame, *bianma*.
Square stool, *fangdeng*.
Square tables of various sizes, *fangzhuo*.
Standing spandrel, *zhanya*.
Stepped apron moulding, *tuosai*.
Stepped chair stretchers, *bubugao gancheng*.
Stool, *deng* or *wudeng*.
Straight form, *simianpingshi*.
Straight leg, *zhizu*.
Straight shoulder joint, *qijianbang*.
Straight stretcher, *zhicheng*.
Stretcher, *chengzi*.
String moulding, *xianwen*.
Stylized hornless dragon design, *chiwen*.
Stylized hornless dragon design in medallion, *tuanchiwen*.
Sugar-cane squeezer, *ganzhechuang*.
Sword-ridge moulding, *jianjileng*.

Tables, *zhuoan*.

Tea table, *chaji*.

Tenon-bearing frame member, *dabian*.

Three-dimensional carving, *yuandiao*.

Three-drawer coffer, *liansanchu*.

Three joined pieces, *sanjie*.

Three spandrels to one leg, *yituisanya*.

Three spandrels to one leg and a humpbacked stretcher, *yituisanya luoguocheng*.

Thrice attached, *zhensanshang*.

Throne, *baozuo*.

Throne-type mirror platform, *baozuoshi jingtai*.

Tieli wood, *Mesua ferrea*, *tielimu*.

Tiers, *zhuang*.

Tongue, *bianhuang*.

Tongue-and-groove joint, *longfengsun*.

Top rail *da'nao*.

Transverse brace, *dai*.

Trestle table, *jiaji'an*.

Trousseau coffer, *jiadi*.

Truth-bringing incense, *jiangzhenxiang*.

Twice attached, *zhenliangshang*.

Twisted rope pattern, *ningmahua* or *shengwen*.

Two-drawer coffer, *lianerchu*.

Two-incense-stick beading, *liangzhuxiang*.

Two-seater bench, *errendeng*.

Unmitred joint of apron and leg, *qiyatiao*.

Up-and-down lotus flower design, *yangfu lianwen*.

Up-and-down mountain design, *yangfu shanzi*.

Upper part of a compound wardrobe in four parts, *dingxiang*.

Upward-folding stool, *shangzheshi jiaowu*.

Upward-tapering member, *haoziyi*.

Waist, *suoyao*.

Waisted, *yousuoyao*.

Waistless, *wusuoyao*.

Waistless narrow rectangular table, *tiaoji*.

Wan motif, *wanzi*.

Wanli display cabinet, Wanli *gui* or Wanli *ge*.

Washbasin stand, *aimianpenjia* or *mianpenjia*.

Washbasin stand with towel rack, *gaomianpenjia*.

Water-stopping moulding, *lanshuixian*.

Wave lattice, *bowen*.

Well lattice, *jingzi lingge*.

Wide corner-leg writing table with drawers, *shuzhuo*.

Wide *kang* table, *kangzhuo*.

Wide trestle writing table on stands with drawers, *jiaji shu'an*.

Windmill lattice, *fengcheshi*.

Wine table, *jiuzhuo*.

Wood-hinged cabinet, *muzhoumengui*.

Wood inlay, *muqian*.

Wood or bamboo nail, *xiaoding*.

Writing chair, *wenyi*. See also **Rose chair.**

Zitan wood, *Pterocarpus santalinus*, *zitan*. See also **Rosewood.**

Zuo wood, *Quercus dentata*, *zuomu*.

Chinese terms and their definitions

It was decided to base the romanization on Beijing craftsmen's pronunciation in the few instances where it differs from standard pronunciation of these characters. Examples are the character *mo* 抹 which, in certain terms, craftsmen pronounce *ma* (as in *matou* and *bianma*; but *wumomen*, not *wumamen*), the character *shu* 束 which they pronounce *suo* (as in *suoyao*, *yousuoyao* and *wusuoyao*), and the character *wei* 委 which they pronounce *wo* (as in *wojuexian*).

ailao 矮老　Pillar-shaped strut.

aimianpenjia 矮面盆架　Washbasin stand. See also *mianpenjia*.

aizhuozhantuishi 矮桌展腿式　Low table with extended legs. Low waisted table which is transformed into a high table by adding round extensions to the square legs.

an 案　Recessed-leg table.

anchouti 暗抽屜　Hidden drawers, opened by raising from underneath rather than with a pull.

aomian 凹面　Concave moulding; also *dawa* or *wamian*.

babuchuang 拔步牀　Alcove bedstead.

baibaoqian 百寶嵌　One-hundred-precious-material inlay.

bancaodi 半槽地　Half-and-half relief. The most common type of relief carving with relief and ground occupying about the same amount of space.

banzhuo 半桌　Half table, slightly larger than half an Eight Immortals table.

baogu 抱鼓　Embracing drums. The drum-shaped elements at the top of a shoe-foot used to hold the spandrels of screens, clothes racks and lampstands in position.

baojiansun 抱肩榫　Embracing-shoulder tenon. A mitred joint used in waisted furniture of the corner-leg construction to attach the leg and apron. A concealed triangular-shaped tenon in the apron fits into a mortise in the leg. Simultaneously a concealed long and vertical dovetailed tenon slides into a mortise in the apron.

baotawen 寶塔紋　Pagoda pattern. Term used in Suzhou to describe the natural grain of *ju* wood.

baoxiang 包鑲　Complete veneer, a hardwood veneer covering the entire piece of furniture.

baozuo 寶座　Throne, for emperor or god.

baozuoshi jingtai 寶座式鏡台　Throne-type mirror platform.

bawangcheng 霸王根　Giant's arm brace, extending from the leg to the underside of the table top at a 45° angle.

baxianzhuo 八仙桌　Eight Immortals table. Square table suitable for seating eight people.

bianhuang 邊簧　Tongue, on four sides of the floating panel of a table top.

biankuang 邊框　Frame.

bianma 邊抹　Square or rectangular frame, consisting of two sides with tenons (*dabian*) and two sides with mortises (*matou*).

biaojiao 鰾膠　Fish glue, the best cabinetmaker's glue made from the air bladder of the yellow croaker fish.

bingpanyan 冰盤沿　Ice-plate edge. General term for all

inward-sloping mouldings.

bowen 波紋   Wave lattice. Term found in *Yuan ye* (*The Art of the Garden*) and also used for furniture.

bubugao gancheng 步步高趕棖   Stepped chair stretchers. Chair stretchers which are arranged with the front one lowest, the side ones higher, and the back one highest, so that the joints do not overlap.

cai 踩   Lowering the surface of the wood. General term popular among craftsmen.

caolong 草龍   Curling limbed dragon. Stylized dragon pattern in which the legs and tail turn into curls, derived from the curling tendril design.

cejiao 側脚   Splayed legs. Term borrowed from ancient architecture (where it describes the splay of pillars at the base) to describe the slight splay of furniture legs at their base.

chaji 茶几   Tea table. High table derived from the Ming incense table and popular in Qing times.

chajiansun 插肩榫   Inserted shoulder joint. One of the essential joints of the recessed-leg construction. The upper part of the leg is split to form two tenoned pieces; the front one is made shoulder-like so that it can be inserted into cavities in the apron. When the joint is in place the surfaces of leg and apron are flush.

chandi fudiao 鏟地浮雕   Relief carving on smoothed ground.

changdeng 長櫈   Long bench, general term.

changfangdeng 長方櫈   Rectangular stool.

chanzhi lianwen 纏枝蓮紋   Scrolling lotus design.

chaoyigui 朝衣櫃   Court costume cabinet. Compound wardrobe in four parts with side panels. A kind of *sijiangui* with panels between the doors and outer frames which make the wardrobe wide enough for court costumes to be placed inside without being folded.

chapingshi zuopingfeng 插屏式座屏風   Removable-panel screen set in a stand, the panel having tongues which can be slid in and out of grooves in the vertical pillars.

chengzi 棖子   Stretcher. Member used mainly to connect two legs.

chihu nao lingzhi 螭虎鬧靈芝   Hornless dragons intertwined with *lingzhi* fungus.

chiwen 螭紋   Stylized hornless dragon design.

choutijia 抽屜架   Drawer frame, put inside a cabinet or shelf to hold the drawers.

choutilian 抽屜臉   Front of a drawer.

choutizhuo 抽屜桌   Narrow table with drawers.

chu 櫥   Cabinet, southern term for *gui*, which is more current in the north.

chuandai 穿帶   Penetrating transverse brace, which fits into a groove in the floating panel.

chuang 牀   Bed, which in China is used for daytime sitting as well as sleeping. General term for both large and small beds.

chuangweizi 牀圍子   Railing on Luohan and canopy bed.

chuanyijing 穿衣鏡   Full-length mirror, a type derived from a screen set into a base which became popular during the Qing dynasty.

chundeng 春櫈   Large bench. In south China the term refers to a bench for two or more people. Northerners use this term only for a bench for more than two people.

cuan 攢   To join.

cuan dou 攢鬥   Latticework. Literally joining the straight and assembling the curved, two methods of making lattice. General term which is a contraction of *cuanjie* and *doucu*.

cuan yazi 攢牙子   Apron or apron and spandrel made by joining the straight.

cuanbian dacao zhuangban 攢邊打槽裝板   Assembling a mortised-and-tenoned frame with floating panel. This is done by first making a groove all around the inner edge of the frame and then inserting the tongue of the panel.

cuanbian zhuangban weizi 攢邊裝板圍子   Railing of a Luohan bed consisting of frames with inset panels.

cuanjie 攢接   Joining the straight. Term used for the method of making a lattice from short straight pieces of wood, placed vertically, horizontally, and sometimes diagonally, and mortised and tenoned together. The resulting lattice may have square or rounded corners.

cuanjie weizi 攢接圍子   Bed railing made by joining the straight.

daban shu'an 搭板書案   Board and stand desk, consisting of a top resting on two separate stands with drawers which originally were not intended to be used apart from the table.

dabian 大邊   Tenon-bearing frame member. If the frame is rectangular the term refers to the two long pieces with tenons; if square, it indicates the two tenon-bearing members; if round, each piece is called a *dabian*.

dafang gangxiang 大方扛箱   Large square box carried on a pole. Term used in *Lu Ban jing* (*Lu Ban's Classic*) for a large picnic box.

dai 帶   Transverse brace, which always connects the tenon-bearing frame members. General term which includes the penetrating transverse brace and the curved transverse brace.

daikou 帶口   Dovetailed groove for the penetrating transverse brace on the back of a floating panel.

dalishi 大理石   Marble, and in particular Dali marble, from Mount Diancang 點蒼 in the Dali District of Yunnan Province.

da'nao 搭腦   Top rail. Highest rail on the back of a chair. The term also refers to the highest horizontal member of any frame, such as a clothes rack or towel rack.

dangban 擋板   Inset panel on a recessed-leg table with side panels. It usually has openwork carving finished on both sides and sits on a side floor stretcher or base stretchers.

daoleng 倒棱   Rounding the edges. Procedure done to soften the sharp edges of a member.

dawa 打窪   Concave moulding; also called *aomian* or *wamian*.

dayeyu 大葉榆   Large leaf elm, a kind of *ju* wood; also called *juyu*.

deng 櫈   Stool. Also *wudeng*.

dengcaoxian 燈草線   Beading, a rounded moulding. *Dengcao* are rushes used as lampwicks.

dengguayi 燈掛椅   Lamp-hanger chair. Side chair with a high narrow back resembling the bamboo lamp hangers commonly used in south China.

diaoke 雕刻   Carving.

diaopai 吊牌　　Metal pull.

diaotou 吊頭　　Protruding end. The part of the top of a recessed-leg table which extends beyond the leg towards the sides.

dicheng 地栿　　Lowest stretcher on a cabinet.

dingxiang 頂箱　　Upper part of a compound wardrobe in four parts.

dingxiang ligui 頂箱立櫃　　Compound wardrobe in four parts, consisting of two lower cabinets and two upper cabinets; also called *sijiangui*.

diping 地平　　Platform. Large low wooden platform, usually square, placed in a room to hold furniture. When used for an alcove bed it is slightly larger than the bed. Very large ones are for a screen and throne.

dou 鬥　　Assembly of more than two members.

doubainan 鬥栢楠　　Burl of *nan* wood; also *toubainan*, the term used in *Gegu yaolun* (*The Essential Criteria of Antiquities*).

doucu 鬥簇　　Assembling the curved, a term for the method of making a lattice unit from large or small curved pieces of wood joined together by loose tenons.

doucu weizi 鬥簇圍子　　Luohan bed railing lattice made by assembling the curved; or Luohan bed railing lattice made by assembling the curved together with joining the straight.

dougongshi 斗拱式　　Bracket model, a type of spandrel inspired by architectural members.

duanwen 斷紋　　Crack patterns, the fortuitous designs formed of small cracks on the surface of aged lacquer.

dubanmian 獨板面　　Solid board top, found most often on narrow rectangular tables with recessed legs, trestle tables, and benches whose top is not made with a frame.

dubanweizi 獨板圍子　　Solid board railing.

duchengpan 都承盤 or 都丞盤 , *dushengpan* 都盛盤 or *duzhenpan* 都珍盤　　Desk tray or desk treasure tray, for holding the treasures (the paraphernalia used in calligraphy and painting) on a scholar's desk.

dunzi 墩子　　Shoe-foot. Horizontal, usually bridge-shaped, piece of wood supporting a vertical member of a screen, clothes rack or lampstand. It tends to be large and includes the embracing drum.

duobian 垛邊　　Frame-thickening inserts. Separate pieces of wood added, mainly for aesthetic reasons, beneath the four sides of a frame of a table top in order to increase its height. They are commonly found on tables and stools, often on the type with leg-encircling stretcher, or with three spandrels to one leg, and a humpbacked stretcher. The inserts are less deep than the frame members and thus give the illusion of a thick frame without having its weight.

duoyun shuangchiwen 朵雲雙螭紋　　Cloud surrounded by confronting dragons motif.

ebo 鵝脖　　Gooseneck front posts. Curved posts of an armchair which are often made from the same piece of wood as the front legs.

errendeng 二人櫈　　Two-seater bench.

fangdeng 方櫈　　Square stool.

fangjiaogui 方角櫃　　Square-corner cabinet. Usually a metal hinged cabinet with very little or no splay, and in which each of the four corners forms a right angle.

fangzhuo 方桌　　Square table. Term refers to tables of various sizes.

fengcheshi 風車式　　Windmill lattice. Patterned on the shape of the windmill motif used in Chinese paper toys.

fenxinhua 分心花　　Dividing-the-heart motif, the cusp in the middle of an apron.

fudiao 浮雕　　Relief carving.

fudiao toudiao jiehe 浮雕透雕結合　　Relief and openwork carving. Term used when both types of decoration occur in a single piece.

fushou 扶手　　Arms of a chair.

fushouyi 扶手椅　　Armchair.

gaimian 蓋面　　Convex surface or moulding. Term used in *Yingzao fashi* (*Building Standards*) and by cabinetmakers today; also called *hunmian* and *tumian*.

gancheng 趕根　　Changing the level of stretchers, in order to spread out the mortises. The term usually refers to the lower stretchers of chairs.

ganzhechuang 甘蔗牀　　Sugar-cane squeezer.

gaogong luoguocheng 高拱羅鍋根　　High humpbacked stretcher. Stretcher which often appears on the type of table with three spandrels to one leg and on rectangular tables with recessed legs.

gaomianpenjia 高面盆架　　Washbasin stand with towel rack. The two back legs are extended to form the towel rack.

gaosuoyao 高束腰　　High waist. On some examples the influence of a Buddhist pedestal is still discernible.

gaozhuo 高桌　　High table.

gejian 格肩　　Mitre, single or double.

gejiansun 格肩榫　　Double-mitred tenon.

gongan 供案　　Recessed-leg altar table.

gongzhuo 供桌　　Corner-leg altar table.

gouguadiansun 勾掛墊榫　　Hook-and-plug tenon joint, used to attach a giant's arm brace to the leg. The slightly hooked tenon is secured in the mortise by a small block of wood placed beneath it.

gualengxian 瓜棱線　　Melon-shaped moulding, a ridge-shaped moulding used on legs. (When the leg is seen in section, it resembles the section of a fluted melon.) It is often found on waistless square tables and round-corner cabinets. Also called *tiangualeng*.

guanjiaocheng 管脚根　　Base stretcher, a bar placed just above the feet of a piece of furniture to hold the legs in position.

guanmaoyi 官帽椅　　Official's hat armchair. Term includes the official's hat armchair with four protruding ends and the southern official's hat armchair. See also *nanguanmaoyi*.

guanpixiang 官皮箱　　Dressing case, usually having a base with drawers, which are often behind doors, and a top consisting of a lidded tray.

guaxiao 掛銷　　Hanger tenon. Dovetail-shaped tenon on the top of a leg on which to hang the apron, usually as long as the apron.

guaya 掛牙　　Hanging spandrel. Spandrel whose length is greater than its width, and which narrows towards its lower edge.

guayan 掛檐　Canopy lattice, around the top of a canopy bed.

guding 鼓釘　Bosses, the nail motifs on a drum stool.

gudun 鼓墩　Drum stool; also called *zuodun*.

gui 櫃　Cabinet, northern term for *chu*, which is more current in the south.

guibang 櫃幫　Side of a cabinet. Craftsmen's term.

guimao 櫃帽　Cabinet's cap, the top of a round-corner cabinet which protrudes beyond the side posts to allow for the wood hinged construction and which usually has rounded edges.

guimian 鬼面　Devil's face. Term used in *Gegu yaolun* (*The Essential Criteria of Antiquities*) to describe a particular formation in the grain of *huanghuali* wood.

guisai 櫃塞　One-drawer coffer, literally the plug between two cabinets, because the coffer is often placed between a pair of cabinets or compound wardrobes in four parts.

guitang 櫃膛　Hidden compartment, occupying the space below the door and above the bottom board of a cabinet.

gundeng 滾凳　Roller stool. Stool with movable rollers, used to exercise the feet.

guotuicheng 裹腿根　Leg-encircling stretcher. Stretcher continuing around the entire circumference of a piece, passing over the outside edges of the legs.

guotuizuo 裹腿做　Leg-encircling.

gutui 鼓腿　Bulging leg.

gutui pengya 鼓腿彭牙　Convex apron and bulging leg ending in a horse-hoof foot. Term used by Beijing cabinetmakers and in the Qing Regulations.

hainantan 海南檀　*Dalbergia hainanensis*, the scientific name previously given to *huanghuali* wood.

haitangshi 海棠式　Begonia-shaped.

haoziyi 耗子尾　Upward-tapering member, such as the side posts of an armchair.

hengcheng 橫根　Side stretcher, on rectangular tables.

hengguaizi 橫拐子　Short horizontal members on the base of a washbasin stand.

heye 合頁　Metal hinge.

heyetuo 荷葉托　Lotus-leaf support, often occurring on mirror stands.

hongmu 紅木　*Hong* wood. There are two kinds: old *hong* wood was the principal hardwood used by furniture makers from mid Qing times to the first quarter of the 20th century, and new *hong* wood is one of the main hardwoods used by furniture factories today.

huaan 畫案　Recessed-leg painting table. Large, wide rectangular table without drawers.

huali 花梨　*Huali* wood, *Ormosia henryi*. One of the main hardwoods used for furniture after the mid Qing dynasty.

hualü 花櫚　*Huali* wood. Pre-Ming way of writing the term which at that time referred mainly to *huanghuali* wood.

huanghuali 黃花梨　*Huanghuali* wood, *Dalbergia odorifera*, the principal hardwood used for furniture from mid Ming until the first part of the Qing dynasty.

huangyang 黃楊　Boxwood, *Buxus microphylia*, a dense yellowish wood.

huazhuo 畫桌　Corner-leg painting table, a large, wide rectangular table without drawers.

huchuang 胡牀　Barbarian seat. Earliest name for a cross-legged stool. It was imported from the west in the Eastern Han and is the ancestor of the folding stool and the folding armchair.

huiwen 回紋　Angular spirals, based on a motif resembling the archaic form of the character *hui* 回 , repeated continuously.

hunmian 混面　Convex surface or moulding. Term used in *Yingzao fashi* (*Building Standards*) and by cabinetmakers today. Also called *gaimian* and *tumian*.

huoxiao 活銷　Loose tenon.

huyanqian 護眼錢　Hole-protecting coin, a round coin-shaped metal disc used between the metal pivot and the surface of a piece of furniture as a protective device against abrasion.

ji 几　Narrow waistless table, each side of which usually consists of a board meeting the top at right angles.

jiadi 嫁底　Trousseau coffer, a common name for a coffer since a bride's trousseau was placed in it, tied with red strings, and carried to her new home.

jiage 架格　Shelf; also *tiban*.

jiaji'an 架几案　Trestle table. Long table supported by two separate stands.

jiaji shu'an 架几書案　Wide trestle writing table on stands with drawers.

jiangxiang huangtan 降香黃檀　*Huanghuali* wood, *Dalbergia odorifera*, new name given by Cheng Junqing.

jiangzhenxiang 降眞香　Truth-bringing incense. A type of incense with which *huanghuali* wood is often compared in old texts.

jianjileng 劍脊棱　Sword-ridge moulding. Moulding which slopes downwards from a central ridge. *Lu Ban jing* (*Lu Ban's Classic*) calls it *jianjixian* 劍脊線 .

jianjin 鋄金　Gold designs hammered into iron.

jianyin 鋄銀　Silver designs hammered into iron.

jiaochuang 脚牀　Footstool. Song dynasty name for the footstool in front of chairs and beds. Also *jiaota* and *tachuang*.

jiaoquan 交圈　Continuous flow. The continuous connection (upwards, downwards, sideways) of mouldings or the surfaces of different members in order to give the piece of furniture a unified appearance. This term is also used by architects and other craftsmen, especially for four-sided and curved forms.

jiaota 脚踏　Footstool. Also *jiaochuang* and *tachuang*.

jiaowu 交杌　Folding stool; most commonly *mazha*.

jiaoya 角牙　Spandrel.

jiaoyi 交椅　Folding chair.

jiasanshang 假三上　Pseudo thrice attached. See *zhenliangshang*.

jiatousun 夾頭榫　Elongated bridle joint. This and the inserted shoulder joint are the two basic joints of the recessed-leg construction. The top of the leg has tenons, fitting into mortises in the tenon-bearing frame of the top, and a slot, into which the apron and apron-head spandrel can be inserted. Sometimes there are false elongated bridle

joints, with the outward appearance of an elongated bridle joint but constructed in other ways.

jiazichuang 架子牀   Canopy bed.

jichimu 鸂鶒木   *Jichi* wood. Hardwood with purplish-brown patterns, belonging to the *Ormosia* family.

jichimu 鷄翅木   Chicken-wing wood, another name for *jichi* wood.

jiezhuo 接桌   Extension table. When one Eight Immortals table is not enough, a table slightly larger than half its size, similar to a half table, is added to extend it.

jindi fudiao 錦地浮雕   Relief carving on diaper ground.

jingjia 鏡架   Mirror stand.

jingtai 鏡台   Mirror platform.

jingxiang 鏡箱   Mirror box.

jingzi lingge 井字欞格   Well lattice. Lattice of a design centred around the character *jing* 井 (well), and its variations.

jinshu shijian 金屬飾件   Metalwork ornaments.

jitui jiage 几腿架格   Shelf supported by two separate stands.

jiuwo 臼窩   Door pivot mortise.

jiuzhuo 酒桌   Wine table. Small rectangular table used for wine and food.

jixiangcao 吉祥草   Lucky grass. Leaves forming a round motif which is often found on a decorative strut.

juancaowen 卷草紋   Curling tendril design.

juanshu 卷書   Scroll termination. Termination which appears on the sides of narrow waistless tables and splats or top rails of chairs. The term refers to the resemblance of the termination to a soft book when rolled up.

jumu 椇木   *Ju* wood, ancient simplified form of *ju* 櫸 , *Zelkova schneideriana*, one of the semi-hard furniture woods imported in the Ming dynasty; known as southern elm in north China.

juyu 櫸榆   Large leaf elm, a kind of *ju* wood; also called *dayeyu*.

kaiguang 開光   Medallion, which may be empty or filled with carving or a recessed wood or stone panel.

kang 炕   Chair-level bed, which is also sat on during the day, built-in against the wall of a room in north China. It is hollow and made of wood, bricks, or, in poorer households, unbaked clay with a brick top. Brick and clay *kang* can be heated from within. In the case of wooden *kang* which were used in the palace, the specially-made brick floor of the entire room was heated from underneath.

kang'an 炕案   Narrow recessed-leg *kang* table.

kanggui 炕櫃   *Kang* cabinets. Pair of small cabinets placed on the *kang*.

kangji 炕几   Narrow *kang* table, with either corner legs or solid board legs.

kangzhuo 炕桌   Wide *kang* table. The usual proportion of the long to the short sides is three to two.

kanmian 看面   Front, literally the show side of a piece of furniture or one of its members.

kaobei 靠背   Back of chair or throne, either splat or whole back.

kaobeiyi 靠背椅   Side chair.

kaolaoyang 栲栳樣   Basket back. Song dynasty term referring to the armchair with circular armrest.

kuancai 款彩   The technique often used to decorate folding screens whereby lacquer is applied overall to a flat surface, and in areas within the outlines of the design a layer of lacquer is dug out and the resulting cavity is filled in with coloured lacquer or oil paint. Term used in *Xiushilu* (*A Record of Lacquer Art*) for what antique dealers call *dadiaotian* 大雕填 . In the West, such pieces were known first as Bantam work, after the Dutch East India Company's port in Java, and from the 19th century as Coromandel lacquer, after the port on the southeast coast of India.

kunmen 壼門   Ornamental openings or medallions with cusped upper edges. In the Tang and Song dynasties these often appear on the platform construction and on Buddhist pedestals.

kunmen'an 壼門案   Large tables with ornamental openings on four sides. They existed as early as the Tang dynasty, as may be seen in, for example, the painting "The Court Musicians".

kunmenchuang 壼門牀   Box-construction bed, having a box-like base with wide panels containing ornamental openings with cusped upper edges or a single panel with one cusped upper-edge opening.

lan'gan 欄杆   Railing.

lanshuixian 攔水線   Water-stopping moulding. High moulding around the edge of a table to prevent spilt water or wine from soiling the user's clothes.

laojichimu 老鸂鶒木   Old *jichi* wood.

laotang 落堂   Recessed.

laotang caigu 落堂踩鼓   Floating panel with raised centre and recessed sides, so that despite its thickness it will still fit into the grooves of the frame. It is most often found on pieces dating from the mid Qing dynasty and later.

lashou 拉手   Pull, of any shape.

lianbanggun 聯幫棍   Side posts of an armchair, literally the handle of a sickle; also *liandaoba*.

liandaoba 鎌刀把   Side posts of an armchair, usually slightly curved and upward tapering; also *lianbanggun*.

lianerchu 聯二櫥   Two-drawer coffer.

liangge 亮格   Open shelf.

lianggegui 亮格櫃   Display cabinet, a cupboard with one or more open shelves.

liangjiao 亮脚   Brightening-the-feet opening, found on the bottom of chair splats, and under folding screens and railings of Luohan beds.

liangjuan xiangdi 兩卷相抵   Abutting curls. Pair of back-to-back curls, often found on spandrels and stretchers.

liangmianzuo 兩面做   Double-faced openwork, on which the carving is finished to the same degree on both sides.

liangzhuxiang 兩炷香   Two-incense-stick beading. Double row of beading down the centre of the leg of a recessed-leg table.

liansanchu 聯三櫥   Three-drawer coffer.

ligui 立櫃   Lower part of a compound wardrobe in four parts.

lingzhiwen 靈芝紋   *Lingzhi* fungus motif.

liufangyi 六方椅   Hexagonal-seat chair.

liuxianzhuo 六仙桌   Six Immortals table. Medium-sized square table.

liuzhuchuang 六柱牀   Six-post canopy bed. Southern name for a canopy bed with front railings.

lizhu 立柱   Post.

longfengsun 龍鳳榫   Tongue-and-groove joint, in which a long dovetail-shaped mortise and tenon is used to join two long boards. Literally dragon-and-phoenix joint.

longwen 龍紋   Dragon design.

luodianqian 螺鈿嵌   Mother-of pearl inlay; also *qian-luodian*.

luoguocheng 羅鍋棖   Humpbacked stretcher.

luoguocheng jia ailao 羅鍋棖加矮老   Humpbacked stretcher with pillar-shaped struts.

luoguocheng jia qiazihua 羅鍋棖加卡子花   Humpbacked stretcher with decorative struts.

luohanchuang 羅漢牀   Luohan bed. Bed with railings on three sides.

manmian putao 滿面葡萄   Allover grape pattern. Term used in *Gegu yaolun* (*The Essential Criteria of Antiquities*) for the pattern on the burl of *nan* wood.

mati 馬蹄   Horse-hoof foot, which may be inward or outward curving.

matibian 馬蹄邊   Horse-hoof edge.

matou 抹頭   Mortise-bearing frame member. If the frame is rectangular the term refers to the two short pieces with mortises; if square, it indicates the pieces with mortises. On the thick top boards of most trestle tables there is a *matou* at each end but no tenon-bearing frame member. In this instance the tenons, and sometimes also a tongue, are on the top board itself. Sometimes an everted flange is made from the same piece of wood. Also a short horizontal frame member, connecting the two long vertical members of a screen, partition or door.

mazha 馬閘   Folding stool. Common term for *jiaowu*.

meiguiyi 玫瑰椅   Rose chair. Small armchair with back and armrests at right angles to the seat. See also *wenyi*.

mencang 悶倉   Hidden storage, in a coffer.

menhuchu 悶戶櫥   Coffer. General term for a coffer, which may have one, two or three drawers and hidden storage below.

mensun 悶榫   Hidden tenon.

menweizi jiazichuang 門圍子架子牀   Canopy bed with front railings.

menzhou 門軸   Door pivot of a round-corner cabinet. It is the tenon-bearing frame member of the door extended outward, upward and downward to fit into mortises in the top and the stretcher below.

menzhu 門柱   Door pillars, the two pillars on the front of the alcove of a canopy bed.

mianpenjia 面盆架   Washbasin stand. Term which includes both the simple washbasin stand and the washbasin stand with towel rack.

miantiaogui 面條櫃   Noodles cabinet. Common name for round-corner cabinet.

mianxin 面心   Floating panel, inset in a frame.

mianye 面葉   Face plate. Large back plate for pulls and pierced knobs.

mingsun 明榫   Exposed tenon.

muqian 木嵌   Wood inlay.

mushubei 木梳背   Comb-back, the back of a chair having many vertical straight rods under the top rail.

muzhoumengui 木軸門櫃   Wood-hinged cabinet.

nanbai 南栢   Southern cypress.

nanguanmaoyi 南官帽椅   Southern official's hat armchair. Armchair whose back does not have protruding ends.

nanmu 楠木   *Nan* wood, *Phoebe nanmu*.

nanyu 南榆   *Ju* wood, name used in the north.

ningmahua 擰麻花   Twisted rope pattern. Form of moulding resembling a fried dough twist; also called *shengwen*.

niubi 鈕鼻   Lock knob. Knob with a hole through which the rod of a lock passes. Also *suobi*.

niumaoduan 牛毛斷   Ox hair crack pattern, found on the surface of aged lacquer.

niutou 鈕頭   Pierced knob. Metal knob with hole through which a lock or securing rod passes; found on boxes and cabinets.

niutoushiyi 牛頭式椅   Ox head side chair. Chair whose top rail bends backwards resembling the horns of an ox.

paizi 拍子   Hasp. Hinged racket-shaped metal plate usually used to fasten the lid of a chest.

paizishi jingtai 拍子式鏡台   Collapsible mirror platform.

paozhangtong 炮仗筒   Fire-cracker-shaped opening. Southern craftsmen's name for a kind of *yumendong* opening which is the shape of a long oval and used as a motif on the waist.

pengya 彭牙   Outward-curving apron.

penmianshi 噴面式   Protruding top.

pietui 撇腿   Frontward-curving legs; also called *xianglutui* (incense burner legs).

piliao 劈料   Split moulding. Convex moulding made from a single piece of wood which is usually divided evenly into two (also three or four in late Qing times) segments.

pingdi 平地   Smoothed ground of an area with relief decoration.

pingfeng 屏風   Screen. General term which includes folding screens and screens set in a stand.

pingfengshi jingtai 屏風式鏡台   Screen-type mirror platform.

pingji 憑几   Armrest.

pingtouan 平頭案   Flat-top narrow recessed-leg table, without everted flanges.

pingxiang 平鑲   Flush. Term referring, on furniture, to the relationship between the floating panel and its frame or between metalwork and the surrounding wood surface. Also *pingzhuang*.

pingxin 屏心   Central panel of a screen set in a stand.

pingzhuang 平裝   Flush; also *pingxiang*.

pinzi lingge 品字欞格   Alternating-square-openings lattice, the pattern resembling the character *pin* 品 .

pishui yazi 披水牙子   Slanted apron. Craftsmen's term derived from architectural masonry; used on screens and

late Cantonese furniture.

pitiaoxian 皮條線　Leather-strip moulding. Moulding which is rather flat and broad.

pitiaoxian jia wa'er 皮條線加窪兒　Leather-strip moulding and beaded moulding with concave centre.

qiangweimu 薔薇木　Rosewood, *Pterocarpus indicus*, another name for one type of *zitan* wood.

qianluodian 嵌螺鈿　Mother-of-pearl inlay; also *luodian-qian*.

qiaotou 翹頭　Everted flange.

qiaotouan 翹頭案　Recessed-leg table with everted flanges.

qiazihua 卡子花　Decorative strut.

qibianxian 起邊線　Edge beading.

qijianbang 齊肩膀　Straight shoulder joint. The T-shaped joint of two members, so called because the tenon-bearing piece has a straight edge and is not mitred.

qilin songzi 麒麟送子　Boy riding a *qilin*, an auspicious motif used on wedding paraphernalia in the hope of its auguring the birth of a good child.

qingtingtui 蜻蜓腿　Dragonfly leg, the long slender cabriole legs of incense stands.

qinzhuo 琴桌　Narrow rectangular table with corner legs; also *tiaozhou*. This is the more common meaning of the term and refers to tables of various sizes. Also lute table, a small narrow rectangular table specially made for playing the lute.

qipingfengshi luohanchuang 七屏風式羅漢牀　Luohan bed with seven-panel screen. Bed whose back and sides have seven panels.

qisimao 氣死猫　Food cupboard, for storing food and kitchen utensils, usually of unfinished wood with lattice on doors and sides. The name means literally vexing the cat.

qiyatiao 齊牙條　Unmitred joint of apron and leg. The joint used in the form of waisted table in which the two ends of the aprons meet the legs in vertical lines.

qizhuo 棋桌　Chess table, with removable top under which there are usually a double-sided chess board and a board for playing the game of Double Sixes.

qizimu 杞梓木　A variant name of *jichimu*.

quankou 圈口　Four-sided inner frame.

quankou 券口　Arch-shaped inner frame. Three-sided frame usually found under the seat of a chair or on open shelves.

quankou yazi 券口牙子　Arch-shaped apron, beneath the seat of a chair.

quanti 筌蹄　Hourglass-shaped stool.

quanyi 圈椅　Armchair with curved rest; also *yuanyi*.

quchi lan'gan 曲尺欄杆　Railing decorated with carpenter's-square lattice, which is in the shape of the square used by carpenters to make right angles.

quchishi 曲尺式　Carpenter's-square lattice, in the shape of the square used by carpenters to make right angles.

queti 雀替　Bracket, architectural term for a weight-bearing member which has some similarities with the apron on furniture. See also *tatou*.

ruanti 軟屜　Soft mat seat made of cane, palm or woven silk, for stools, chairs and beds. See also *tengti*.

ruyiyun baogu quhua zhanya 如意雲抱鼓葉花站牙　Shoe-foot with cloud ends, flower-patterned embracing drums, and standing spandrel. Term used in the Qing Regulations to describe the base of screens and lampstands.

sanjie 三接　Three joined pieces. Term referring to the curved rest of an armchair formed of three pieces of wood with two joints.

sanpingfengshi luohanchuang 三屏風式羅漢牀　Luohan bed with three-panel screen. Bed whose back and sides have three panels.

sanwantui 三彎腿　Cabriole leg, an S-shaped leg ending in an outward-curving horse-hoof foot.

shangzheshi jiaowu 上折式交杌　Upward-folding stool.

shanhuo 扇活　Completed part. General term applicable to all kinds of structures.

shanmianzhuo 扇面桌　Fan-shaped table. Two can be put together to form a hexagonal table.

shengwen 繩紋　Twisted rope pattern. Form of moulding resembling a fried dough twist; more commonly called *ningmahua*.

shige 食格　Food box. Term used in *Lu Ban jing* (*Lu Ban's Classic*) for a medium-sized picnic box.

shizicheng 十字棖　Crossed stretchers.

shu'an 書案　Recessed-leg writing table with drawers.

shuan'gan 閂杆　Central removable stile, between two doors of a cabinet.

shuangfeng chaoyang 雙鳳朝陽　Pair of phoenixes facing the sun.

shuanghunmian ya bianxian 雙混面壓邊線　Double convex moulding with flat edges.

shuangtaohuan qiazihua 雙套環卡子花　Decorative strut in the form of double interlocking circles.

shuchu 書櫥　Book cabinet, Suzhou name for a medium-sized round-corner cabinet.

shuge 書格　Book shelf, another name for *shujia*.

shujia 書架　Book shelf, another name for *shuge*.

shuzhuo 書桌　Wide corner-leg writing table with drawers.

sichutou guanmaoyi 四出頭官帽椅　Armchair with four protruding ends.

sicuyunwen 四簇雲紋　Four-cloud motif, carved from a board or made by assembling the curved.

sijiangui 四件櫃　Compound wardrobe in four parts, consisting of two lower cabinets and two upper cabinets; also called *dingxiang ligui*.

simianpingshi 四面平式　Straight form. Term used to describe furniture with straight flat sides derived from the box construction.

sixianzhuo 四仙桌　Four Immortals table. Small square table suitable for four.

sizhuchuang 四柱牀　Four-post canopy bed.

suncao 榫槽　Groove, such as that in which the tongue of a floating panel is inserted.

sunmao 榫卯　Mortise and tenon.

suobi 鎖鼻　See *niubi*.

suoxiao 鎖銷　Lock tongue. The bolt of a lock which engages with the lock receptacle to secure a drawer.

suoyao 束腰　Waist. Inset panel between the top and the apron.

ta 榻   Daybed, a light bed without railing.

tachuang 踏牀   Footstool, a Song dynasty term. Also *jiaochuang* and *jiaota*.

tajiaocheng 踏脚根   Footrest stretcher, usually referring to the front stretcher of a chair. When used in the context of a stool, it refers to the base stretcher.

taohuanban 縧環板   Ornamental panel.

tatou 楂頭   Bracket. Term used in *Yingzao fashi* (*Building Standards*) for what was called *queti* in Qing times.

tayao 塌腰   Sag. Condition caused when the top of a piece of furniture droops due to overloading. Occurs mostly in long pieces of furniture of inferior material and craftsmanship.

tengti 籘屜   Soft mat seat, made from woven cane. See also *ruanti*.

tiangualeng 甜瓜棱   Melon-shaped moulding. See *gualengxian*.

tiaoan 條案   Narrow rectangular table with recessed legs.

tiaodeng 條櫈   Long narrow bench.

tiaoji 條几   Waistless narrow rectangular table, usually made from three thick boards meeting at right angles.

tiaozhuo 條桌   Narrow rectangular table with corner legs. See also *qinzhuo*.

tiban 屜板   Shelf; also *jiage*.

tielimu 鐵力木, 鐵梨木 or 鐵栗木   *Tieli* wood, *Mesua ferrea*. Wood which resembles *jichi* wood but which is slightly inferior in colour and grain.

tihe 提盒   Hand-carried box. Term used by Beijing craftsmen for a small picnic box.

tihuan 提環   Handle.

toubainan 骰柏楠   Burl of *nan* wood. Term used in *Gegu yaolun* (*The Essential Criteria of Antiquities*). Also *doubainan*.

toudiao 透雕   Openwork carving.

touguang 透光   Opening.

tuanchiwen 團螭紋   Stylized hornless dragon design in medallion.

tumian 凸面   Convex surface or moulding. Term used in *Yingzao fashi* (*Building Standards*) and by cabinetmakers today; also called *gaimian* and *hunmian*.

tuoni 托泥   Continuous floor stretcher, to the top of which the legs are joined and below which there are separate small feet.

tuosai 托腮   Stepped apron moulding. Term used in the Qing Regulations and by craftsmen for a moulding between the waist and the apron, which may be in one with the apron or made from a separate piece of wood.

tuozi 托子   Side floor stretcher. Stretcher on the short sides of a table with recessed legs. At each end are usually low feet which are sometimes separate pieces of wood attached with glue.

waifanmati 外翻馬蹄   Outward-curving horse-hoof foot. Type of foot which often terminates a cabriole leg.

waishuacao 外刷槽   Floating panel with lowered edges on the outside. Panel which slopes gently towards the sides in order to retain a certain thickness and at the same time to allow it to fit into the grooves of the frame. It is often used in floating panels with raised centres.

wamian 窪面   Concave moulding; also *aomian* or *dawa*.

wandai 彎帶   Curved transverse brace, used under a soft mat seat.

Wanli *gui* 萬曆櫃   Wanli display cabinet. Display cabinet consisting of a cupboard with open shelf above, resting on a separate low stand. Also called Wanli *ge* 萬曆格.

wanzi 卍字   *Wan* motif. Auspicious motif based on the character *wan* 卍.

wanzi lan'gan 卍字欄杆   Endless *wan* motif railing. Railing decorated with continuous pattern of auspicious motifs based on the character *wan* 卍.

waque 挖缺   Carpenter's-square leg. Leg from which about one-half is cut away from the inside so that in cross-section it resembles a carpenter's square. This type of leg preserves more traces of the platform construction than legs terminating in horse-hoof feet.

watangdu 窪堂肚   Lowered centre apron, often found on chairs with an arched apron.

weiping 圍屏   Folding screen.

weizi 圍子   Seat railing, on beds and chairs.

wenyi 文椅   Writing chair. Southern name for rose chair. See *meiguiyi*.

wocao pingxiang 臥槽平鑲   Flush metalwork.

wojuexian 委角線   Indented corner moulding.

wudeng 杌凳   Stool. Term more commonly used in north China than *deng*.

wujie 五接   Five joined pieces. Term applied to curved rest of an armchair formed of five pieces of wood with four joints.

wumomen 五抹門   Door with five horizontal members.

wumu 烏木   Ebony.

wupingfengshi luohanchuang 五屏風式羅漢牀   Luohan bed with five-panel screen. Bed whose back and sides have five panels.

wusuoyao 無束腰   Waistless. Type of furniture without inset panel between the top and the apron, a tradition derived from wooden architectural construction.

xiang 箱   Chest.

xiangji 香几   Incense stand.

xianglutui 香爐腿   Frontward-curving legs in the manner of legs on incense burners; also called *pietui*.

xiangqian 鑲嵌   Inlay.

xiangsimu 相思木   Alternative name for *jichi* wood, sometimes translated as boxwood.

xianjiao 線脚   Moulding. General term for all types of moulding.

xianwen 弦紋   String moulding, on round stools.

xiaoding 銷釘   Wood or bamboo nail.

xiaoxiang 小箱   Small chest.

xiedingsun 楔釘榫   Peg tenon joint, used on curved members.

xieju 血櫸   Blood *ju* wood, a kind of *ju* wood which is reddish and comes from old trees.

xiewanzi 斜卍字   Slanted *wan* motif.

xinhuali 新花梨   New *huali* wood. See *huali*.

xinjichimu 新鸂鶒木   New *jichi* wood. See *jichimu*.

xiudun 繡墩   Embroidery stool, another name for *zuodun* and *gudun* (drum stool).

xumizuo 須彌座   Buddhist pedestal, a waisted pedestal.

yabianxian 壓邊線   Flat edges of a moulding.

yangfu lianwen 仰俯蓮紋   Up-and-down lotus flower design. Ornament consisting of two lotus blossoms, one upright and the other inverted, with the top of their petals touching.

yangfu shanzi 仰俯山字   Up-and-down mountain design. Ornament consisting of two *shan* 山 characters .

yanping 硯屏   Inkstone screen.

yaoxiang 藥箱   Medicine chest.

yaqian 牙嵌   Ivory inlay.

yatiao 牙條   Apron.

yatou 牙頭   Apron-head spandrel. Spandrel attached to the apron.

yazi 牙子   Apron and spandrels. General term which includes aprons, apron-head spandrels, spandrels and hanging spandrels.

yi 椅   Chair.

yideng 椅櫈   Seat.

yifengshushi 一封書式   One-part square-corner cabinet. Type of square-corner cabinet, resembling in shape a case (*tao* 套) of traditional Chinese books.

yijia 衣架   Clothes rack.

yikuaiyu 一塊玉   Solid piece of jade. Term used to describe a single piece of wood for the top of a piece of furniture, especially a trestle table or narrow rectangular table with recessed legs.

yindingsun 銀錠榫   Dovetailed tenon.

yingmu 癭木   Burl wood.

yingmu 影木   Shadow wood, another name for burl wood.

yingjimen 硬擠門   Cabinet without a central removable stile.

yingti 硬屜   Hard seat. Category of seats which includes wooden and hard mat seats.

yingzi 癭子   Burl wood, alternative name for *yingmu*.

yinnang 隱囊   Cushion.

yinxing 銀杏   Ginkgo wood, *Ginkgo biloba*.

yiquan 椅圈   Curved rest of a chair.

yituisanya 一腿三牙   Three spandrels to one leg. Type of corner where one leg joins two apron-head spandrels and an additional spandrel along the outer edge.

yituisanya luoguocheng 一腿三牙羅鍋根   Three spandrels to one leg and a humpbacked stretcher. A feature that commonly occurs on a type of square table.

yizhuxiang 一炷香   One-incense-stick beading. Single row of beading down the centre of the leg of a recessed-leg table.

yousuoyao 有束腰   Waisted. Type of furniture with inset panel between the top and the apron, tradition derived from Buddhist pedestals.

yuandeng 圓櫈   Round stool.

yuandiao 圓雕   Three-dimensional carving.

yuanhoubei jiaoyi 圓後背交椅   Folding chair with curved rest.

yuanjiaogui 圓角櫃   Round-corner cabinet. Splayed wood cabinet with hinged doors and rounded-edged top which protrudes beyond the side posts.

yuanyi 圓椅   Armchair with curved rest. Term used in *Sancai tu hui* (*Pictorial Encyclopaedia of Heaven, Earth and Man*) for *quanyi*.

yuedongshi dachuang 月洞式大牀   Large bed with full-moon opening.

yueliangmen 月亮門   Full-moon opening.

yueyazhuo 月牙桌   Half-moon table.

yumendong 魚門洞   Decorative opening, generally found on the waist. General term which includes different specific shapes such as rectangular openings with stepped corners and the long oval openings referred to as *paozhangtong*. Term used in the Qing Regulations, and more popular in south China.

yuntouwen 雲頭紋   Cloud-head design, a symmetrical motif.

yunwen 雲紋   Cloud design.

yusaiban 餘塞板   Outer panel. Panel between the door and outer frame of a cabinet.

zaisun 栽榫   Planted tenon. Tenon which is not made from the same piece of wood as the member but is a separate piece fitted into the member.

zaohuomen 竈火門   Opening with cusped upper edge. Term used by Beijing craftsmen because of the resemblance of the opening to that of a country stove.

zasun 扎榫   Slide lock tenon. Southern name for *zoumaxiao* (running horse tenon).

zhanya 站牙   Standing spandrel. Any two spandrels facing each other against a post, such as those found on stands, clothes racks and screens.

zhedieshi jingtai 折叠式鏡台   Folding mirror platform.

zhedieshi mianpenjia 折叠式面盆架   Folding washbasin stand.

zhedieta 折叠榻   Folding daybed.

zhendeng 枕櫈   Bench-shaped pillow.

zhenliangshang 眞兩上   Twice attached. Term used when the waist and apron are made of two separate pieces of wood. Also refers to the method of construction whereby the apron and the apron moulding are made from a single piece of wood and the waist from another piece of wood. Used interchangeably with *jiasanshang*.

zhenping 枕屏   Pillow screen. Small screen placed on beds.

zhensanshang 眞三上   Thrice attached. Method of construction whereby the waist, stepped apron moulding and apron are each made from a separate piece of wood. Most post-Qianlong period furniture is made by this method of construction, which is not as strong as the twice-attached method.

zhezhihua 折枝花   Floral sprays.

zhicheng 直根   Straight stretcher.

zhihoubei jiaoyi 直後背交椅   Folding side chair.

zhizu 直足   Straight leg. Leg without a horse-hoof foot.

zhongpaizi 中牌子   Central panel of a clothes rack or washbasin stand with towel rack. Cabinetmakers' term.

zhouding 軸釘   Metal pivot, the metal rod put through the legs of a folding chair as a pivot.

zhuang 撞   Tiers. Southern term.

zhuangban 裝板   Panel tongued-and-grooved into a frame. Panel may be flush or recessed.

zhujiewen 竹節紋   Bamboo-shaped.

zhuo 桌   Corner-leg table.

zhuoan 桌案   Tables. Term referring to both corner-leg and recessed-leg tables.

zhuodi guanjiaocheng 着地管脚根   Floor base stretcher.

Combination of the base stretcher and side floor stretchers on recessed-leg tables.

zikuang 仔框   Inner frame.

zikou 子口   Indented box lid. Box lid which has a narrow indentation along its inner edge; the edge of the box has a wider indentation along its outer edge so that the lid can be securely closed.

zitan 紫檀   *Zitan* wood, *Pterocarpus santalinus*. Purplish wood, one of the most important furniture woods.

zongjiaosun 棕角榫   Mortise-and-tenon joint at which three square members meet at one corner. Name derived from the resemblance of the joint to the corners of parcels of sticky rice wrapped in leaves which are eaten at the Dragon Boat Festival.

zoumaxiao 走馬銷   Running horse tenon. Planted tenon which is tapered and stepped at one end. It is inserted in the larger end of the mortise and slid to the smaller end, thereby locking the joint. To separate the two members the tenon must be pushed back to the large end of the mortise. See also *zasun*.

zuomu 柞木   *Zuo* wood, *Quercus dentata*. Type of oak which is semi-hard and yellowish-brown in colour, with grain lines a few centimetres long and pointed at both ends.

zuopingfeng 座屏風   Screen set in a stand.

Bibliography

Bao Liang 保亮 *et al.* (Qing), *Gongbu xuzeng zuofa zeli* 工部續增做法則例(*Additional Manufacturing Regulations for the Ministry of Works*) (Beijing: Ministry of Works, 1819).

Chen Hezhi 陳和志 (editor, Qing), *Zhenze xian zhi* 震澤縣志(*Gazetteer of Zhenzi Xian*) (1893 edition).

Chen Pengnian 陳彭年 (revised by, Song), *Yu pian* 玉篇 (*The Jade Book*, a lexicon) (privately published in 1850 by the Deng 鄧 family after the Song edition).

Chen Rong 陳嶸, *Zhongguo shumu fenlei xue* 中國樹木分類學 (*A Classification of Chinese Woods*) (Shanghai: Science and Technology Press 科學技術出版社, 1959, 2nd revised edition).

Cheng Junqing 成俊卿, *Zhongguo redai ji yaredai mucai* 中國熱帶及亞熱帶木材 (*Tropical and Sub-tropical Woods of China*) (Beijing: Science Press, 1980).

Cui Bao 崔豹 (Jin), *Gu jin zhu* 古今註 (*Explanation of Ancient and Modern Matters*) (Sibu congkan 四部叢刊, 1935 edition).

Dong Shining 董世寧 (editor, Qing), *Wu Qing Zhen zhi* 烏青鎮志 (*Gazetteer of Wuzhen and Qingzhen*) (1760 edition).

Dunhuang Wenwu Yanjiu Suo 敦煌文物研究所 (Dunhuang Research Institute), *Dunhuang bihua ji* 敦煌壁畫集 (*Dunhuang Wall Paintings*) (Beijing: Wenwu Press, 1975).

Ecke, Gustav, *Chinese Domestic Furniture* (Peking: Henri Vetch, 1944).

Ellsworth, R.H., *Chinese Furniture, Hardwood Examples of the Ming and Early Ch'ing Dynasties* (New York: Random House, 1971).

Fan Lian 范濂 (Ming), *Yunjian jumu chao* 雲間據目抄 (*Record of Things Seen in Yunjian*) (Biji xiaoshuo daguan 筆記小說大觀 lithographic edition).

Fang Yizhi 方以智 (Ming), *Tong ya* 通雅 (*Compendium of My Knowledge*) (Qing Fushancizangxuan 浮山此藏軒 edition).

Fu Weilin 傅維鱗 (Qing), *Ming shu* 明書 (*Ming History*) (Jifu congshu 畿輔叢書, 1913 edition).

Fu Yunzi 傅芸子, *Zhengcangyuan kaogu ji* 正倉院考古記 (*Notes on the Antiquities in the Shosoin*) (Tokyo: Bunkyūdō 文求堂, 1941).

Gao Lian 高濂 (Ming), *Zun sheng ba jian* 遵生八箋 (*Eight Volumes on Nourishing Life*) (Qing woodblock edition).

He Shijin 何士晉 (compiler, Ming), *Gongbu changku xuzhi* 工部廠庫須知 (*What One Ought to Know about the Workshops and Storehouses of the Ministry of Works*) (Xuanlantang congshu xubian 玄覽堂叢書續編, 1947 edition).

Hou Kuanzhao 侯寬昭 *et al.*, *Guangzhou zhiwu zhi* 廣州植物誌 (*Record of the Plants of Guangzhou*) (Beijing: Science Press, 1956).

Huang Cheng 黃成 (Ming), *Xiushilu* 髹飾錄 (*A Record of Lacquer Art*) (private edition, 1927).

Ji Cheng 計成 (Ming), *Yuan ye* 園冶 (*The Art of the Garden*) (Beiping: Zhongguo Yingzao Xueshe 中國營造學社, 1932).

Jiangsu Sheng Wenwu Guanli Weiyuanhui 江蘇省文物管理委員會 (CPAM, Jiangsu Province), "Nanjing jinjiao Liuchao mu de qingli 南京近郊六朝墓的清理" ("The Excavation of Six Dynasties Tombs in the Suburbs of Nanjing"), *Kaogu xuebao* 考古學報, 1957:1, pp. 187-91.

Lee Yu-kuan, *Oriental Lacquer Art* (New York and Tokyo: Weatherhill, 1972).

Li Dou 李斗 (Qing), *Yangzhou huafang lu* 揚州畫舫錄 (*Record of the Yangzhou Pleasure Boats*) (1795 edition).

Li Jie 李誡 (Song), *Yingzao fashi* 營造法式 (*Building Standards*) (Shanghai: Commercial Press, 1954 reprint of Wanyou Wenku 萬有文庫 edition).

Li Shizhen 李時珍, *Bencao gangmu* 本草綱目 (*Compendium of Materia Medica*) (Shanghai: Commercial Press, 1930).

Li Tiaoyuan 李調元 (Qing), *Nanyue biji* 南越筆記 (*Notes on Nanyue*) (1882 edition).

Li Yu 李漁 (Qing), *Li Liweng yijiayan quanji* 李笠翁一家言全集 (*Complete Collection of Li Liweng's Sayings*) (Beiping: Zhongguo Yingzao Xueshe, 1931).

Liu Sheng 劉勝, "Wen mu fu 文木賦" ("Prose Poem on the Beauty of Wood Grains"), in Yan Kejun 嚴可均 (editor), *Quan shanggu Sandai Qin Han Sanguo Liuchao wen* 全上古三代秦漢三國六朝文 (*Complete Collection of Essays From Earliest Times Through the Six Dynasties Period*) (Beijing: Zhonghua Shuju 中華書局, 1958), *juan* 12, pp. 190-1.

Longmen Baoguan Suo 龍門保管所 (Longmen Preservation Institute), *Longmen shiku* 龍門石窟 (*The Longmen Caves*) (Beijing: Wenwu Press, 1980).

Ming Yi 明誼 *et al.* (Qing), *Qiongzhoufu zhi* 瓊州府志 (*Gazetteer of Qiongzhoufu* [Hainan Island]) (1841 edition).

Qu Dajun 屈大均 (Qing), *Guangdong xinyu* 廣東新語 (*New Remarks on Guangdong Province*) (1700 edition).

Schafer, Edward H., "Rosewood, Dragon's Blood and Lac", *Journal of the American Oriental Society*, vol. 77, no. 2, pp. 129-36.

Shang Chengzuo 商承祚 *Changsha chutu Chu qiqi tulu* 長沙出土楚漆器圖錄 (*Illustrated Catalogue of the Chu*

Lacquer Excavated at Changsha) (Shanghai: Chinese Classical Art Press 中國古典藝術出版社, 1957).

Shanghaishi Wenwu Baoguan Weiyuanhui 上海市文物保管委員會 (CPAM, the City of Shanghai), "Shanghaishi Luwan Qu Ming Pan Shi mu fajue baogao 上海市盧灣區明潘氏墓發掘報告" ("Report on the Excavation of the Ming Dynasty Tomb of the Pan Family in the Luwan District, Shanghai"), *Kaogu*, 1961:8, pp. 425-34.

Tianlaige jiu cang Songren huace 天籟閣舊藏宋人畫冊 (*Album of Song Paintings Formerly in the Tianlaige Collection*) (n.p., n.d.).

Tomita Kojiro, *Portfolio of Chinese Paintings in the Museum of Fine Arts, Boston* (*Han to Sung Periods*) (Cambridge, Mass.: Harvard University Press, 1938).

Tu Long 屠隆 (Ming), *You ju jian* 游具箋 (*Notes on Equipment for Excursions*) (Meishu congshu 美術叢書 edition, Part II, Section 9; 1920s).

Wang Shixiang 王世襄

"*Lu Ban jing jiangjia jing* jiaju tiaokuan chushi 魯班經匠家鏡家具條款初釋" ("Preliminary Explanatory Notes on the Furniture Entries in *Lu Ban's Classic, A Mirror for Craftsmen*"), *Gugong Bowuyuan yuankan* 故宮博物院院刊 1980:3, pp. 55-65; and 1981:1, pp. 74-89.

"Ming shi jiaju de pin yu bing 明式家具的'品'與'病'" ("The Merits and Defects of Ming and Early Qing Furniture"), *Wenwu*, 1980:4, pp. 74-81; 1980:6, pp. 75-9; and *Artist*, 1980, overall no. 13, pp. 44-51; overall no. 15, pp. 75-9.

"Tan Qingdai de jiangzuo zeli 談清代的匠造則例" ("On the Qing Dynasty Regulations for Various Craftsmen"), *Wenwu*, 1963:7, pp. 19-25.

Xiushilu jieshuo 髹飾錄解說 (*Commentary on A Record of Lacquer Art* by Huang Cheng 黃成, preface 1625) (Beijing: Wenwu Press, 1983).

Wang Shixing 王士性 (Ming), *Guang zhi yi* 廣志繹 (*On a Variety of Subjects*) (Taizhou congshu 台州叢書, Jiaqing edition).

Wang Siyi 王思義 (Ming), *San cai tu hui* 三才圖會 (*Pictorial Encyclopaedia of Heaven, Earth and Man*) (Ming edition).

Wang Zuo 王佐, *Xinzeng Gegu yaolun* 新增格古要論 (*Revised and Enlarged Edition of The Essential Criteria of Antiquities* by Cao Zhao 曹昭, 1388) (1462; Xiyinxuan congshu 惜陰軒叢書, 1846 edition).

Wen Zhenheng 文震亨 (Ming), *Zhangwu zhi* 長物志 (*Notes on My Belongings*) (Meishu congshu 美術叢書 edition, Part III, Section 9; 1920s).

Wu Rong 午榮 (Ming), *Lu Ban jing jiangjia jing* 魯班經匠家鏡 (*Lu Ban's Classic, A Mirror for Craftsmen*) (Wanli edition).

Xie Zhaozhe 謝肇淛 (Ming), *Wu za zu* 五雜組 (*Compendium of Knowledge Classified into Five Parts*) (Beijing: Zhonghua Shuju 中華書局, 1959).

Yang Dingjian 楊定見 (editor, Ming), *Zhongyi shuihu quanzhuan* 忠義水滸全傳 (*The Complete Story of the Loyal Heroes of the Water Margin*) (Ming edition).

Zhang Duanyi 張端義 (Song), *Gui er ji* 貴耳集 (*Precious Ear Collection*) (Congshu jicheng chubian 叢書集成初編 edition).

Zhao Rukua 趙汝适 (Song), *Zhufan zhi* 諸蕃志 (*Record of Foreign Lands*) (Xuejin taoyuan 學津討原, 1805 edition).

Zhongguo Shehui Kexue Yuan Kaogu Yanjiusuo 中國社會科學院考古研究所 (Institute of Archaeology, Central Academy of Social Sciences), *Huixian fajue baogao* 輝縣發掘報告 (*Report on the Excavations at Huixian*) (Beijing: Science Press, 1958).

Zhou Qiyuan 周起元, preface to Zhang Xie 張燮 (Ming), *Dong xi yang kao* 東西洋考 (*Studies on Countries to the East and West*) (Congshu jicheng chubian 叢書集成初編 edition).

Author's Biography

1914	Wang Shixiang was born on 25 May in Beijing. His ancestors were from Fujian Province. His mother, Jin Zhang 金章, was a celebrated painter in the genres of fish and aquatic plants and of birds and flowers.
1938	Graduated as Bachelor of Arts from Yenching University.
1941	Obtained his Master of Arts from Yenching University.
1943-45	Served as Assistant Research Fellow in Zhongguo Yingzao Xueshe (the Society for Research in Chinese Architecture) in Lizhuang, Sichuan Province.
1945-46	Served as Assistant Representative of the Beiping-Tianjin Regional Office of the Bureau for the Recovery of Cultural Relics Lost During the Sino-Japanese War, a bureau under the Ministry of Education.
1946-47	Was assigned to Japan from December 1946 to February 1947 as a Member of the Fourth Team of the Chinese Mission to Japan whose duty it was to negotiate the return of the rare books taken by the Japanese during the war.
1947-48	Served as Curator of the Department of Antiquities in the Palace Museum, Beijing.
1948-49	Travelled for one year on a Rockefeller Foundation Fellowship to study museums and collections in the U.S.A. and Canada.
1949-53	Resumed the curatorship of the Department of Antiquities in the Palace Museum in 1949 and later served as Head of the Museum's Exhibition Department.
1953-62	Served as Associate Research Fellow, Institute of Chinese Music. Also taught a course in the history of Chinese furniture styles at the Central Academy of Arts and Crafts in 1961.
1962-80	Served as Associate Research Fellow in the Institute of Research on Cultural Relics and Museums and in the Research Institute for the Conservation of Cultural Property.
1980-	Serving as Senior Research Fellow in the Research Institute of Ancient Texts of the Cultural Relics Bureau of the Ministry of Culture. Concurrently serving as Member of the Chinese People's Political Consultative Conference.

Afterword

As the Chinese have given us one of the world's great cuisines, they have also created one of the major traditions in furniture. Both are basic arts of daily use, on which people depend for their practical needs in everyday life. When pragmatic and aesthetic considerations in these arts are felicitously combined, as in the furniture of the Ming and early Qing dynasties, the result is both functional and beautiful. Although the tradition of Chinese furniture goes back to at least the 4th century BC — and a few rare pieces of early furniture have indeed survived — the great period of extant examples is Ming and early Qing. This period of splendour is covered in this volume by Wang Shixiang, the world's foremost authority on Chinese furniture.

Wang Shixiang has diverse expertise and is, like the furniture he studies and illuminates, something of an authentic relic, no longer made today. This is to say, he is a traditional Chinese intellectual with immense knowledge in all the arts, including literature and calligraphy. He has written major treatises on Chinese music, painting, ancient lacquer, and bamboo carving and his studies range from Fujian handcrafts to pigeon whistles. Appropriate to the humanist Eastern tradition he represents, he is also famous in Beijing as a gourmet cook, and served as an adjudicator in the recent national cuisine competition (establishing the hierarchy of chefs in China), which, to be sure, he recorded in an article on Chinese cuisine.

From a family of scholars and diplomats, Wang Shixiang was educated at the American School in Beijing and Yenching University, becoming part of a bilingual and bicultural circle of Chinese intellectuals. During World War II he left Beijing to join the community of refugee scholars in Sichuan. Here he worked with Liang Sicheng, the great historian of Chinese architecture, who was trained at the University of Pennsylvania. Later Wang applied Liang's careful methodology to the study of Chinese furniture. As a result of this experience with Liang's work, he has also been very much aware of the close relationship between architecture and furniture, in their forms, structure, development, and even terminology. In the late forties, he travelled in America and Canada as a Rockefeller research fellow, studying the Chinese art collections in their museums.

After working in the Palace Museum and in the Institute of Research in Chinese Music, during the bleak years of the Cultural Revolution, Wang Shixiang was sent, along with most Chinese intellectuals and artists, "down to the countryside", where he took care of pigs and oxen. Now a senior fellow at the Research Institute of Ancient Texts, Cultural Relics Bureau, he is the international authority on Chinese furniture and in 1983 went to the Victoria and Albert Museum in London for consultation and to lecture. In his capacity as art historian he accompanied in 1980 the "Great Bronze Age of China" exhibition, which was shown in several museums in the United States.

Furniture is the centre of Wang Shixiang's world. During more than forty years of dedication to furniture, he has acquired, restored and now possesses the most important private collection of Chinese furniture in the world. Much of his time he has spent searching for rare pieces, which he has photographed and documented when unable to purchase them. Many of the pieces illustrated in this book come from his own choice collection. These he has lived with, studied, and taken apart to have measured drawings made showing their construction.

Wang Shixiang has acquired knowledge of furniture by going to the living sources, the cabinetmakers. When repairs were necessary he carefully watched cabinetmakers at work in order to learn the secrets of their craft. The living tradition has until now been largely oral, but from the makers Wang Shixing has learned and recorded the rich technical vocabulary of their art. Some of these terms appeared in earlier texts, such as the Qing dynasty manufacturing regulations and *Lu Ban Jing jiangjia jing*, (*Lu Ban's Classic: A Manual for Craftsmen*). These sources were sometimes inexact or even erroneous, and so he published studies in which he corrected the texts and standardized a specific furniture lexicon.

Classic Chinese Furniture is Wang Shixiang's first full-length volume on furniture. It will be followed in the near future by a larger and more detailed volume in the same area. All the pieces illustrated in *Classic Chinese Furniture* are in Chinese collections and most are published in English for the first time. Wang's work is actually the first major scholarly book in the field written in Chinese; prior to this all significant volumes on Chinese furniture were put together by Western art historians. His tome continues and expands the work begun in the 1940s by Gustav Ecke and George Kates, who together with other foreign residents of Beijing at that time bought classic Chinese furniture to furnish their homes. Later, in the 1970s, R.H. Ellsworth and Michel Beurdeley, two dealers and collectors, published illustrated books with some background information.

In *Classic Chinese Furniture*, Wang Shixiang makes seminal contributions to these earlier studies. He arranges the pieces so as to show the development of types and styles, beginning with the simplest, followed by their more complicated variations, and ending with their transformations. He divides all furniture into waisted and waistless categories, thus showing their distinct forms and origins. He even includes detailed investigations of the historical background and of the places of manufacture.

An original and very special contribution to the history of Chinese furniture is Wang Shixiang's definition of the numerous terms used in the old texts and by cabinetmakers. As co-translator of Wang's text, I had to find, invent and sometimes magically concoct an English equivalent for the huge technical vocabulary given to us by the author; this was surely my most formidable task. At times an unavoidable awkwardness enters the English text, which I have tolerated for the sake of consistency. In all, I construed an English glossary of about one thousand terms, for this book and Wang's forthcoming larger volume.

I wish to thank the Committee for Scholarly Communications with the People's Republic of China (CSCPRC) for the fellowship which has permitted me to do research in China and undertake the co-translation of Wang Shixiang's pioneer work.

Sarah Handler
Beijing, 1985

Index

Numbers in italics indicate plates and their relevant notes.